4

FAVORITE STORIES AND SONGS

THE
CHILDREN'S
HOUR

CHANDLER

GROLIER INCORPORATED, DANBURY, CONNECTICUT 06816

1979

International Standard Book Number: 0-7172-8125-6

Library of Congress Catalogue Card Number: 78-68720

Manufactured in the U.S.A.

ACKNOWLEDGEMENTS Volume IV

Grateful acknowledgement and thanks are extended to the following publishers, authors, periodicals, and individuals for permission to reprint copyrighted material:

Beechurst Press, Inc.—"The Princess Bird" from *The Old Aztec Story-Teller,* by J. A. Rickard, Illus. by William Brady, copyright, 1944, by Bernard Ackerman, Inc.

Coward-McCann, Inc.—"The Discontented Village" by Rose Dobbs, with illustrations by Beatrice Tobias. Copyright, 1946, by Rose Dobbs. Reprinted by permission of Coward-McCann, Inc.

Dial Press, Inc.—Illustrations by Steele Savage for "Pandora's Box," "The Miraculous Pitcher," "The Golden Touch," "The Voyage of Ulysses," "Circe the Enchantress," "The Perils of Ulysses," from *Stories of the Gods and Heroes* by Sally Benson, copyright, 1940, by Sally Benson. Used by permission of the publishers, The Dial Press, Inc.

Doubleday & Company.—"Why the Cat and the Dog Are Not Friends" from *Tales of a Korean Grandmother* by Frances Carpenter, copyright, 1947, by Frances Carpenter Huntington, reprinted by permission of Doubleday & Company, Inc. "Billy, the Dog That Made Good" from *Wild Animal Ways* by Ernest Thompson Seton, copyright, 1916, by Ernest Thompson Seton, reprinted by permission of Doubleday & Company, Inc. "The Yellow Shop" from *The Yellow Shop* by Rachel Field, copyright, 1931, by Rachel Field, reprinted by permission of Doubleday & Company, Inc.

Ruth Sawyer Durand—"Juan Cigarron."

Muriel Fellows—"Sah-me and the Rabbit Hunt" from *The Land of Little Rain* by Muriel Fellows, published by The John C. Winston Company.

Grosset & Dunlap, Inc.—Frontispiece by Earle Goodenow from *"The Arabian Nights,"* illustrated by Earle Goodenow, copyright, 1946. Used by permission of the publisher.

Harcourt, Brace and Company, Inc.—"The Tiger's Tail" by Harold Courlander, from *Kantchil's Lime Pit and Other Stories from Indonesia,* by Harold Courlander, copyright, 1950, by Harcourt, Brace and Company, Inc.; Balto's Race Against Death, from *Perilous Journeys,* by Irma H. Taylor, copyright, 1940, by Harcourt, Brace and Company, Inc.

Hart Publishing Company, Inc.—"The Apples of Youth," Baldur the Beautiful," "Thor and the Giants," from *Legends Children Love* by Joanna Strong, copyright, 1950, by Hart Publishing Company.

Henry Holt & Company, Inc.—"Talk," "Kassa, the Strong One," "Guinea Fowl and Rabbitt Get Justice," from *The Cow-Tail Switch and Other West African Stories,* by Harold Courlander and George Herzog, with illustrations by Madye Lee Chastain, copyright, 1947, by Henry Holt & Company, Inc. Used by permission of the publishers.

Thomas Nelson & Sons—"The Goat That Went to School" by Ellis Credle. First published in Story Parade Magazine. Reprinted by permission of Thomas Nelson & Sons. "The Cat Who Became Head Forester" by Arthur Ransome, from *Old Peter's Russian Tales* by Arthur Ransome. Reprinted by permission of Thomas Nelson & Sons, Ltd.

Random House, Inc.—"The Wise King and the Little Bee," by Rose Dobbs, with illustrations by Flavia Gág, copyright, 1950, by Random House, Inc. Also for illustrations for "The Lion-Makers," by Flavia Gág from the same book.

Charles Scribner's Sons—"The Baker's Neighbor," "Sumé," "Our Holy Lady of Good Grace," from *Stories from the Americas,* collected and translated by Frank Henius with illustrations by Leo Politi, copyright, 1944, by Charles Scribner's Sons. Reprinted by permission of the publisher.

Grace Thompson Seton—"Billy, the Dog That Made Good" from *Wild Animal Ways* by Ernest Thompson Seton, copyright, 1916. by Ernest Thompson Seton.

Armstrong Sperry—"The Ghost of the Lagoon."

Story Parade, Inc.—"Juan Cigarron" by Ruth Sawyer, illustrated by Fritz Eichenberg, copyright, 1941, by Story Parade, Inc. "Coronado's Ghost" by Robert M. Hyatt, copyright, 1937, by Story Parade, Inc. "The Goat That Went to School" by Ellis Credle, copyright, 1939, by Story Parade, Inc. "The Peddler's Clock" by Mabel L. Hunt, copyright, 1936, by Story Parade, Inc. "Storm Flight" by Rutherford C. Montgomery, copyright, 1939, by Story Parade, Inc. "The Royal Greens" by Russell Gordon Carter, copyright, 1941, by Story Parade, Inc. All reprinted by permission of Story Parade, Inc.

The University of Chicago Press—"The Lion-Makers," by Arthur Ryder, from *Gold's Gloom,* copyright, 1925, by The University of Chicago Press. Reprinted by permission.

In a few instances, where no acknowledgement is made, the compilers have made every effort to find sources and get permissions from them to reprint, but without success.

A Word to Parents about this Volume

FAVORITE STORIES AND SONGS

OUR children are living in an exciting and perilous time—the Atomic Age. It will be their task to build a new and, we hope, a better world than the one we have left them.

To do so they must have an understanding of people whose customs and ways of thinking may be very different from their own.

Thanks to radio and television, we all now get on-the-spot reporting from lands around the globe. Airplanes whisk more and more of us to faraway places. So we are all, today, more familiar with the ways of "foreigners" than we used to be.

But we are still a long way from understanding why certain cultures differ so radically from ours nor do we always realize how like us, in many ways, are some of the people who seem so different.

This volume, FAVORITE STORIES AND SONGS, is planned to give our children a background for such understanding. Here, first, are the "Greek and Roman Myths and Legends" to give us an insight into "the glory that was Greece and the grandeur that was Rome"—our classical heritage in literature and art.

"Sagas of the Old Norsemen" shed light on people of very different character: those in the cold Scandinavian countries who have been nurtured on tales of the Nibelungs and other hardy Norsemen.

Still farther afield, in Asia and Africa, we get folk tales of the yellow, brown, and black races—tales that give us an idea of the values and customs of these vivid and varied peoples.

In "Old Favorites from the Old Country" we find a wealth of stories, universally popular with Europeans of many countries.

In "Latin American Legends" we taste the particular flavor of the Americas south of the equator.

"North American Stories" range all the way from Louisa May Alcott's tale of an American Indian, *Onawandah,* to *The Yellow Shop,* Rachel Field's delightful story of free enterprise in New England.

The "Singing Games and Favorite Songs," many of which are played and sung all over the world, speak a universal language.

Children will sing these songs out of joyous familiarity and read the stories out of curiosity. We hope that this volume will help them to understand that people may be different but that they can still live and work and play peaceably together.

Table of Contents

NOTE: The **Section Headings** follow the order of their appearance in the book. But under each **Section Heading** the titles of stories, rhymes, etc. appear in *alphabetical* order to make them easier to locate.

ALPHABETICAL INDEX of the **contents of all 9 volumes** will be found *at the end* of Volume 9.

Stories of North America

Singing Games

Favorite Songs

In this volume the titles are listed in alphabetical rather than in numerical order under each section heading.

Illustrators of this Volume

Cyrus Leroy Baldridge, *The Bell of Atri*

De Los Blackmar, *Androcles and the Lion; The Sword of Damocles; The Two Great Painters; The Tiger's Tail; The Poor Count's Christmas*

Elinore Blaisdell, *The Wonderful Weaver, The Cat Who Became Head Forester; Balto's Race Against Death; Onawandah; The Royal Greens*

William Brady, *The Princess Bird*

Rafaello Busoni, *The Wise Man Who Lived in a Tub; The Arrow and the Apple; King Alfred and the Cakes; Horatius at the Bridge; Thor and the Giants; Siegfried; The Wonderful Mallet; The Alligator and the Jackal; A Dream of Paradise; The Peddler's Clock; The Arabian Nights Entertainment: Aladdin and the Wonderful Lamp; Sindbad the Sailor; The Fisherman*

Madye Lee Chastain, *Kassa, the Strong One; Guinea Fowl and Rabbit Get Justice; Talk*

Harry R. Daugherty, *Cornelia's Jewels, The Wooden Horse; Ghost of the Lagoon; The Wise King and the Little Bee; Billy, the Dog That Made Good*

Lawrence Dresser, *Grinding the Ax; Coronado's Ghost*

Fritz Eichenberg, *Juan Cigarron*

Phoebe Erickson, *The Cap That Mother Made; The Goat that Went to School*

Flavia Gag, *The Lion-Makers*

Earle Goodenow, Frontispiece, *Arabian Nights*

Harper Johnson, *Bruce and the Spider*

Ursula Koering, *Sah-mee and the Rabbit Hunt*

Leo Politi, *The Baker's Neighbor; Our Holy Lady of Good Grace; Sumé*

Julie C. Pratt, *Sir Cleges and His Gift*

Virginia Rupp, *Aladdin and the Wonderful Lamp, To A Butterfly, On the Grasshopper and the Cricket*

Steele Savage, *Pandora's Box; The Miraculous Pitcher; The Golden Touch; The Wanderings of Odysseus*

Harold Sichel, *The Stone in the Road; The Last Class; The Porcelain Stove*

Mary Stevens, *The Yellow Shop*

The Stevensons, *Master of All Masters*

Beatrice Tobias, *The Discontented Village*

Sigismund Vidbergs, *The Apples of Youth; The Blind Men and the Elephant; King Canute and His Courtiers*

Kurt Wiese, *The Endless Tale; Why the Dog and the Cat are not Friends; The Dutch Boy and the Dike*

Cover illustrations by Adrian Rappin

VIII

Greek and Roman Myths and Legends

Cornelia's Jewels

By James Baldwin

ONE bright summer morning, in the city of Rome many hundred years ago, two boys stood watching their mother as she strolled with another lady through the garden of their home.

"Did you ever see a lady as pretty as our mother's friend?" asked the younger boy, holding his tall brother's hand. "She looks like a queen."

"But she is not as beautiful as our mother," said the elder boy. "She has a fine dress, to be sure; but her face is not noble and kind. It is our mother who is the queenly one."

"You are quite right," said the other boy. "No woman in all of Rome is so queenly as our own dear mother."

Soon Cornelia, their mother, came down the walk to speak with them. She was simply dressed in a plain white robe. Her feet were bare, as was the custom in those days; there were no rings on her hands and no chains glittering about her neck. Long braids of soft brown hair, coiled about her head, were her only crown, and a tender smile lit up her noble face as she looked into her sons' proud eyes.

"My sons," she said, "I have something to tell you."

They bowed before her, as Roman lads were taught to do. "What is it, mother?" they asked.

"You are to dine with us today, here in the garden; and then our guest is going to show us those wonderful jewels you have heard so much about."

The brothers looked shyly at their mother's friend. Was it possible that she had other rings besides those on her fingers? Could she have still more gems than those which sparkled in the chains about her neck?

When the simple outdoor meal was over, a servant brought the jewel-box from the house. The lady opened it. How dazzling to the eyes of the boys were the jewels they saw there! There were ropes of pearls, white as milk and smooth as satin; heaps of shining rubies red as glowing coals; sapphires as blue as the summer sky; and diamonds that flashed and sparkled like the sunlight.

The brothers looked long at the gems.

"Ah!" whispered the younger, "if our mother could only have such beautiful things!"

At last the jewel-box was closed and carried carefully away.

"Is it true, Cornelia, that you have no jewels?" asked her friend. "Is it true, as I have heard it whispered, that you are poor?"

"No, I am not poor," answered Cornelia, and as she spoke she drew her two boys to her side. "Here are *my* jewels," she said proudly. "My boys are worth far more to me than all the gems in the world."

The boys never forgot their mother's pride in them, or her great love. Years later, indeed, when they had become famous men in Rome, they often thought of this scene in the garden. And even today the world still likes to hear the story of Cornelia's jewels.

Alexander and the Horse Bucephalus

Many hundreds of years ago the country we now call Greece was divided into several separate states, each with its own ruler.

One of these states in the north of Greece was called Macedon, and the King who ruled it was named Philip. Macedon, a land of wide grassy plains and rivers, was famous for its horses which were especially strong and so swift they could outrun the wind. These horses, however, were so wild and free that it was sometimes very hard to tame and ride them.

King Philip of Macedon had a son, Alexander. The boy was a bold and skillful rider not only because he was strong and fearless, but because he loved horses and knew how to handle them.

One day some dealers came to Philip's palace leading a superb black horse with a single white star on his forehead. On the horse's flank was a small mark in the shape of an oxhead. For this reason the horse was called "Bucephalus," the Greek word meaning ox-headed.

"There is not a horse anywhere that can equal his speed," the dealers told Philip.

But Bucephalus was so wild and savage that no man could mount him. He reared and plunged, and threw off everyone who tried to get on his back until there was no one left who was willing even to go near him.

"Take away this beast," the King ordered angrily. "He rears and bucks. He is vicious. No one will ever be able to ride him."

Young Alexander, the King's son, had been watching what was going on. He stepped forward eagerly.

"Father," he said, "it would be a pity to lose so fine a horse just because these men do not know how to handle him. I think *I* can ride that horse."

King Philip laughed, "Do you believe that you, a boy, can *ride* this horse when my best horsemen cannot even mount him?"

"Yes," answered Alexander. "I do. If you will leave him entirely to me."

The horse dealers frowned. The grooms looked worried. King Philip hesitated.

Then something in Alexander's eyes made the King say, "Very well, you may try. But if you fail, what then?"

"Then I will pay you the full price of the horse, Father," answered Alexander.

Now Alexander had been watching Bucephalus carefully. At that hour of the day the sun shone very brightly and the shadow of the horse was sharp and black on the white sand of the palace courtyard. It looked very different from the way it had on the green grassy plains where Bucephalus had been raised. As he pranced and reared about, the black shadow pranced and reared with him. It was his huge black shadow that was causing him to shy. Bucephalus was afraid of his own shadow! His nostrils flared, his proud mane tossed.

While the King and his men watched with bated breath, Alexander quietly moved toward the horse. He began speaking gently to him and took the bridle rein in his hand. Then stroking the animal's head, he slowly turned Bucephalus about so that he faced the sun. The shadow lay behind the horse and Bucephalus could not see it now.

Alexander continued to talk to Bucephalus in a low quiet voice till the horse grew calm and still. Then patting him softly with his hand, the boy moved close to the horse's side and sprang lightly on his back.

Bucephalus plunged forward. Alexander pressed his knees gently but firmly against the horse's sides, keeping him still facing toward the sun, and talking to him all the while in low caressing tones.

Suddenly, like an arrow speeding from a bow, the horse shot off in a wild gallop. The King groaned and closed his eyes. The grooms shuddered. Alexander would be thrown and killed!

But soon the horse and his rider safely reached the end of the field. They turned, and to the King's amazement, there was Alexander not only sitting securely on Bucephalus but guiding him

back at an easy trot! In a few moments they were back at the place where Alexander's father, the King, was standing.

When his son calmly slipped from the horse's back, King Philip caught the boy in his arms. The grooms cheered and shouted, "Long live Prince Alexander!"

"My son," said the King, "Macedon is too small a place for you. Soon you will have to find yourself a kingdom worthy of you. Now you may have the horse for your own!"

Alexander threw his arms about his horse. "Bucephalus," he whispered, "you belong to me. We'll go everywhere together, always."

And so it was. For when one was seen, the other was sure not to be far away. And the horse would never allow anyone to mount him except his master.

Alexander became one of the most famous kings and warriors that history has known, and that is why he is always called Alexander the Great.

Bucephalus carried him through many countries and through battle after battle. In one fierce fight the wonderful horse saved his wounded master's life by carrying him off to safety behind the lines.

When Bucephalus died, Alexander buried him with great pomp and ceremony and gave him a monument such as no other horse had ever received. He built a beautiful city and named it Bucephala in honor of the magnificent black charger he had loved so well.

The Wise Man Who Lived In a Tub

At Corinth, in Greece, in the days of Alexander the Great, there lived a very wise man whose name was Diogenes. He wandered from town to town telling people how little they really needed, and how simply they should live. He did not believe in luxury or soft living. Fine clothes and magnificent houses were, he thought, not at all important.

And so he did not live in a house, but would sleep in doorways or in the porches of temples and was content with the scantiest of clothing and the poorest of food.

Diogenes carried his teachings wherever he could and wandered about till he found a great round wooden tub shaped like a barrel, and that tub became his home for many years. He could roll the tub from place to place and would spend his days sitting in the sun and saying wise things to any who would listen. Many did come from far and wide to hear him.

Many stories are told of his sayings. One day at noon he was seen walking through the streets and market-places of the city with a lighted lantern in his hand. He was looking carefully all about him as if in search of something.

"Why are you carrying a lighted lantern when the sun is shining?" someone asked Diogenes.

"I am looking for an honest man," he said.

When Alexander the Great as a young King visited Corinth, all the foremost men of the city came to greet him with gifts and praise. For Alexander had by that time conquered nearly every nation in Europe and Asia. But Diogenes, the most famous citizen of Corinth, did not come and he was the only man in the city for whose opinion Alexander cared.

Diogenes continued to pay no attention to Alexander's being in the city and gave no sign of moving from his tub.

And so, since the wise man would not come to see the King, the King went to see the wise man.

With his retinue of officers the young King who longed to conquer the whole world, walked to the part of the city where he heard Diogenes was.

Diogenes, wearing rags, was sitting beside his tub enjoying the warmth and light of the sun. He did not even look up for he was absorbed in his thoughts. Diogenes appeared not to notice the man who had made millions tremble.

Alexander approached and stood in front of Diogenes so that his shadow fell across the old man.

The King watched him for a few moments and then said, "Diogenes, I have heard a great deal about your wisdom. Is there anything I can do for you?"

"Yes," said Diogenes looking up for the first time. "Stand to one side so that you won't keep the sun off me."

This answer was so different from what Alexander expected that he was much surprised. But it did not make him angry. It only made him admire the strange man all the more.

As he turned away, he said to his officers, "Say what you will, if I were not Alexander, I would like to be Diogenes."

Androcles and the Lion

By James Baldwin

IN ROME, many centuries ago, there lived a poor slave whose name was Androcles. His master was a cruel man, and so unkind to him that one day Androcles ran away.

He hid himself in a wild wood for many days. But there was no food to be found, and Androcles grew so weak and sick that he thought he would die. At last he crept into a cave and lay down, and soon he was fast asleep.

After a while a great noise woke him up. A lion had come into the cave, and was roaring loudly. Androcles was badly frightened, for he felt sure the beast would kill him. Soon, however, he saw that the lion was not angry, but that he limped as though his foot hurt him.

Then Androcles lost his fear. He took hold of the lion's lame paw to see what was the matter. The lion stood quite still, and rubbed his head against Androcles' shoulder. He seemed to say, "I know you will help me."

Androcles lifted the lion's paw from the ground, and saw that there was a long, sharp thorn sticking into it. He took the end of the thorn in his fingers; then he gave a strong, quick pull, and out it came. The lion was much relieved and very grateful. He jumped about like a dog, and licked the hands and feet of his new friend.

Androcles was not at all afraid after this; and when night came, he and the lion lay down and slept side by side.

For a long time, the lion brought food to Androcles every day; and the two became such good friends that Androcles found his new life a very happy one.

One day some soldiers who were passing through the wood found Androcles in the cave. They knew who he was, and quite brutally they pulled him away and dragged him back to Rome.

It was the law at that time that every slave who ran away from his master should be made to fight a hungry lion. So a fierce lion was shut up in a cage for a while without food, and a time was set for the fight.

When the day came, thousands of people crowded to see the fight. They considered such things as sport! They went to see such shows, at that time, very much as people nowadays go to see a circus or a game of baseball.

The door of the cage was opened, and poor Androcles was brought in. He was almost dead with fear, for the roars of the hungry lion could already be heard. Androcles looked up, but he saw no pity in the thousands of faces around him.

Then the hungry lion rushed in. With a single bound he reached the poor slave. Androcles gave a great cry; but it was a cry not of fear, but of gladness. It was his old friend, the lion of the cave!

The people who had expected to see the man killed by the lion, were filled with wonder. They saw Androcles put his arms around the lion's neck. They saw the lion lie down at his feet, and lick them lovingly. They saw the great beast rub his head against the slave's face as though he wanted to be petted. They could not understand what it all meant.

After a while they called to Androcles demanding that he explain. So Androcles stood up before them, and, with his arm around the lion's neck, told how he and the beast had lived together in the cave.

"I am a man," he said; "but no man has ever befriended me. This poor lion alone has been kind to me; and we love each other as brothers."

The people were not so bad that they could be cruel to the poor slave now. They began to feel sorry for him. "Live and be free!" they cried. free!"

Others cried, "Let the lion go free too! Give both of them their liberty!"

So they set Androcles free, and they gave him the lion to keep as his friend. And Androcles and the lion lived together in Rome for many happy years.

9

Pandora's Box

By Nathaniel Hawthorne

LONG, long ago, when this old world was still very young, there was a boy named Epimetheus. He had neither father nor mother; and to keep him company, a little girl, who, like himself, had no father or mother, was sent from a far country to live with him and be his playmate. Her name was Pandora.

The first thing Pandora saw when she came to the cottage where Epimetheus lived, was a great wooden box. "What have you in the box, Epimetheus?" she asked.

"That is a secret," answered Epimetheus, "and you must not ask any questions about it. The box was left here to be kept safely and I myself do not know what is in it."

"But who gave it to you?" asked Pandora. "And where did it come from?"

"That's a secret, too," answered Epimetheus.

"How tiresome," Pandora pouted, "I wish that ugly box were out of the way!" And she looked very cross.

"Oh come, don't think of it any more," cried Epimetheus. "Let's play games outdoors with the other children."

It is thousands of years since Epimetheus and Pandora were alive. Then, everybody was a child. The children needed no fathers and mothers to take care of them because there was no danger or trouble of any kind. There was always plenty to eat and drink. Whenever a child wanted his dinner he found it growing on a tree, and he could see next morning's breakfast just getting ready to be plucked.

Most wonderful of all, the children never quarreled among themselves, nor did they ever cry. Those ugly little winged monsters called Troubles had never yet been seen on earth. Probably the worst annoyance that a child had ever experienced was Pandora's at not being able to find out the secret of the mysterious box.

At first this was only the shadow of a Trouble, but it grew bigger every day.

"Where could the box have come from?" Pandora kept saying. "And what in the world can be inside it."

"Always talking about that box!" said Epimetheus. "I do wish you'd talk of something else. Come, let's go and gather some ripe figs and eat them under the trees for our supper. And I know a vine that has the juiciest, sweetest grapes you ever tasted."

"Always talking about grapes and figs!" cried Pandora peevishly.

"Well, then," said Epimetheus, "let us run out and have a merry time with our playmates."

"I am tired of merry games! This ugly box! I think about it all the time. You must tell me what is in it!"

"As I have said fifty times over, I do not know," replied Epimetheus, now a little provoked.

"You might open it," said Pandora, looking sideways at Epimetheus.

Epimetheus looked so shocked at the idea of opening a box that had been given to him in trust, that Pandora thought it best not to suggest it any more. "At least," she said, "you could tell me how it came here."

"It was left at the door," replied Epimetheus, "just before you came, by a person who looked very smiling and intelligent. He could hardly keep from laughing as he put it down. He wore an odd kind of cloak and a cap that seemed to be made partly of feathers so that it looked as if it had wings."

"What sort of staff had he?" asked Pandora.

"Oh, the most curious staff you ever saw!" cried Epimetheus. "It seemed like two serpents twisting around a stick, and was carved so naturally that, at first, I thought the serpents were alive."

"I knew him," said Pandora thoughtfully. "It was Mercury. No one else has such a staff. He brought me here as well as that box. I am sure he meant the box for me, and perhaps there are pretty clothes in it for us to wear and toys for us to play with."

"It may be so," said Epimetheus turning away, "but until Mercury comes back and tells us so, we have neither of us the right to lift the lid of the box."

For the first time since Pandora had come there, Epimetheus went out without asking her to go with him. Pandora stood gazing at the box. Although she had called it ugly a hundred times, it actually was very handsome and would have been an ornament in any room.

It was made of beautiful dark wood so highly polished that Pandora could see her face in it. The edges and corners were wonderfully carved. Around the margin there were figures and faces of graceful men and women and pretty children playing among the leaves and flowers. All were combined in a design of exquisite harmony. But here and there, peeping out from among the carved leaves, Pandora once or twice imagined she saw a face not quite so lovely. When she looked more closely, however, and touched the spot with her fingers, she could discover nothing of the kind.

But the most beautiful face of all was the one in the center of the lid. It had a wreath of flowers around its brow. Pandora had looked at this face a great many times. Some days she thought it had a very grave look which made her rather afraid, while at other times its expression was lively and mischievous.

The box was not fastened with a lock and key like most boxes, but with a strange knot of gold cord. There never was a knot so queerly tied. It seemed to have no beginning and no end, but was twisted so cunningly, with so many ins and outs, that not even the cleverest fingers could undo it.

Pandora began to examine the knot to find out how it had been made. "I believe I am beginning to see how it is done," she said to herself. "I am sure I could tie it up again after undoing it. There would be no harm in that, surely. I needn't open the box even if I undo the knot."

First, however, Pandora tried to lift the box. It was heavy—too heavy for her. She could only raise one end of the box a few inches from the floor and let it fall again with a loud thump. A moment afterwards, she thought she heard something stir inside the box. She put her ear as close to the box as possible and listened. There did seem to be a kind of low murmuring within! Or was it only the ringing in Pandora's ears? Her curiosity was greater than ever.

She took the golden knot in her fingers and without quite intending it, she was soon busily trying to undo it.

Meanwhile the bright sunshine came through the open window. She could hear the happy voices of the children playing in the distance. What a beautiful day it was! Perhaps she should leave the troublesome knot alone and run out to join her playmates.

All this time, however, her fingers were busy with the knot. Then she happened to glance at the flower-wreathed face on the lid. The face seemed to be grinning at her!

"That face looks very mischievous," thought Pandora. "I wonder if it is smiling because I am doing wrong! I have a good mind to leave the box alone and run away."

But just at that moment she gave the knot a little shake. As if by magic the gold cord untwined itself, and there was the box without any fastening.

"This is the strangest thing I have ever known," said Pandora, a little frightened. "What will Epimetheus say? And how can I tie it up again?"

She tried once or twice, but the knot would not come right. It had untied itself so suddenly that she could not remember how the strings had been twisted together. So there was nothing to be done but to let the box remain unfastened until Epimetheus should come home.

"But," thought Pandora, "when Epimetheus finds the knot untied, he will know I did it. How shall I ever make him believe I haven't looked into the box?"

And then the thought came into her naughty head that since Epimetheus would believe she had looked into the box, she might as well do so.

She looked at the face with the wreath, and it seemed to smile at her invitingly, as if to say, "Do not be afraid. What harm can there possibly be in raising the lid for a moment?" And she thought she heard within more distinctly than before, the murmur of small voices that seemed to whisper, "Let us out, dear Pandora, let us out."

"What can it be?" said Pandora. "Is there something alive in the box? Yes, I must see. Only one little peep and the lid will be shut down as safely as ever. There cannot be any harm in just one little peep!"

All this time Epimetheus had been playing with the other children in the fields, but he did not feel happy. This was the first time he had played without Pandora, and he was so cross and discontented that the other children could not think what was the matter with him. Up to this time, you see, everyone in all the world had always been happy. No one had ever been ill or naughty or unhappy for the world was still new and beautiful.

Epimetheus could not understand what was the matter with him and he decided to go back to Pandora. On the way, he gathered roses, lilies, and orange blossoms to make a bouquet for her. He noticed in the sky a great black cloud which was creeping nearer and nearer the sun. Just as Epimetheus reached the cottage door, the cloud went right over the sun and made everything look dark and sad.

Epimetheus entered quietly for he wanted to surprise Pandora with the bouquet. Pandora had put her hand on the lid of the box and was just going to open it. Epimetheus saw this quite well, and if he had cried out at once it would have given Pandora such a fright she would have let go the lid.

But now, Epimetheus was just as curious as Pandora to see what was inside. If there was anything pretty or valuable in the box he meant to take half for himself.

As Pandora raised the lid, the cottage grew very dark, for the black cloud now covered the sun entirely and a heavy peal of thunder was heard. But Pandora was too busy and excited to notice this. She lifted the lid right up, and at once a swarm of creatures with wings brushed past her as they flew out of the box.

At the same instant she heard Epimetheus cry out in pain, "Oh, I am stung! I am stung!"

Pandora let the lid fall with a crash and looked up to see what had happened to Epimetheus. The thunder-cloud had so darkened the room that she could scarcely see. But she heard a disagreeable buzz-buzzing, as if a great many huge flies had flown in, and soon she saw a crowd of ugly little winged shapes darting about like bats, and armed with terribly long stings in their tails. One of these had stung Epimetheus, and it was not long before Pandora herself began to scream in pain and fear. An ugly little monster had settled on her forehead and would have stung her if Epimetheus had not run forward and brushed it away.

Now these ugly creatures were the whole family of earthly Troubles. There were bad tempers; there were a great many kinds of cares; there were more than a hundred and fifty sorrows; there were more kinds of naughtiness than it would be of any use to talk about. In fact all the sorrows and worries that have since troubled the world had been shut up in that mysterious box. It had been given to Epimetheus and Pandora to be kept safely. If only these two had obeyed Mercury and left the box alone, all would have gone well. No grown person would ever have been sad, and no child would have had cause to shed a single tear from that hour until this moment.

It was impossible for the two children to keep the ugly swarm in their own little cottage. The first thing they did was to fling open the windows and doors in hopes of getting rid of them. And, sure enough, away flew the winged Troubles and so pestered and tormented the small people everywhere that none of them so much as smiled for many days afterwards.

Meanwhile Pandora and Epimetheus remained in their cottage. Both of them had been grievously stung. Epimetheus sat down sullenly with his back to Pandora while Pandora flung herself sobbing on the floor and rested her head on the lid of the fatal box.

Suddenly there was a gentle tap-tap inside.

"Who are you?" asked Pandora. "Who are you inside this horrid box?"

A sweet voice spoke from within: "Only lift the lid and you shall see."

"No, no," answered Pandora, again beginning to sob, "I have had enough of lifting the lid! There are plenty of your ugly brothers and sisters already flying about the world. You need not think I would be so foolish as to let you out!"

"Ah, but I am not one of these," the sweet voice said. "They are no brothers or sisters of mine, as you will see, if only you will let me out!"

The voice sounded so kind and cheery that it was almost impossible to refuse it anything. Pandora's heart had grown lighter at every word. Epimetheus, too, had heard the voice.

"Dear Epimetheus," cried Pandora, "shall I lift the lid again?"

14

"Just as you please," said Epimetheus. "You have done so much mischief already that perhaps you may as well do a little more. One other Trouble can make no great difference."

"You might speak a little more kindly!" murmured Pandora.

"Ah, naughty boy," laughed the little voice from within the box. "He knows he is longing to see me. Come, dear Pandora, lift the lid. I am in a great hurry to comfort you."

"Epimetheus," exclaimed Pandora, "come what may, I am resolved to open the box!"

"As the lid seems very heavy," cried Epimetheus, running across the room, "I will help you."

This time both children opened the box. Out flew a bright, sunny, fairylike creature that hovered about the room throwing a light wherever she went. She flew to Epimetheus and with her finger touched his brow where the Trouble had stung him, and immediately the pain was gone. Then she kissed Pandora and her hurt was better at once.

"Pray, who are you, beautiful creature?" asked Pandora.

"I am called Hope," answered the sunshiny figure. "I was packed into the box so that I might comfort people when that swarm of ugly Troubles was let loose among them."

"What lovely wings you have!" exclaimed Pandora. "They are colored like the rainbow!"

"Yes, they are like the rainbow," said Hope, "because, happy as my nature is, I am made of tears as well as smiles."

"And will you stay with us?" asked Epimetheus, "forever and ever?"

"Yes, I shall stay with you as long as you live," said Hope. "There may come times when you will think I have vanished. But again and again, perhaps when you least dream of it, you shall see the glimmer of my wings on the ceiling of your cottage. But you must trust my promise that I will never leave you."

"Yes, we do trust you," cried both children.

And all the rest of their lives when Troubles would come back and buzz about their heads, they would wait patiently till Hope, the fairy with the rainbow wings, came back to heal and comfort them.

—*Adapted from* A WONDER BOOK

The Sword of Damocles

By James Baldwin

THERE was once a King whose name was Dionysius. He was so unjust and so cruel that everyone knew him for what he was, a tyrant. He knew how he was hated too, and so he lived in constant dread lest someone should kill him.

But he was very rich, and he lived in a fine palace where there were many beautiful and costly things, and he was waited upon by a host of servants who had to be ready always to do his bidding.

One day a friend of his, whose name was Damocles, said to him, "How happy you must be! You have everything that any man could wish."

"Perhaps you would like to change places with me," said the tyrant.

"O King!" said Damocles. "It seems to me that if I could have your riches and your pleasures for only one day, I should not want any greater happiness."

"Very well," said the tyrant, "you shall have them."

And so, the next day, Damocles was led into the palace, and all the servants were bidden to treat him as their master. He sat down at a table in the banquet hall, and rich foods were placed before him. Nothing was wanting that could give him pleasure. There were costly wines, and beautiful flowers, and rare perfumes, and delightful music. He rested among soft cushions, and felt that he was the luckiest man in all the world.

Then he chanced to raise his eyes toward the ceiling. What was that

shining blade dangling above him, its point almost touching his head?

It was a sharp sword, and it was hung by only a single horse-hair.

What if the hair should break? There was danger every moment that it would

The smile faded from the lips of Damocles. His face became ashy pale. His hands trembled. He wanted no more food; he could drink no more wine; he took no more delight in the perfumes or the music. He wanted only to be out of the palace, and away, he cared not where.

"What is the matter?" said the tyrant.

"That sword! that sword!" cried Damocles. He was so badly frightened that he dared not move.

"Yes," said King Dionysius, "I know there is a sword above your head, and it may fall at any moment. But why should that trouble you? *I* have a sword over my head all the time. I am every moment in dread lest something may cause me to lose my life."

"Let me go," cried Damocles. "I now see how mistaken I was; the rich and powerful are not always as happy as they seem. Let me go back to my old home in the poor little cottage among the mountains!"

And so, as long as he lived, Damocles never again wished to be rich, or to change places, even for a moment, with Dionysius or any other King.

Two Great Painters
By James Baldwin

THERE was once a painter whose name was Zeuxis. He could paint pictures so lifelike that they were mistaken for the real things which they represented.

At one time he painted the picture of some fruit which was so real that the birds flew down and pecked at it. This made him very proud of his skill.

"I am the only man in the world who can paint a picture so true," he said.

There was another famous artist whose name was Parrhasius. When he heard of the boast which Zeuxis had made, he said to himself, "I will see what I can do."

So he painted a beautiful picture which seemed to be covered with a curtain. Then he invited Zeuxis to see it.

Zeuxis looked at it closely. "Draw the curtain and show the picture," he said.

Parrhasius laughed and answered, "The curtain is the picture."

"Well," said Zeuxis, "you have beaten me this time, and I shall boast no more. I deceived only the birds, but you have deceived me, a painter."

Some time after this, Zeuxis painted another wonderful picture. It was that of a boy carrying a basket of ripe red cherries. When he hung this painting outside of his door, some birds flew down and tried to carry the cherries away.

"Ah! this picture is a failure," he said. "For if the boy had been as well painted as the cherries, the birds would have been afraid to come near him."

17

Horatius at the Bridge

ONCE, long ago, there was a war between the people of Rome and the Etruscans who lived in the towns on the other side of the Tiber River. This river ran through the great city of Rome.

Lars Porsena, the tyrant King of the Etruscans, had gathered a huge army and was marching toward Rome. His soldiers, sure that they would conquer Rome, thought of all the wealth and treasure in the city that they could take away, and of the people they could carry off to be their slaves. So they marched along confidently. Rome had never been in such great danger.

The Romans did not have very many fighting men at that time, and they knew they were not strong enough to meet the Etruscans in open battle. Therefore they kept within their city walls, and set guards to watch the roads.

One morning the army of Lars Porsena, thousands strong, was seen sweeping over the hills near Janiculum, a town to the north, in a surprise advance. They were horsemen and footmen armed with spears and javelins and all the people in the country through which they marched were fleeing before them into the city of Rome.

The Roman soldiers stationed on that side of the Tiber herded the frightened people on toward the city before Porsena and his men could overtake them.

The invading soldiers were coming closer. They were marching straight toward the wooden bridge that spanned the Tiber River at Rome.

The white-haired Senators of Rome, the men who ruled that city, did not know what to do. Their army was not strong enough to hold the land on the far side of the river.

But there was the crowded bridge. "Once Porsena's men gain the bridge, we cannot stop them from crossing over," said the Senators. "And what hope will there be for Rome, then?" They shook their heads mournfully.

They thought of cruel Lars Porsena and the sorrow and ruin his conquering army would bring to their people and their beloved land. Already they could see, looking toward Janiculum, the smoke of the fires that rose from burning homes and villages. The invaders left not a house or a fence or a barn untouched.

Still the crowds of women and children, old people and farmers from the plains around, pushing their flocks and herds of sheep and cattle before them, kept coming on over the bridge.

Not far behind them came the soldiers of the Roman garrison running hard to get to the bridge, while Lars Porsena's men raced quickly to cross with them and capture Rome.

Now, among the guards at the bridge there was a brave man named Horatius. He was on the farther side of the river and could see in the bright noonday sun, through the rolling clouds of dust, the gleaming helmets and spears of the approaching army.

He could hear the trampling of thousands of feet and the blare of trumpets proclaiming the victory the Etruscan invaders saw ahead of them.

There was only one thing to do. Horatius turned toward the Romans who were behind him. In a loud voice he called, "Hew down the bridge with all the speed you can! I, with two men to stand by me, will hold the enemy at bay!"

Two brave Romans stepped beside him. Then, with their shields before them, their long spears in their hands, the three men stood at the head of the bridge and kept back the first horsemen Porsena had sent forward to take it.

On the bridge the Romans hewed away at its beams and posts. Axes rang and the chips flew loosening the props that held the bridge in place.

The Senators and the people watched as Horatius and his two companions silently prepared for the next attack. The enemy hordes came rolling forward with banners flying and trumpets sounding. The sun flashed and glittered on helmets, spears and swords.

When the foremost ranks saw the three Romans standing at the head of the bridge, a great shout of laughter went up among them. Three Etruscan horsemen sprang from their horses, drew their swords, and with shields raised high, rushed forward to attack the Romans who barred their way.

But it was they who fell, not the three Romans. And the same fate met others of the enemy who came forward. The enemy army watched in grim amazement. The Etruscans could not advance while the three Romans held the head of the bridge for only three had room to battle in that narrow passageway. On the city side the citizens of Rome were working desperately to destroy the bridge.

A mighty roar of anger rose from the invaders and the crowd of soldiers seethed with rage. Horatius was wounded by a spear thrust but the three men fought on. At last the trumpet's blare died down and the enemy army began to shrink back.

Now the bridge was tottering, ready to fall. "Come back! Come back and save your lives!" the people shouted to Horatius and the two men with him.

But just then some of Porsena's horsemen dashed toward them again.

"Run for your lives!" cried Horatius to his friends. "I'll keep guard. No one shall go through!"

The two darted across the bridge. They had hardly reached the other side when there was a great crashing of beams and timber. The bridge toppled over to one side and fell with a great splash into the Tiber.

19

When Horatius heard the crash of the bridge, he knew his city was safe. A shout of triumph rose from the opposite bank.

With his face still toward the enemy Horatius moved slowly backward till he stood on the river's bank. A dart thrown by one of Porsena's men put out his left eye, but Horatius did not stop. He hurled his spear at an oncoming horseman and then turned quickly around. He saw the white porch of his own home among the trees on the other side of the stream.

Horatius sheathed his sword and plunged into the deep swift stream. He was still wearing his heavy armor when he sank out of sight and not a Roman nor an Etruscan thought he would ever be seen again.

The wounded weary man fought hard to keep afloat in the swirling yellow waters. But Horatius was a strong man and the best swimmer in Rome. Soon his crest and helmet appeared above the waves and a great cheer rang out from the Roman side. He was half-way across the river and safe from the spears and darts which Porsena's soldiers had hurled after him.

As Horatius reached the far side friendly hands stretched out to draw him to the shore. Joyful shouts burst from every Roman throat as he climbed upon the bank. Then, even Porsena's men shouted, for they had never seen a man so brave and strong as he was. He had kept them out of Rome but in so doing he had performed a deed they could not help but praise.

As for the Romans, Senators and citizens thronged about him to press his hands and thank him. The young men took him up and put him on their shoulders. Then they carried him through the roaring crowds to his home.

Horatius had given no thought to his own safety. He had thought only of his city and how it could be saved.

With weeping and with laughter,
  Still was the story told,
How well Horatius kept the bridge
  In the brave days of old.
                                    Macaulay

The Miraculous Pitcher

By Nathaniel Hawthorne

LONG, long ago, a good man and his wife lived in a little cottage on a hilltop. Their names were Philemon and Baucis. They were old and very poor, and they worked hard to earn their living, but they were happy all day long for they loved one another dearly.

They lived on their hilltop looking after their small garden and their bee-hives and tending their cow. They seldom had anything more to eat than bread and milk and vegetables, with sometimes a little honey from their bee-hives, or a few ripe pears or apples from the garden.

They were two of the kindest old people in the world, and would gladly have gone without their dinner any day rather than refuse a slice of bread or a cupful of milk to any hungry traveler who might stop at their cottage.

A beautiful village lay in the valley below the hilltop where the cottage of Philemon and Baucis stood. The valley, shaped like a bowl, was fertile with green meadows, gardens and orchards. But, sad to say, the people living in this pleasant fertile valley were selfish and hard-hearted, with never a thought of pity or kindness for the friendless or needy.

These villagers taught their children to be just as unkind as they were. They kept large fierce dogs, and whenever unfortunate strangers appeared in the village, the dogs would rush out barking and snarling at them. The children, too, were encouraged to run after them pelting them with stones and jeering at their shabby clothes.

What made it even worse was that if the strangers were rich people attended by servants, the villagers would be extra polite and would bow and scrape before them. If the children happened to be rude to these wealthy visitors, they had their ears boxed. As for the dogs, if a single dog dared as much as to growl at anyone who was rich, that dog was beaten and tied up without any supper.

One evening, Philemon and Baucis were sitting on a bench outside their doorway, talking quietly about their garden and enjoying the sunset.

Suddenly they were interrupted by the shouts of children and the angry barking of dogs in the village. The noise grew louder and louder until Philemon and Baucis could hardly hear each other speak.

"I have never heard the dogs bark so savagely," said Baucis.

"Nor the children shout so rudely," answered old Philemon.

They sat shaking their heads sorrowfully as the noise came nearer and nearer until they saw two strangers coming along the road on foot. Both travellers were very plainly dressed and looked as if they had no money for food or a night's lodging. Close behind them came the fierce dogs snarling at their heels and a little farther off ran a crowd of children who screamed shrilly and flung stones at the strangers.

"Good wife," said Philemon to Baucis, "I will go to meet these poor people while you prepare something for them to eat. Perhaps they feel too heavy-hearted to climb the hill."

And he hastened forward saying heartily, "Welcome, strangers! Welcome!"

"Thank you," answered the younger of the two travellers. "Yours is a kind welcome, very different from the one we just got in the village."

Philemon took a good look at him and his companion. The younger of the two strangers was slim and dressed in an odd kind of way. Though the evening was mild, he wore his cloak wrapped tightly about him. He had a cap on with a brim that stuck out over his ears. There was something queer, too, about his shoes, but as it was growing dark, Philemon could not see exactly what they were like.

Another thing struck Philemon. The younger stranger was so wonderfully light and active that it seemed as if his feet sometimes rose from the ground of their own accord and could be kept on

the ground only with difficulty. He carried, besides, a staff which was the oddest Philemon had ever seen. It was made of wood and had a little pair of wings near the tip. Two snakes carved in wood were twisting around the staff and these were so finely made that the old man almost thought he could see them wriggling.

The elder of the two strangers was very tall and walked calmly along. He seemed not to have noticed the barking dogs or the screaming children.

When they reached the cottage, Philemon said, "We are poor folk and haven't much to offer, but all we have is yours."

The strangers sat down on the bench and the younger one dropped his staff on the grass. And then a strange thing happened. The staff seemed to get up by itself and, spreading its little pair of wings, half-hopped and half-flew to lean itself against the wall of the cottage.

Before Philemon could ask any questions, the elder stranger said, "Was there not a lake long ago that covered this place where the village now stands?"

"Not in my time," said Philemon, "nor in my father's or grandfather's. There have always been meadows and gardens just as there are now and I suppose there always will be."

"That I am not so sure of," answered the stranger. "Since the people of that place have forgotten how to be kind, it might be better perhaps if a lake should be rippling over that village again." He looked sad and stern.

Philemon was sure now that he was not an ordinary wanderer. His clothes were old and shabby. Perhaps he was a learned man who wandered about the world seeking wisdom and knowledge.

Philemon turned to the younger traveller. "What is your name, my friend?" he asked.

"I am called Mercury," he said.

"Does your companion have as strange a name?" asked Philemon.

"You must ask the thunder to tell you," replied Mercury. "No other voice is loud enough."

Philemon did not quite know what to make of this, but the strangers appeared to be so kind and friendly that he began telling them about his good wife Baucis, and what fine butter and cheese she made. He told them how happy they were in their little cottage and how they hoped that when they died, they might die together. The elder of the travellers listened to all this with a gentle smile on his stern face.

Now Baucis had the supper ready and called her husband to invite their guests to come in. "Had we known you were coming," she said, "my husband and I would have been happy to have gone without our supper, to give you a better one."

"Do not trouble yourself about that," said the elder of the strangers. "A cordial welcome is better than the best food and we are so hungry that whatever you have to offer will be a feast."

Then they all went into the cottage. As they turned into the doorway, that staff of Mercury's that had been leaning against the cottage wall opened its small wings and hopped up the steps and tap-tapped across the floor. It stopped behind the chair where Mercury sat. But Baucis and Philemon did not notice this. They were too busy attending to their guests.

On the table was half a loaf of brown bread and a bit of cheese, a pitcher with some milk, a little honey, and a bunch of purple grapes. Baucis filled two bowls with milk from the pitcher. "What delicious milk, Mother Baucis!" exclaimed Mercury. "May I have more? This has been such a warm day I am very thirsty."

"I am so sorry," said Baucis, "but there are barely a few drops left in the pitcher. If only we hadn't used so much milk for our supper before!"

"Let me see," said Mercury picking up the pitcher. "Why, there certainly *is* more milk here." And he poured out a bowlful for himself and another for his companion.

Baucis could hardly believe her eyes.

In a few moments Mercury said, "Your milk is really the most delicious I have ever tasted. I must have just a little more."

As Baucis lifted the pitcher to pour out what she thought would be the very last drop of milk into the stranger's bowl, a wonderful stream of rich, fresh milk fell bubbling into it and overflowed on to the table. The more Baucis poured, the more milk remained. The pitcher was always filled to the brim.

And so it was with the bread. Though it had been rather dry when Philemon and Baucis had had it for their supper, it was now as fresh and tasty as if it had just come from the oven. Baucis could hardly believe this was the loaf she had baked with her own hands.

Baucis sat down beside Philemon. "Did you ever hear of anything so wonderful?" she whispered.

" No, I never did," answered Philemon. "Perhaps you are imagining all this, my dear."

"Just one more bowl of milk, please," Mercury asked. This time Philemon lifted the pitcher himself and peeped into it. There wasn't a drop in it. Then all at once a little white fountain of milk gushed up from the bottom and soon the pitcher was filled again to its very brim.

In his amazement Philemon nearly dropped the miraculous pitcher. "Who are you?" he cried, gazing wide-eyed at the wonder-working strangers.

"We are your guests and your friends, my good Philemon," replied the elder traveller in his deep voice. "May that pitcher never be empty for yourselves or for any needy wayfarer."

The old people did not like to ask any more questions. They gave their beds to the strangers and they themselves lay down to sleep on the hard kitchen floor. In the morning they rose with the sun to help their guests make ready to continue their journey.

"If the villagers only knew what a pleasure it is to be kind to strangers, they would tie up their dogs and never allow their children to fling another stone," said Philemon.

"It is a sin and a shame for them to behave that way, and I mean to tell them so this very day," declared Baucis firmly.

"I'm afraid," said Mercury smiling, "that you will find none of them home." And he pointed to the foot of the hill.

The old people looked at the elder traveller. His face had grown very grave and stern. "When men do not feel towards the poorest stranger as if he were a brother," he said in his deep voice, "they do not deserve to remain on earth."

Philemon and Baucis turned toward the valley where just the evening before they had seen meadows, houses, gardens and streets. But now there was not a sign of the village—or even of the valley.

"Alas! What has become of our poor neighbors?" asked the kind-hearted old people.

"They are not men and women any longer," answered the elder traveller in a voice like thunder. "Those wicked people of the valley have had their punishment. As for you, good Philemon and Baucis, your reward shall be anything you may wish for."

Philemon and Baucis looked at one another and whispered together for a moment. Then Philemon spoke to the gods. "Our wish, O great gods from High Olympus," the old man said slowly, "is that we may live the rest of our lives together. Neither of us wishes to live without the other."

"So be it," said the elder stranger who was the god Jupiter. As he spoke, he and his companion vanished from sight like mist in the morning sun.

When Baucis and Philemon turned to go back to their little cottage, it had disappeared. In its place stood a white marble palace with a beautiful park around it. The kind old people lived there for many years, and to every traveller who passed that way they offered a drink from the ever bubbling pitcher.

Baucis and Philemon grew very very old. Then one summer morning when guests came to visit them, neither Baucis nor Philemon could be found. The guests looked everywhere but it was of no use. Suddenly one of them noticed two large beautiful trees in the garden just in front of the doorway of the palace. One was an oak tree and the other a linden, and their branches were entwined so that they seemed to be embracing one another.

No one could remember having seen them before. While the guests wondered how such fine trees could possibly have grown up in one night, a gentle wind blew up that set the branches stirring.

A mysterious voice whispered from the oak, "I am Philemon." And from the linden came, "I am Baucis." Then the voices seemed to speak together.

Now the people knew that the good couple would live on for many many years in the lovely trees. They would cast a pleasant shade for the weary traveller who rested under their branches, and they seemed to be forever saying, "Welcome, dear travellers, welcome."

Adapted from A WONDER BOOK.

The Wonderful Weaver

By James Baldwin

THERE was a young girl in Greece whose name was Arachne. Her face was pale but fair, and her eyes were big and blue, and her hair was long and like gold. All that she cared to do from morn till noon was to sit in the sun and spin; and all that she cared to do from noon till night was to sit in the shade and weave.

And oh, how fine and fair were the things which she wove in her loom! Flax, wool, silk—she worked with them all; and when they came from her hands, the cloth which she had made of them was so thin and soft and bright that men came from all parts of the world to see it. And they said that cloth so rare could not be made of flax, or wool, or silk, but that the warp was of rays of sunlight and the woof was of threads of gold.

Then as, day by day, the girl sat in the sun and spun, or sat in the shade and wove, she said: "In all the world there is no yarn as fine as mine, and in all the world there is no cloth so soft and smooth, nor silk so bright and rare."

"Who taught you to spin and weave so well?" someone asked.

"No one taught me," she said. "I learned how to do it as I sat in the sun and the shade; but no one showed me."

"But it may be that Athena, the queen of the air, taught you, and you did not know it."

"Athena, the queen of the air? Bah!" said Arachne. "How could she teach me? Can she spin such skeins of yarn as these? Can she weave goods like mine? I should like to see her try. I can teach her a thing or two."

She looked up and saw in the doorway

26

a tall woman wrapped in a long cloak. Her face was fair to see, but stern, oh, so stern! and her gray eyes were so sharp and bright that Arachne could not meet her gaze.

"Arachne," said the woman, "I am Athena, the queen of the air, and I have heard your boast. Do you still mean to say that I have not taught you how to spin and weave?"

"No one has taught me," said Arachne, "and I thank no one for what I know." And she stood up, straight and proud, by the side of her loom.

"And do you still think that you can spin and weave as well as I?" said Athena.

Arachne's cheeks grew pale, but she said: "Yes. I can weave as well as you."

"Then let me tell you what we will do," said Athena. "Three days from now we will both weave; you on your loom, and I on mine. We will ask all the world to come and see us; and great Jupiter, who sits in the clouds, shall be the judge. And if your work is best, then I will weave no more so long as the world shall last; but if my work is best, then you shall never use loom or spindle or distaff again. Do you agree to this?"

"I agree," said Arachne.

"It is well," said Athena. And she was gone.

When the time came for the contest in weaving, all the world was there to see it, and great Jupiter sat among the clouds and looked on.

Arachne had set up her loom in the shade of a mulberry tree, where butter-flies were flitting and grasshoppers chirping all through the livelong day. But Athena had set up her loom in the sky, where the breezes were blowing and the summer sun was shining; for she was queen of the air.

Then Arachne took her skeins of finest silk and began to weave. And she wove

a web of marvelous beauty, so thin and light that it would float in the air, and yet so strong that it could hold a lion in its meshes; and the threads of warp and woof were of many colors, so beautifully arranged and mingled one with another that all who saw were filled with delight.

"No wonder that the maiden boasted of her skill," said the people.

And Jupiter himself nodded.

Then Athena began to weave. And she took of the sunbeams that gilded the mountain top, and of the snowy fleece of the summer clouds, and of the blue ether of the summer sky, and of the bright green of the summer fields, and of the royal purple of the autumn woods, —and what do you suppose she wove?

The web which she wove in the sky was full of enchanting pictures of flowers and gardens, and of castles and towers, and of mountain heights, and of men and beasts, and of giants and dwarfs, and of the mighty beings who dwell in the clouds with Jupiter. And those who looked upon it were so filled with wonder and delight that they forgot all about the beautiful web which Arachne had woven. And Arachne herself was ashamed and afraid when she saw it; and she hid her face in her hands and wept.

"Oh, how can I live," she cried, "now that I must never again use loom or spindle or distaff?"

And she kept on, weeping and weeping and weeping, and saying, "How can I live?"

Then, when Athena saw that the poor maiden would never have any joy unless she were allowed to spin and weave, she took pity on her and said:

"I would free you from your bargain if I could, but that is a thing which no one can do. You must hold to your agreement never to touch loom or spindle again. And yet, since you will never be happy unless you can spin and weave, I will give you a new form so that you can carry on your work with neither spindle nor loom."

Then she touched Arachne with the tip of the spear which she sometimes carried; and the maid was changed at once into a nimble spider, which ran into a shady place in the grass and began merrily to spin and weave a beautiful web.

I have heard it said that all the spiders which have been in the world since then are the children of Arachne; but I doubt this. Yet, for all I know, Arachne still lives and spins and weaves; and the very next spider that you see may be Arachne herself.

The Wooden Horse of Troy

About four thousand years ago, a great city stood on the shores of the Aegean Sea, near the mouth of the Hellespont. That great city is entirely gone and people in our time have found relics of it by digging deep into the ground. And the name Hellespont, like the name of the city—Troy—is part of ancient legends and writings. The actual waterway still exists and is called The Dardanelles, which you can find on the map; but Troy is no more.

The walls of this great city were so high that no enemy could climb over them. And they were so thick and strong that no enemy could break through them or batter them down. And the gates of the city were well defended by its ablest and bravest soldiers.

Yet, proud and glorious though its history had been, and confident as the Trojans were that their city would live forever, Troy at last fell upon evil days. This was because Paris, a prince of Troy, stole Helen, the most beautiful woman in the world, away from her husband Menela′us, a king of the Greeks.

To avenge this great wrong, Menelaus called together all the heroes and great warriors of his country, among them the wise and courageous Ulysses. In two years of preparation, the Greeks assembled a tremendous army. They set sail for Troy in a fleet of a thousand ships. They landed on the beaches of the coastal plain before the city, and there the heroes made camp. The Trojans, too, were well prepared for battle, and their old king, Priam, gathered many brave fighters and chieftains about him. The Greeks defied the Trojans to engage in battle.

For nine long years the Greeks laid siege to Troy. Many fierce battles were fought outside the gates, and many were the noble heroes who were slain on both sides, for the chief warriors would engage in single combat as their armies stood by, and the old people and children of Troy would come out to watch the contests from the city's walls. On both sides, the warriors were equally valiant, so that the Trojans could not rid their beaches of the invaders, nor could the Greeks force their way into the city. Both sides suffered and struggled and the weary siege dragged on and on. Finally the Greeks began to despair of ever conquering Troy in outright battle.

"For nine years we have been laying siege to Troy. Our bravest comrades are dead. Still the city is not ours, and Menelaus has not been avenged for the theft of Helen," the Greek soldiers grumbled.

"To fight any longer is useless. Let us give up this hopeless struggle! Our wives and children will learn to forget their husbands and fathers. We long to see our homes once more," they whispered at night among themselves.

Agamem'non, chief of the Greek army, came to Ulysses. "Surely you, with your great cleverness and wisdom, can find a way to subdue the Trojans and save us," he urged.

After long consideration, Ulysses thought of a plan which the Greek chieftains decided to carry out.

Ulysses ordered his men, with the aid of a Greek sculptor, to build a colossal horse of wood. It was so huge and spacious that it could hold a hundred armed men within its hollow body. It was fitted with a door so skillfully concealed, that no one could possibly notice it. One night, under the cloak of darkness, Ulysses, Menelaus, Agamemnon, and others of the Greek heroes, fully armed, crept into the wooden figure. The door was shut upon them, and the rest of the Greek army broke up camp and set sail, leaving the enormous wooden horse on the beach.

The Greeks pretended they were abandoning the siege and were sailing for home. But once out of sight of Troy, they anchored behind a somewhat distant neighboring island, where they were well hidden from their enemies.

When the sun rose the next morning, there was not a Greek ship to be seen on the shore, and not a single tent on the plain. Only the huge wooden horse remained. Like wildfire, the exciting news spread throughout the city. "The Greeks have fled! The Greeks have fled! They have left at last!" cried the people. Hundreds of eager men, women, and children ran toward the city's walls, and gazed with happy, straining eyes toward the last straggling ship as it disappeared around the bend of the distant island.

Then the Trojans went wild with delight. The long years of siege were over, they thought. Everywhere there were embraces, kisses and joyous shouts of laughter.

The newly found peace and liberty were wonderful to a people long besieged. They surged forward to the city gates which were soon flung wide open and quickly the crowds streamed over the site of the deserted enemy camp.

Now they saw the great wooden figure of the horse, resting on a wide platform of wood. Slowly they drew near it. Gazing and wondering, they walked round and round the colossal image. Touching it curiously, as little children will a strange object, they marveled at its tremendous height and girth.

"Perhaps it is a peace offering from the Greeks to the goddess, Athene," said one Trojan to another. A few cautious ones continued to be afraid of the strange wooden creature, but others, becoming bolder, thought it should be carried back into the city as a war trophy.

At this, Laoco'ön, priest of Neptune, god of the sea, came forward. "Trojans," warned the old man, "put no trust in this horse. Have you so soon forgotten the sad years of siege and suffering? Whatever this is, I fear the Greeks, even when they bear gifts," he cried.

Suddenly a great uproar was heard, the priest's warning was drowned in the hubbub that followed. "It's a Greek! A Greek!" A poor wretched fellow wearing Greek garments, was dragged forward, his hands tightly bound. The

ragged, badly beaten captive had been found by some shepherds hiding among the reeds along the shore.

The captured Greek in reality was Sinon, a trusted friend of the crafty Ulysses, and he had been left behind by his companions to deceive the Trojans into taking the wooden horse within their gates.

"Do not kill me," he begged his Trojan captors. "It is true that I am a Greek, but I escaped from my cruel countrymen when they were about to sacrifice me to the gods."

Sinon was brought before the Trojan chiefs, who promised to spare his life if he would tell them the truth about the wooden horse. "The Wooden Horse," he told them, "was built by my countrymen as an offering to appease the goddess, Athene. It was made so large so that you would be unable to take it within your walls." "For," he went on lying craftily, "those who own this wooden horse will gain the favor and protection of Athene. If once the horse stands within the walls of Troy, the city can never be captured!"

At first the Trojans doubted the spy's story, but after a while Sinon convinced them that if they took the sacred object the Greeks had left behind them into their city, they would have happiness and prosperity forever.

Soon they devised a scheme for taking the huge figure into the city. Putting rollers under the wooden platform on which the horse stood, they fastened long ropes about its legs and began dragging the immense image across the plain toward the walls of Troy.

Again, out of the crowd, came the voice of the aged priest, Laocoön. "Men of Troy," he cried, "beware, beware of the treacherous Greeks. Cast the horse into the sea, or burn it, for it will bring you only misery and ruin!" As he spoke, he hurled his spear against the side of the horse, and it resounded with a hollow clang of armor.

While some people were again per-

31

suaded to doubt, and were standing about discussing the priest's warning, an event occurred before their very eyes which seemed an omen direct from the gods. Out of the sea rose two immense serpents. With rearing heads, their eyes and tongues flashing flames before them, they swiftly glided through the terrified, panic-stricken crowd and made straight for Laocoön and his two sons.

Before they could escape, the two serpents entwined their coiling, slimy bodies about the three unfortunate men, and crushed them to death. The monsters then slipped silently away again into the sea.

The Trojans, frozen with horror at this dreadful scene, were sure that this punishment had come to Laocoön for his words against the wooden horse. "He has been doomed for his sacrilege against this gift," they cried. "We will offer thanks to our protector Athene and bring the sacred image into our city."

Amid great acclaim, many willing hands dragged and pushed the great horse on its rolling platform over the plain, and little by little it approached the gate. When it was reached, they found that the opening was too narrow to admit the horse. So they pulled down part of the wall and made a breach to allow the wooden horse to be brought into the city. "Now," said the Trojans, "our city is safe from every enemy," and they draped garlands of flowers around the horse.

That night they had a great feast of wild merrymaking to celebrate the end of nine years of anxious watching and suffering. For the first time in nine years, no one was on guard on the walls of Troy. On that night all went to sleep, secure in the belief that the gods were on their side.

When the noises of the city had died down, and the streets were quiet and empty, Sinon, as had been planned, opened the cunningly concealed trap door in the side of the wooden horse. Out of it came the hero Ulysses, Menelaus, and the many other hidden Greeks. They set up a beacon light as a signal to the Greek army, for during the night the ships that had anchored behind the island had sailed back again toward Troy.

Soon, thousands of Greek soldiers swarmed through the streets of a proud city sunken in darkness and sleep. It was to the sounds of battle that the Trojans awoke from their dreams of peace. So the prophecy of Laocoön was fulfilled.

Priam, the king, and his noblest warriors were killed. Greek soldiers robbed the palaces and plundered the city of all its wealth and treasure. Helpless, the Trojans watched as their glorious city, set to the torch, burned to its very foundations.

Then the Greeks set sail for their own country taking with them many Trojan captives. With them they took also the fair Helen, for whose sake the dreadful war had been waged. At last she had awakened from the spell that the goddess Venus had cast upon her, and she was eager to behold again her native land.

But the glory of Troy was gone forever. Nothing but smouldering ruins and the everlasting renown of its valiant heroes remained of the wondrous, rich city on the shores of the Aegean.

33

The Golden Touch

By Nathaniel Hawthorne

O NCE upon a time there lived a very rich King whose name was Midas. He was fonder of gold than of anything else in the whole world. But he loved dearly, also, his little daughter who played so merrily around the palace.

The more Midas loved his daughter, the more he wished to be rich for her sake. This foolish man thought that the best thing he could do for his child was to leave her the biggest pile of glittering gold that had ever been heaped together since the world began. So he gave himself up to dreams of gold.

When his little daughter ran to him with her hands full of buttercups and dandelions, he used to say, "Ah, child, if only these flowers had been made of real gold, they would have been worth gathering!"

He had been fond of gardening once, but now if he looked at his roses at all, it was only to calculate how much the garden would be worth if each rose petal were a thin plate of gold. At length he could hardly bear to see or touch anything that was not made of gold.

He made it his custom, therefore, to spend a large part of each day in a dreary basement dungeon with his bags of golden coin, bars of gold, and vases and statues, all of gold. Sometimes he would carry a boxful of gold dust from the dark corner where it lay and he would look at the shiny heap by the light that came from a tiny window.

To Midas' greedy eyes there never seemed to be half enough. He was quite discontented. "How happy I would be," he said one day, "if only the whole world were made of gold and if it all belonged to me!"

Just then a shadow fell over his gold. Midas looked up with a start to see a young man with a cheerful rosy face standing in the narrow strip of sunlight that came through the window. Midas was sure he had carefully locked the door before he opened his treasures, so he knew his visitor must be other than mortal to get into the room.

The stranger seemed so friendly and pleasant that Midas felt he must surely have come to do him a favor.

"You are a rich man, friend Midas," said the visitor. "I doubt if any other room in this whole world has as much gold in it as this."

"I've done fairly well," said Midas in a discontented voice, "but I wish it were much more. No one lifetime is long enough, though. If only I could live for a thousand years, then I might become really rich."

"What?" exclaimed the stranger. "What would satisfy you?"

Midas looked at his visitor for a moment, and then said, "I am tired of having to take so much trouble to get money. I wish everything I touched might turn to gold."

The stranger smiled, and his smile seemed to fill the room like a flood of sunshine.

"The golden touch!" he exclaimed. "But are you quite sure, Midas, that this would make you happy?"

"Quite sure," said Midas. "I ask nothing more to make me perfectly happy."

"Be it as you wish, then," said the stranger. "From tomorrow at sunrise you will have your desire—everything you touch will be changed to gold."

The figure of the stranger grew brighter and brighter so that Midas had to close his eyes. When he opened them again, he saw only one yellow sunbeam in the room, and all around him the glittering precious gold he had spent his life in hoarding up.

Midas could scarcely sleep that night. How he longed for the dawn! As soon as the night began to fade, he reached out eagerly and touched a chair by his bed. When he saw that nothing happened, he nearly cried. The chair remained just as it was. The stranger had failed him, thought Midas. Or had the whole thing been only a dream? His spirits sank.

But just then the sun rose. Its first rays fell on the brocaded cover of his bed which gleamed in the golden rays.

Midas sat up and looked more closely. To his delight he saw that the bedcovers on which his hands rested had become a cloth of purest and brightest gold. The golden touch had come to King Midas with the first sunbeam!

Midas leaped up in a frenzy of joy and ran about touching everything. He caught hold of the bedpost. Instantly it became a golden pillar. He pulled aside the window-curtain and the tassel he pulled it by became a heavy mass of gold! He picked up a book from a table, and at his first touch it became a bundle of gold pages with nothing to read on them. His clothes became magnificent robes of gold cloth.

Midas had to admit that all these golden things were somewhat heavy. Nevertheless he was delighted with his good fortune. He took his spectacles from his pocket and put them on, so that he might see more distinctly what he was about. To his surprise he could not see through the spectacles at all. The clear glass had turned to gold, and though they were worth a great deal of money, they were useless as spectacles.

Midas found this inconvenient, but surely, he thought, the golden touch was worth the sacrifice of a pair of spectacles. His spirits rose as he went down the palace stairs and saw the railing become a bar of shining gold as he rested his hand on it!

The garden was very lovely. In the old days Midas had been fond of flowers and had spared no effort in getting rare trees and plants to make his garden even more beautiful. But since he had become so fond of gold, he had lost all pleasure in his garden. He did not even see how lovely it was this morning.

He was thinking only of the wonderful gift the stranger had granted him and he was sure he could make the garden of far more value than it had ever been. So he went from bush to bush, touching the flowers. And the beautiful colors faded from them and the petals became stiff glittering flakes of gold—gold glistening so brightly in the sunshine that Midas had to shade his eyes from the glare of them.

However, he was quite satisfied with the morning's work and went back to the palace feeling very happy and with a hearty appetite for breakfast.

Just then he heard his little daughter sobbing as if her heart would break. "Look, Father," she said as she came running toward him holding out one of the golden roses. "All the beautiful blossoms that smelled so sweetly are spoiled. They have grown stiff and yellow and ugly, and they have no fragrance at all. What can be the matter?" And she cried bitterly.

Midas was ashamed to confess that he had caused her unhappiness, so he said, "Pooh, my dear, don't cry about it. Sit down and eat your bread and milk."

They sat down at the table. The King was very hungry and poured himself a cup of coffee. But the moment he lifted the cup to his lips the coffee turned to molten gold and then hardened into a solid lump.

"Oh, dear me!" exclaimed the King, rather surprised.

"What's the matter, Father?" asked his little daughter.

"Nothing, child, nothing," Midas answered. "Eat your bread and milk."

Then he looked at the nice little fish on his plate, and gently touched its tail with his finger. It was immediately changed into gold.

He took one of the smoking hot cakes and had scarcely broken it when the white flour turned into golden crumbs that gleamed like grains of hard sea-sand.

"I do not see how I am going to get any breakfast," he exclaimed peevishly. And he looked with envy at his little daughter who had dried her tears and was eating her bread and milk eagerly. "I wonder whether it will be the same

at dinner," he thought, "and if so, how am I going to live if all my food is to be turned to gold?"

Midas began to grow very anxious and to think about many things that he had never thought of before. Here was the richest breakfast that could be set before a King, and yet there was nothing he could eat! The poorest laborer sitting down to a crust of bread and cup of water was far better off than King Midas, whose delicate food was really worth its weight in gold.

He began to wonder whether, after all, gold was the only good thing in the world. Yet the glitter of the yellow metal so fascinated him that he would still have refused to give up the golden touch just for some breakfast. But he was so hungry that he could not help groaning.

His little daughter had noticed that her father ate nothing, and at first she sat still gazing at him and trying to find out what it was that troubled him. Then she got down from her chair, and ran with outstretched arms to her father.

Midas bent down and kissed her. As he did so, he suddenly knew that his child's love was a thousand times more precious than all the gold he had gained since the stranger had visited him. "My precious, precious little girl!" he cried.

But there was no answer. Alas, what had he done? The moment his lips had touched his child's forehead, her sweet rosy face, so full of love and happiness, hardened and became a glittering yellow. Her beautiful brown curls hung like golden wires around her head. And her soft tender little figure grew stiff in his arms.

It had always been a favorite saying of Midas that his little girl was worth her weight in gold to him.

Midas began to wring his hands. He wished he were the poorest man in the world if the loss of all his wealth could bring back the flush of life and color to his dear child's face.

In his grief and despair, he suddenly saw a stranger standing near the door.

"Well, friend Midas," said the stranger, "pray how are you enjoying your new power?"

Midas shook his head. "I am very miserable," he replied.

"Very miserable, are you?" exclaimed the stranger. "How does that happen?"

"Gold is not everything," answered Midas, "and I have lost all that my heart really cared for."

"Ah! So you have made some discoveries since yesterday? Tell me truly, which of these things do you really think is worth more—a cup of clear cold water and a crust of bread, or the power of turning everything you touch into gold? Your own little girl, alive and loving, or the statue of solid gold your child has now become?"

"O my little daughter, my dear child!" sobbed Midas, wringing his hands. "I would not have given that small dimple in her chin for the power of changing this whole big earth into gold. And I would give all I own for a

37

cup of cold water and a crust of bread."

"You are wiser than you were, King Midas," said the stranger. "Tell me, now, do you really wish to get rid of your fatal gift?"

"Oh, yes!" exclaimed Midas. "It is hateful to me."

"Go, then," said the stranger, "and plunge into the river that flows at the bottom of your garden. Take a pitcher of that same water and sprinkle it over anything you wish to change back again from gold to its former substance."

King Midas bowed low. When he lifted his head the stranger was gone.

Midas lost no time in snatching up a big earthen pitcher. Immediately it turned to gold. Then he ran toward the river and plunged in without waiting even to take off his royal shoes.

"How delightful!" he said, as he came out with his hair dripping.

Then he dipped the pitcher into the water. How happy he was to see it change from gold into the same earthen pitcher it had been five minutes ago, before he had touched it!

Now he also began to feel a change within himself. A cold heavy weight seemed to have lifted from his heart, and he felt light and happy and human once more. Maybe his heart had been changing into gold, too, and had now softened again and become gentle.

Midas saw a violet growing by the river bank. He touched it and was overjoyed to find that the delicate flower kept its purple hue instead of turning to solid gold.

He hurried back to the palace with his pitcher of water and the first thing he did was to sprinkle it by handfuls over the stiff golden figure of his daughter. At once the rosy color came back to her cheeks and she began to sneeze and cough. And how amazed the little girl was to find herself dripping wet and her father throwing water over her!

You see, she did not know she had been a little golden statue, for she could not remember anything from the moment when she ran with outstretched arms to comfort her poor father.

The King then led his little girl into the garden where he sprinkled all the rest of the water over the rose-bushes and the grass and the trees. In a moment they were blooming as freshly as ever, and the air was filled with the scent of the flowers.

There were only two things left which kept on reminding King Midas of the stranger's fatal gift. One was that from then on the sands at the bottom of the river always sparkled like gold. The other was that his daughter's curls were no longer brown. They had a golden tinge that had not been there before the King had received the fatal gift of the golden touch, and his kiss had changed the precious curls into gold. These two things served to remind King Midas, as long as he lived, that nothing could be worse than the curse of gold.

—*Adapted from* A WONDER BOOK

38

The Wanderings of Odysseus

From the Greek of Homer

"Sing us the song of the hero, steadfast, skillful and strong,
Taker of Troy's high towers, who wandered for ten years long
Over the perilous waters, through unknown cities of men,
Leading his comrades onward, seeking his home again.
Sing us the song of the Wanderer, sing us the wonderful song!"

THE STORY of Odysseus, whom the Romans called Ulysses, is one of the greatest stories of the world. It tells about the craftiest of the warriors who commanded the Greeks at the Siege of Troy. Of all the chieftains he had farthest to travel to the war, and his return was the most adventurous. Well may we say, as we read this version, told as far as possible in the words of Homer himself, what King Alcinous said when he heard it from the hero's own lips, "I could abide even till the bright dawn, so long as thou couldst endure to rehearse me these woes of thine and your wondrous deeds."

It was the wily Odysseus who devised the plan whereby the Trojans permitted the wooden horse, full of Greek soldiers, to enter their city and capture it. The Greeks had brought down the wrath of the gods upon their heads by their cruelty after the victory, and Odysseus, one of the last to set sail, felt the full force of their wrath. Twelve ships he had as he started for home, each carrying fifty men, only half the number that had sailed with him from far-off Ithaca.

While he was away the nobles of Ithaca had filled his house with disorder and violence, wooing his wife, the fair Penelope, in marriage. His son Telemachus grew to manhood, and decided to sail away to find his father and save his home and mother.

In the meantime the goddess Athene had won the consent of heaven to the rescue of Odysseus, the hero. Odysseus had been made prisoner on the island of a beautiful nymph named Calypso. The messenger of the gods, Hermes, was sent to order her to release him.

HOW ODYSSEUS CAME TO THE LAND OF THE SEA-KINGS

So Hermes bound his golden sandals to his feet and leaped down from the sky to the sea and flew over the waves like a cormorant to the far-off island. He went up to the lofty cave and found

Calypso alone within, singing sweetly as she wove at her loom with a golden shuttle.

Hermes entered and Calypso offered him a shining seat and gave him ambrosia and nectar, the food of the Immortals, saying, "Tell me your errand, Hermes, for it is long since you have fared this way." So he told her how Zeus had taken pity on the wandering Odysseus, and now bade her send him on his way. The nymph trembled when she heard this message, and said, "You are jealous of my friend and guest. I saved him when he was left alone clinging to the wreck of his ship. But if it is the will of Zeus I will not hinder his departure."

So Hermes departed, and Calypso went to seek Odysseus.

"Unhappy man," she said, "do not sorrow any more. Come, build a raft and make it strong enough for the sea, and I will give you bread and wine and water for your journey, and a fair wind to follow you and bring you safely home. Such is the will of the gods who are wiser and stronger than I."

They went back to the cave and feasted and talked until dusk.

At last Calypso said, "Odysseus, if you knew what suffering you have in store for you before you see the wife you love, you would remain with me. Am I less beautiful or less noble than your wife?"

And he replied, "Penelope cannot compare with you in form or stature.

She also will grow old and die, yet day and night all my desires end in her sight, and I would endure another shipwreck and untold sorrows to be at home again. I can bear these as I have borne the rest."

When morning came, Calypso dressed herself in a shining robe, lightly woven and graceful, and fastened about her waist a golden girdle. She gave Odysseus a bronze ax and hatchet, and he felled a score of trees, made timbers straight and smooth, and joined them together to build a ship. He stocked the ship well with food and water and wine that Calypso gave him and at length set sail with a joyful heart.

For seventeen days and nights he did not sleep, but steered straight on, watching the Pleiades and keeping on his left hand those great stars that men call the Bear. And on the eighteenth day he sighted the wooded hills of the Sea-King's land, like a shadow upon the misty waters.

But Poseidon, god of the Ocean, saw Odysseus from afar and he was angry. "So!" he cried, "the gods have changed their plans while I was away from Olympus!" Then, grasping his trident, he gathered the clouds, and roused the winds and brought down a storm from heaven.

A huge wave fell upon Odysseus and swept him from his raft, and he was overwhelmed by the surging waters. His garments weighed him down, but at last he rose, clutched at his raft and raised himself onto it.

He would have perished on the raft had not one of the sea nymphs, Ino, the slender-footed, taken pity on him in his need. She rose from the depths in the form of a sea-bird and sat upon the raft. "Fasten my magic veil beneath your breast," she cried, "and swim to land. As soon as you have touched the shore loose it, throw it far back into the sea, and as you throw it, turn away."

Odysseus stripped off the garments which Calypso had given him, wound the sea-nymph's veil around his breast, and plunged into the sea. And the sea-bird dived past his sight into the fathomless abyss of ocean. When the bright dawn was in the sky the wind fell, and from the top of a rising wave he saw the coast. The sight made him as glad as children are who see their father well again after a long sickness. But when he was near enough to hear the thunder of the breakers and see that there was no harbor, only cliffs and jagged reefs, his heart sank within him. He saved himself in the end by swimming along the shore outside the breakers until he found the mouth of a river, free from rocks and sheltered from the wind.

He fell senseless on the shore of the Sea-King's land, and there for a time he lay in a swoon. When at last he came to himself, he remembered the magic veil and threw it back into the water. A great wave came and bore it out to sea where Ino rose and caught it in her white hands. Odysseus sank down among the rushes by the river-bank and kissed the kindly earth. Dead weary he was. He felt that the sea had soaked through his heart.

HOW ODYSSEUS MET THE PRINCESS NAUSICAA

Meanwhile the goddess Athena went up to the City of the Sea-Kings unto the palace of their ruler, King Alcinous, and into a beautiful chamber where his daughter, the young Princess Nausicaa lay asleep. She was fair as the Immortals. On each side of the threshold slept two maidens, lovely as the Graces. The glittering doors were shut. The goddess appeared to Nausicaa in a dream in the likeness of one of her dear companions.

"How heedless you are, Nausicaa!" said the goddess. "Your marriage day is coming soon, when you ought to have beautiful garments for yourself and for your maidens. Let us take the clothes down to the river and wash them early tomorrow morning, for the princes among your people are already suitors for your hand. Ask the king, your father, to give you a pair of mules and a cart, for the river is a long way off."

Then Athena went back to Olympus, home of the gods. There, so men say, no winds blow, no rain falls and snow is never seen. The sky is calm and cloudless and all the air is full of light.

When the young dawn appeared on her glorious throne in the sky the Princess awoke, full of wonder at her dream.

She greeted her mother, who was sitting by the hearth spinning the sea-blue yarn, and she met her father at the door on his way to the council of his lords. Nausicaa ran up to him and said, "Father, there is much fine linen lying soiled in the house. You must have clean robes to wear when you sit at the council among the chiefs, and your fine sons always want fresh linen for the dances. I must think of it all. Will you not lend me a pair of mules and a cart, and I will take it all down to the river and wash it." She was too shy to speak about her marriage, but her father understood, and answered, "You may have the mules, my child, and anything you wish."

So the Princess filled the cart with the garments, and her mother gave her figs and dates, a goatskin full of wine, and olive-oil in a golden flask. Then Nausicaa climbed upon the cart with her maidens. She took the whip and the reins in her hands and they clattered off through the city.

When they came to the flowing river they unyoked the mules and let them feed on the sweet clover. They lifted out the clothes and trod them in the dark water. When they had finished they spread them out on the beach to dry in the sun. Then they bathed and anointed themselves and took their meal beside the river, and afterward they threw aside their veils and played ball, white-armed Nausicaa beginning the pastime with a song.

At last it was time to go home and they harnessed the mules and folded up the clothes. Just then the Princess threw the ball to one of the girls, but it missed her and dropped into the river. They all cried out as they saw it fall. The cry roused Odysseus from his sleep and he sprang up in wonder.

"Where am I?" he asked himself. "Are these the voices of Immortals or of nymphs of the meadows?"

When he came out from his shelter, all rough and naked as he was and caked with brine, they were terrified. They ran away to the end of the curving beach. Only the daughter of Alcinous stood where she was and waited for him without fear. Odysseus considered whether he should fall at the feet of the lovely maiden in supplication, or stand apart. At length he spoke gently to her. "Maiden," he said, "surely you must be Artemis the Huntress, one of the Immortals. Whoever you are, I need your help. I have been wandering over the dark sea for twenty days and nights, tossed to and fro by wave and storm. In kindness, in mercy, show me the way to the city, and give me clothing—perhaps some wrapping that you have used for your linen.

Nausicaa answered the stranger, "You seem to me brave and wise, and since you have asked me for help, you shall have everything you need. This is the land of the Sea-Kings and I am the daughter of their ruler, the great-hearted Alcinous." She called to her maidens, "Come back to me, girls. This man is no enemy, but a shipwrecked wanderer, and we must treat him kindly."

So they took Odysseus to a sheltered place and gave him clothing and the soft olive-oil in the golden flask. And he washed the sea-brine from his limbs and anointed himself and put on the garments. His long curls fell clustering about his shoulders, and the goddess Athena gave him grace and stateliness.

Then the Princess whispered to her maidens, "At first I thought him ill-favored, but now he looks like one of the Immortals. Ah, that such a hero would stay with us, and be my husband. Go now, give him food and drink."

As Nausicaa led the way to the city, she spoke prudently to Odysseus. "As we go through the meadows, follow close behind me, but when we draw near the city, do not come near me, lest the insolent among our folk should say, 'Who is the tall king-like stranger with Nausicaa? Has she found a foreign husband for herself and scorned the noble sea-kings who make suit to her?'"

Odysseus obeyed. He entered the palace alone, and was filled with wonder, for the whole house shone, the walls being of bronze, and doors of gold. Inside were rows of seats spread with fine coverlets, where the sea-kings sat feasting. Before the gates were pear trees and pomegranates and olives and bright apples and sweet figs. There were vineyards and flower-beds on either hand, always in blossom.

Odysseus crossed the threshold and walked through the hall to the place where the King and Queen were sitting. He knelt down on the hearth.

He remained kneeling like a suppliant until at last one old lord, wiser and readier than the rest, spoke out, "Surely it is not seemly, O Alcinous, that a guest should sit among the ashes. Lead him, I pray you, to a seat of honor and let him have food and drink."

So Alcinous took Odysseus by the hand and set him by his side in his own son's place, and the servants washed his hands and spread the table with good things.

Then said Odysseus, "I am no Immortal, Alcinous, but the most afflicted of mortal men, and I can tell a long tale of the sufferings that the gods have given me to bear. But now let me forget my troubles and in the morning make haste to send me on my way, for all I now desire is to see my people and my home again."

"Sir," replied Alcinous, "when the morrow comes, however far you may wish to go, you may have men who will row you quickly over the sea, for we have the best sailors and the finest ships in the world."

HOW ODYSSEUS ESCAPED FROM THE CYCLOPS

The next day Odysseus contended with the sea-kings in their games, and his skill and swiftness were the amazement of them all. And when evening was come, he came again to the hall

where the kings were sitting, and Alcinous said, "Hide your secret no longer. Tell us your name and your country."

Then Odysseus answered, "I am that Odysseus whose fame has gone through the world. My home is the Isle of Ithaca, a rugged land but the cradle of heroes, and now I will tell you the tale of my wanderings and of my sufferings on my way home from Troy.

"From the first, I and my companions had trouble by sea and land. As soon as

44

we had rounded the Cape of Malea, the north winds smote us. Nine days we drifted before the gale, but on the tenth, we came to the land of the lotus-eaters who live on flowers. The lotus-eaters were kind to us and gave us lotus to taste. It is sweet as honey, but all who take it forget their country and long to stay there and to eat it forever. I forced my men back to the ships, and we put to sea.

"Then we sailed on sadly till we came to the land of the Cyclops. They are a savage and lawless race who dwell alone in caves, and each one cares for no one else. I led my crew up to the shore of their island to see what the Cyclops were like. We came to a high cave. It was there that one of the Cyclops penned his flocks at night. A strange monster he was. He had only one eye in the middle of his forehead. He looked more like a mountain peak than a man.

"Twelve of us went up to the giant's cave. The Cyclops was still away at the pasture. Within were sheepfolds crowded with lambs and kids, and piles of wicker baskets loaded with cheeses. So we lit a fire, ate some of the cheeses, and waited.

"At nightfall the Cyclops came home with his herds, carrying a bundle of fagots. He flung the wood down on the ground and drove his sheep into the cave. Then he lifted an enormous stone, so heavy that twenty horses could not move it, and set it against the mouth of the cave. When he had lit his fire, he caught sight of us and cried out. We told

him that we were Greeks homeward bound, and we besought him to treat us as guests. But the giant seized two of my comrades, dashed their heads on the ground, and tore them limb from limb. He devoured them as if they were wild beasts. Then he lay down at full length among his flocks and fell asleep. In my rage I thought to draw my sword and strike him dead, but I remembered that if I killed him none of us could roll away the enormous stone.

"The next morning the giant seized two more of us for a meal, and then lifting away the stone and putting it back, he went off to the mountains, whistling to his herd.

"I was left to scheme for our revenge. The giant had placed his great club in the cave to dry. It was of olive-wood. I cut off a fathom's length and we sharpened it to a point and hid it from sight.

"In the evening he came back with his flocks, and after he had milked the ewes he seized two more of us for his meal. Then I filled a wooden bowl with the wine which we had brought, and gave it to the Cyclops, pleading for mercy. Three times I poured it out, and when the wine began to cloud his thoughts I said to him softly, 'Cyclops, now I will tell you my name and you must give me the gift you promised. Noman is my name.'

"But the Cyclops only answered, 'I will eat Noman last, that shall be his gift.'

"With that he rolled over on his back

and lay there fast asleep. Then I thrust the stake into the fire and four of my men took hold of it with me and we drove it into the monster's eye. The giant gave a terrible cry, so that the whole cliff rang, and he pulled down the stone from the door and shouted to the other Cyclops who lived near him on the windy mountain-peaks.

" 'What ails you, Polyphemus?' they replied. 'Has some one driven off your flocks and tried to murder you?'

"And the Cyclops answered, 'Oh, my friends, Noman is murdering me.'

"Then they replied, 'If no man has hurt you, why do you call for help? Pray to our father, Poseidon.'

"While the giant was groping his way around, moaning in his agony, I considered how we might escape. The rams were big and strong and their fleece was thick with wool. I bound them together in threes, and under each middle ram I fastened a man so that he was protected on either side. When the morning broke and it was time for the sheep to go out to the pasture, their master felt along the backs of the rams as they passed before him, but he had not the wit to suspect that men might be bound underneath.

"So we came out of the cave. We hastened to our ships, and we took our places on the benches and struck our oars into the gray sea-foam. I shouted to the Cyclops as we swept out of earshot, and his anger burst forth. He tore off the top of a mountain and hurled it down at us. Luckily it struck the sea too far off to sink us.

" 'Cyclops, if anyone asks who blinded you, tell them it was not Noman, but Odysseus, who dwells in Ithaca.' Then Polyphemus groaned and said, 'Alas, the old oracle is fulfilled. A prophet told me long ago that Odysseus would take my sight, but I had always looked for a great and valiant hero and now it is a puny nobody who has deceived me.' Then the giant called upon Poseidon, the blue-haired god of the sea.

HOW ODYSSEUS WAS HELD IN THE HOUSE OF CIRCE

"At last we came to the island where lives Circe, the bright-haired daughter of the sun.

"I went up to the top of a craggy hill, and there I saw the whole island beneath me, and in the midst of the forest below I could see smoke coming up from the house of Circe.

"I divided my company into two bands, and we cast lots, and the lot fell on Eurylochus, the captain of the second band.

"While I and my company waited, Eurylochus and his company went up to the house of Circe. They could hear her singing with a sweet voice inside, and they could see her as she worked at a wonderful loom, weaving a texture subtle and glorious, worthy of an immortal goddess.

"So they called out to her and she

came and opened the shining doors and bade them welcome, and in their folly they obeyed. Only Eurylochus stayed outside, for he feared some mischief.

"She led them in and seated them on couches, and prepared for them a drink of wine and yellow honey, but into it she mixed deadly drugs. Now when they had drunk, suddenly she struck them with a wand and they were changed into swine. She shut them up in a sty, and threw before them beech-nuts and acorns, fit food for swine.

"Eurylochus hastened back to me, perplexed and affrighted. He could tell me only of a palace and a woman singing at her work, and gates guarded by lions. His companions had vanished. Then I slung my bow over my shoulder and took my silver-studded sword and ordered him to lead the way, although he fell on his knees and entreated me not to go.

"So I went up into the enchanted valley, and as I drew near the house of the sorceress, the god Hermes met me and gave me warning. He said, 'Take this magic herb in your hand.' It was a small plant with a black root and a milk-white flower, and the gods call it Moly. It is sovereign against enchantments. And Hermes continued, 'When she has mixed you a drink, she will afterward strike you with her wand. Then you must draw your sword and rush upon her as though to kill her, but before you go any farther make her swear a solemn oath by the blessed gods that she will

do you no harm.' So I went into the house of Circe and I did as the god had directed me and I made Circe swear me an oath as I commanded.

"Now in the house of Circe there are four maid-servants. They are the daughters of the sylvan springs and sacred woods and of the lonely rivers that flow toward the sea. They prepared for me a feast and a bath to take away the weariness from my limbs and the hurt from my heart. But I had no taste for food and my thoughts were far away. So when I had explained my sorrow to Circe, she took her wand and went through the hall, opened the doors of the sty, and drove out those creatures that looked like swine. She went among them and sprinkled them with another charm and they became men again, even comelier than before.

"Then I brought all my companions up to the house of Circe, although they were afraid, and we sat together at the banquet. So there we lived together in all comfort until a whole year had passed. But at the year's end, my comrades called me apart, and bade me remember our native country.

"The sorceress would fain have detained me in the island as her husband, making new delights for me every day. Also she told me of the terrors that were before me, for I must visit the House of Death and there seek counsel.

"When I heard this, my heart sank, and I no longer wished to look upon the sun. 'Who will be my pilot, Circe, upon such a voyage? No ship has ever touched that shore.'

"She told me that I would need no pilot, and directed me fully upon my way.

"So we talked through the night, and when morning came I aroused my comrades and said to them, 'Awake! and let us go upon our journey.' "

HOW ODYSSEUS PASSED BY THE SIRENS AND SCYLLA

Odysseus told Alcinous how he had gone down to the House of Death, and what had been revealed to him there as to his future, and how he had said farewell in that shadowy home to the old heroes, his companions in the war against Troy. He returned to Circe, who had told him how to escape from the Sirens he would meet.

"Thus," said Odysseus to the King, "the night passed away, and when morning came I went down to my ship, and Circe of the braided tresses sent a friendly breeze to help us. So we sat at ease while the ship sped on, and then I said to my crew, 'Comrades, you must hear of the counsel which Circe gave me. She bade us beware of the Sirens and their magic song and the flowering meadow where they sit. I, alone, may listen, but you must bind me to the mast so that I cannot move. And if I beg you to set me free, bind me tighter than before.'

"So the good ship ran on to the Sirens' Island, and as the wind had dropped, my crew hauled down the sails and took out the oars. I made plugs of wax and stopped their ears with them, and they bound me hand and foot to the mast.

"When we came within earshot of the shore, the Sirens caught sight of our ship and began their magic song.

"I heard the wonderful music and my heart was entranced, and I made frantic signs to my comrades to set me free. But they, of course unhearing, remained bent to their oars. Two of them even came and bound me tighter than before. And still the Sirens sang, but so we drifted by, and when we had at last left the Sirens behind us and could no longer hear their song, then my comrades took out the wax from their ears and unbound me.

"Hardly were we clear of the island than we saw breakers ahead of us and heard the thunder of the surf. I had not told the men of the perils by Scylla, for I knew that there was no means by which we could fight her. Circe had counseled me that I must not arm myself against Scylla. I put on my harness and stood at the prow to get a first glimpse of the monster. But I could see nothing, though I strained my eyes, searching the face of the shadowy cliff.

"While we looked and trembled as the whirlpool seethed in its center, and the spray dashed high over the cliff, suddenly Scylla darted down and snatched six of my crew, and devoured them at the very mouth of her den, while they

cried to us and stretched out their hands in vain. That was the saddest sight I saw in all my wanderings over the sea.

"But the rest of us sailed away and left the strait behind. Then we came in sight of the Sun-God's beautiful island. Even while we were still some way off I could hear the lowing of his oxen and the bleating of his flocks, and I remembered the warning that Circe had given me, that we ought not to land lest we be tempted to kill the oxen of the Sun-God.

"But my men were weary in spirit, and Eurylochus said angrily, 'Have you no pity, Odysseus? We are wearied to death and yet you would drive us out again to wander all night over the dim waters. Darkness is here already, and surely we may as well sleep on the beach tonight, and tomorrow we can set sail once more.'

"It would have been impossible to land anyway, because after midnight a storm arose, and it blew without ceasing a whole month long. And by that time we had eaten everything in the ship. We tried to catch fish and birds, and almost died of hunger. Then one day, when I was apart from my comrades, Eurylochus gave evil counsel to them. 'Come,' he said, 'let us choose the best of the herd and sacrifice to the gods. When we reach home again we can build a stately temple and make votive offerings to the Sun-God.'

"Thus he persuaded them, and they killed the oxen and made a burnt offering. But even as the fire was burning, the flesh moved and groans were heard coming from the altar.

"On the seventh day the storm abated and we hoisted our white sails again and stood out to sea. As soon as we were out of sight of land a black cloud gathered overhead, darkening the waves. Thunder pealed on every side, lightning struck the boat and sent her reeling, and my men were washed overboard. I lashed myself to the mast and drifted before the gale. Nine days I drifted thus, and on the tenth I came to the island where lives Calypso, the bright-haired goddess, who took me to her home and cared for me. But I told you of that yesterday, and what need is there to speak of it again? I have no love for a twice-told tale."

ODYSSEUS REACHES ITHACA

So they learned from the mouth of the hero the sorrows that this much-suffering man had borne, and his telling made the life that flowed around them seem very sweet.

Then Odysseus said, "Alcinous, fare you well, and may Heaven grant you a happy home and every blessing." And to Queen Arete he said, "May I but find my wife safe and sound at home. And, lady, may you live happily with your husband and children and this people until old age comes to you and death, which must come to all."

And as he went out of the hall, Nausicaa stood in her beauty beside the door, and she looked at him with sadness and said, "Farewell, stranger. Remember me sometimes, even when you are at home again in your own native land."

And Odysseus said, "Princess, I will think of you there, and you will always be like a goddess to me, for it was you who gave me back my life. May the gods give you a princely husband and from you two spring blessings to this state."

Then Odysseus went down to his ship, and the rowers took their places on the benches. The wonderful ship leaped forward, and the great dark waves roared round the stern. As she sped on, the man who had suffered so much and was as wise as the gods, lay peacefully asleep, and forgot his sufferings.

When the bright star rose that tells

of the approach of day, the ship drew near the Island of Ithaca. There is a harbor there between two steep headlands. At the head of it there is an olive-tree, and beneath it a shadowy cave where the water-fairies come and tend their bees and weave their sea-blue garments on hanging looms. There the mariners landed him gently, not willing to wake him.

When the godlike Odysseus awoke, he did not know that he had reached his native land. The goddess Athena met him and told him that this was his own country. And she said that she would turn him into a wretched old beggar, and that he must stay with Eumanes, who tended his swine, until his son Telemachus returned from Sparta.

So Athena gave him the shape of a beggar man, and she put on him filthy rags and gave him a staff. She hung a wallet from his shoulders.

She departed, and Odysseus went to the house of Eumanes, the swine-herd. When Odysseus came near, the dogs ran upon him and would have harmed him had not the swineherd run forth and driven them away. He brought the old man in and gave him a seat with a great goatskin over it.

And Odysseus said, "Zeus will repay thee for this kindness."

Eumanes told him how the suitors of the queen were devouring the substance of Odysseus. The false beggar asked him about the King, but Eumanes said, "We hear nothing true about him. Whenever any vagabond comes to this island our Queen must see him and ask him many things, weeping all the while. Odysseus, I know, is dead, and either the fowls of the air or the fishes of the sea have devoured him."

When Eumanes asked the stranger who he was, Odysseus invented a long story of marvelous adventure.

In the meantime, Athena had gone to Telemachus in Sparta and warned him to return to his home immediately, because the suitors were devouring his father's wealth, and because Penelope, his mother, was being much pressed to marry one of them.

So Telemachus returned to Ithaca and came to the dwelling of the swineherd. And Odysseus heard the steps of a man, and since the dogs barked not, he said, "Here comes some comrade or friend."

"Who is this stranger?" asked Telemachus of the swineherd.

Then the swineherd told him the story as he had heard it, and said, "I will give the stranger food and clothing, but let us not permit him to go among the suitors, so violent are they."

When Eumanes had gone away, Athena came to Odysseus in secret and told him to hide nothing from his son. "Plan with him how he may slay the suitors, for, behold I am with you."

So she made his garments white and fair again and his body lusty and strong, and when Telemachus looked upon him, he thought he was a god. Odysseus answered, "I am no god, but only thy father whom thou hast so long desired to see." They threw their arms about each other and both wept together for a while. Then Odysseus asked him how many suitors there were and whether they two could fight them alone.

"I know," said Telemachus, "that thou art a great warrior and a wise one, but this we cannot do, for these men are over a hundred in number."

Then said Odysseus, "Go home and mingle with the suitors, and I will come as a beggar. Protect me not, even if they treat me shamefully. Only heed this: take all the arms from the house and hide them, but keep two swords and two spears and two shields, for thee and for me. Only let no one know of my coming back, not even the Queen herself."

ODYSSEUS COMES HOME

The next day Telemachus went to the palace and greeted the old nurse Euryclea and his mother, Penelope, but to them he told nothing of what had happened.

Odysseus and Eumanes followed him, and at the door of the Court lay the old dog Argus, whom in the old days Odysseus had reared with his own hand. When he was strong, men used him in the chase, but now he lay on a dunghill, and vermin swarmed upon him. He knew his master, and though he could not come near him, he wagged his tail and dropped his ears. And as Odysseus spoke a word of pity, wiping away a tear, the old dog Argus died. Twenty years he had waited to see his master once more.

After this Odysseus and Eumanes entered the hall and Telemachus, when he saw them, took bread and meat and commanded that they be carried to the beggar. He told his father to go around among the suitors, asking alms. So Odysseus went stretching out his hand as though he were accustomed to begging, and some gave, having compassion upon him, but most of them laughed him to scorn, and of these Antinous was the most shameless.

That evening the suitors having departed to their dwellings, Telemachus took the arms from the hall. And when the Queen with her maidens came into the hall to make it ready for the morrow Penelope asked the beggar about his family and his country. The false beggar comforted her, saying that Odysseus was still in the land of the Thespatians. He had lost his ship, yet he would speedily return.

Penelope bade her servants make ready a bed for the stranger, and prepare a bath for him. "For," said she, "perchance such even now are the feet and hands of Odysseus himself, for men quickly age with evil fortune."

When the bath had been prepared for his feet, Odysseus sat by the fire as far in the shadow as he might, lest Euryclea, his old nurse, should see a scar that was upon his leg and know him thereby. By this scar at length she did discover that it was Odysseus himself and she cried out, "Odysseus! O my child, to think that I knew thee not!"

And she looked toward the Queen as meaning to tell her. But Odysseus laid his hand on her throat. "Wouldst thou kill me? None must know till I am ready to take vengeance."

After this Penelope slept, but Odysseus watched in the hall.

The next day Penelope went to fetch the great bow of Odysseus from its peg. Sitting down, she laid it on her knees and wept over it, and then brought it to where the suitors sat feasting in the hall.

"Lo! You may give proof of your skill!" she cried. "Here is the bow of the great Odysseus. Whoso shall bend it and shoot an arrow most easily, him will I follow, leaving this house which I shall remember only in my dreams." For the suitors had pressed her to make a choice among them and this was the promise that she now made.

By the grace of Athena never had Penelope appeared so comely as on that day, and the suitors were excited beholding so much beauty offered as the price of their skill. And they cried out that if the heroes who sailed for Colchis to capture the golden fleece had seen her, earth's richer prize, they would not have made their voyage, but would have vowed their lives and their manhood to her, for she was altogether faultless.

Telemachus set up the mark and the suitors in turn tried the bow, but they could not draw it. Last of all, Eurymachus took the bow and warmed it at the fire and then he tried to draw it, but could not. "Alas!" he cried, "that we are so much weaker than the great Odysseus. This is indeed shameful!"

Then Odysseus in the guise of the old beggar handled the great bow, though the suitors scorned him. He examined it and found it flawless. Then he strung the bow without effort, as a minstrel fastens a string upon his harp. He tried its tone, and the tone was sweet as the voice of the nightingale. Then he took an arrow from the quiver and laid the notch upon the string and drew it, sitting, and the arrow passed through the mark and stood in the wall beyond. Then he said to Telemachus, "There is yet a feast to be held before the sun go down."

So he nodded the sign to Telemachus. The young man sprang to his side, armed with spear and helmet and shield. Then said Odysseus, "Let me try at yet another mark." And he aimed an arrow at Antinous. The man was just raising a cup to his lips, thinking little of death, when the arrow passed through his neck, and he dropped the cup and fell back from the table.

Then said Eurymachus to his comrades, "This man will never stay his hand. Let us win our way to the door and raise a cry in the city."

He rushed toward the hero, knife in hand, but as he rushed, Odysseus smote him on the breast with an arrow and he fell forward. Then Odysseus and Telemachus and Eumanes and two goatherds sprang upon the suitors. They slew them all except Phemius the minstrel and Medon the herald.

After they had cleansed the hall, Odysseus told Euryclea, his nurse, to go to Penelope and tell her that her husband was indeed returned.

"Awake, Penelope, dear child!" she cried, "that thou mayst see with thine own eyes that which thou hast desired day by day. For Odysseus hath come and hath slain the proud suitors that devoured his house and oppressed his child."

So the Queen went, doubting, and sat down in the twilight by the wall, and Odysseus sat by a pillar with downcast eyes, waiting for his wife to speak to him. But she was sore perplexed, for now she seemed to know him and now she knew him not.

Then Odysseus bathed and anointed himself and put on a splendid mantle and Athena made him statelier than before. When he came back to the hall, he sat down opposite Penelope and said, "Strange wife, the gods have given you a harder heart than any woman living. No other wife would sit like this, when her husband had come home to her at last after twenty years of wandering and grief."

Then Penelope spoke at last. "My lord, I am not proud or heartless. I am utterly bewildered. Go, nurse, and bring out from the chamber the good bedstead that my husband built, and spread it for him."

She said this to try him, but he could bear it no longer and he cried out, "Wife, you cut me to the heart. How could anyone move my bedstead? There was a stout olive-tree growing in the inner court and I built my chamber around it. I smoothed the trunk and shaped it into a bedpost and built the bedstead there."

Then Penelope could doubt no longer, and her heart melted when she saw that it was her husband indeed. She ran to him weeping and threw her arms around his neck and cried, "Be not angry with me, Odysseus, that I did not know you at first as I know you now. I have always feared that some other might come and deceive me, but now you tell me what no one else could know and I believe you and give my heart to you."

So Odysseus held in his arms the wife he loved and wept for joy. And she clung to him as a tired swimmer clings to his own land which he has reached at last after deadly storm and wreck, and her white arms could never loose their hold.

Then Odysseus told her of the message that had come to him when he had gone down to the House of the Dead. There was one more long journey that he must take. "Then," he said, "I shall have rest at last and my people shall be happy. And death will come to me at length from the sea, the gentlest of all, when my strength is gone, at the end of a calm old age."

55

So they talked together while the old nurse was preparing their bed by the light of the blazing torches, and when all was ready she came and led the way to their chamber, torch in hand, as she had done twenty years before. There they now lay down together, and Telemachus stayed the feet of the women from dancing in the courts of the palace, sending them to their chambers through the shadowy halls. And the whole house was still.

The Greeks

By Charles Eliot Norton

It is perhaps the highest distinction of the Greeks that they recognized the indissoluble connection of beauty and goodness . . . I think that a knowledge of Greek thought and life, and of the arts in which the Greeks expressed their thought and sentiment, essential to high culture. A man may know everything else, but without this knowledge he remains ignorant of the best intellectual and moral achievements of his own race.

Sagas of the Old Norsemen

The Apples of Youth

HOW ASGARD'S TREASURE
WAS SAVED

HIGH in the heavens, in the cloud kingdom called Asgard, the Norse gods dwelt under the watchful eye of Odin their king. But the gods, who loved travel and adventure, did not always stay in Asgard. From time to time they liked to disguise themselves and wander on the earth, where men lived, and below the earth, where dwelt their enemies the giants.

One day Odin, weary of governing Asgard, decided to seek release in such a journey. He called upon his brother Hoenir and his half-brother Loki to be his traveling companions. Now Hoenir was a true god, noble and brave and good. Loki, however, was by birth a half giant. As such he was not always to be trusted. Still, Loki could be a gay companion, which was why Odin chose him to go along.

In a merry mood the three gods crossed the rainbow bridge which led down from Asgard to the rest of the world. All that day they traveled over mountains and plains, over great rivers and waste places. Toward nightfall they were ravenously hungry. So they searched until

they caught sight of a herd of oxen feeding in a grassy field. "There!" shouted Loki. "There is our supper!" In a matter of moments an ox was slain and roasting over a crackling fire.

The hungry gods could hardly wait for the meat to be cooked. Finally they judged that it was done, and they lifted it from the fire. But, strange to say, when they cut into it they found the meat as raw as when it was first set on the spit. Loki shrugged and hung up the meat again. The gods heaped more wood on the fire until they had a towering blaze. This time they allowed the meat to roast even longer than before. But again when they began to carve it they found that it was raw!

"Can it be that the meat is bewitched?" asked Hoenir in amazement. Just then they heard a strange sound that seemed to come from a nearby oak tree. Peering up at the top of the tree, they spied an enormous eagle.

"Ho! Ho!" cried the eagle. "The meat *is* bewitched, and it is I who have bewitched it! Give me my share and you will find that the meat will cook as fast as you please."

"Come down and take your share," cried the hungry gods.

The eagle flew down, but instead of taking just a share, he grasped the whole ox in his talons and started to fly away!

"You thief!" roared Loki. "Drop that ox this instant!" He seized a long pole and struck at the eagle with all his might.

Then a strange thing happened. The pole stuck to the eagle and Loki was lifted high into the air. The bewildered Loki clung to the pole with all his strength. If he let go he would be dashed to pieces on the ground! The bird flew toward a far mountain.

"Loki," said the eagle, "no one can help you now except me. But if you will promise to do what I ask, you shall go free."

"Anything!" cried Loki. "Anything you say! Only let me go."

"Though I am disguised as an eagle I am really Thiasse, the giant," continued the bird. "You ought to love me, Loki, for you yourself are partly a giant."

"Oh, yes," moaned the thoroughly miserable Loki. "I dearly love you, but tell me, only tell me what you want of me!"

By this time they had reached the mountain, and Thiasse set Loki down. But he did not release him from the grasp of his strong claws. "I am growing old," said Thiasse. "There is but one thing that can make me young again. I must have the magic apples of youth that Idun keeps in her golden casket. You, Loki, must get them for me."

Loki grew pale as he heard this. "Oh giant!" he cried. "Idun's apples are the most precious treasure in all Asgard. Without them the gods themselves would grow old and die. I could never steal them from Idun. Not only does she guard them better than life itself, but if she should cry out, everyone in all Asgard would rush to her rescue."

59

"How difficult your task is does not interest me," said Thiasse. "I must have the apples and you have promised to do anything I ask. Clever as you are, you will be able to find a way."

Loki thought and thought. He hit upon a terrible but cunning plan. "I will do it, Thiasse," he said. "In one week I will bring you not only the apples, but the fair Idun herself. But you must not forget the terrible risk I shall take. In return, you must allow me to keep young by eating the apples."

"Agreed," said the eagle. He picked up Loki again and fled swiftly back the way he had come. Then, swooping down, he dropped Loki on a soft bed of moss close by Odin and Hoenir. These two gods were glad and surprised to see Loki again. They had feared he might have been devoured by the eagle. The three decided they had had enough of adventuring, and returned to Asgard.

Loki watched for a chance to carry out his wicked plan. A few mornings later he strode to the meadow where the lovely Idun sat amongst the flowers. The golden casket containing the apples was on her knees. Idun greeted Loki pleasantly. "Good morning, Loki," she said. "Have you come for a bite of the magic apples?"

"Whatever for?" answered Loki. "I do not need your apples any longer. This very morning I have found some apples which are sweeter by far, and more magical than yours."

Idun frowned. "That cannot be, Loki," she said. "There are no apples as wonderful as mine. Where have you found these apples of which you speak?"

"Oho, not so fast!" said Loki. "I will not tell anyone the place. I will say, however, that it is in a little wood not very far from here. But no one could ever find it without me."

Idun grew more curious and more anxious than ever. She began to plead and coax. At last Loki said, "Well, all right, then, Idun, I will show you the place. But remember, it must be a secret between you and me."

"Oh, yes," agreed Idun eagerly. "Come, let us go now while no one is looking."

Loki led Idun off. They walked and walked. Suddenly Idun noticed with alarm that they were outside of Asgard. "Oh, Loki," she said, "I mustn't leave Asgard."

"Don't worry," said Loki. "It is not very far." So on they went. Then without a moment's warning there came a rustling of great wings. Down swooped Thiasse in the shape of an eagle. Before Idun could even scream, the eagle fastened his claws in her clothing and flew away toward the land of the giants. Loki waited till nightfall to slink back into Asgard, hoping that no one had seen him.

The next morning when the gods looked for Idun she was nowhere to be found! They were terribly frightened. If Idun and her apples were not quickly found, all the gods of Asgard would

grow old and die. A great council was called.

Finally one of the gods remembered that the previous morning he had seen Idun walking with Loki. Since she had not been seen afterwards, it became clear that Loki must have had a part in her disappearance. The wrath of the gods was terrible. They seized Loki and threatened to kill him instantly unless he told them what he had done with Idun.

The terrified Loki confessed the truth. Odin said, "If you do not bring back Idun from the land of the giants, you will never escape punishment, and will surely die a horrible death."

Loki trembled. "How can I bring her back?" he asked.

"That is for you to discover," was Odin's only reply.

Loki thought for a moment. Then he said, "If the goddess Freia will lend me her falcon dress, I will bring Idun back. The giant Thiasse dresses as an eagle; therefore I must disguise myself as a bird before I can outwit him." Freia agreed.

When Loki donned the falcon's guise he looked exactly like a great brown hawk. He flapped his wings and off he went. Over mountains and forests Loki flew until finally he arrived at the palace of Thiasse. Luckily for Loki, Thiasse had gone fishing in the sea, and Idun sat weeping and alone, imprisoned in the palace.

Hearing a light tap on her window, Idun looked up and saw a great brown bird on the ledge. She jumped up in fright, but the bird nodded pleasantly and said, "Don't be afraid, Idun. I have come to set you free. I am Loki, your friend."

"Loki!" she cried. "You are no friend of mine."

"You must believe me," said Loki. "I have come to take you back to Asgard. We must hurry before Thiasse returns."

"But how can I get out?" Idun asked. "My door is locked, and this window is barred."

"I will change you into a nut. Then I can lift you through the bars." Idun agreed, and Loki who was a skilled magician quickly turned her into a nut. Grasping the nut in one of his falcon's claws, and the casket in the other, Loki flew off towards Asgard.

In a little while, Thiasse came home. Finding Idun and the magic apples gone, he instantly guessed what had happened. Quickly he put on his eagle dress and set out in pursuit of the falcon.

Now an eagle is bigger and stronger than any other bird, and even though Loki had a good head start, the eagle rapidly shortened the distance between them. Loki was terrified. He was sure the swift flying eagle would overtake him. Finally Asgard loomed ahead. But the eagle was close, dangerously close behind Loki. The gods, who were gathered all along the rainbow bridge, watched breathlessly as the eagle gained on the falcon. Then Odin knew he must do something to save the falcon and its precious burden. He gave rapid orders. Soon all the gods were at work gathering wood and chips and piling them on the walls of Asgard. As soon as Loki had managed to fly over the wall the gods set lighted torches to the pile of wood. In a moment a wall of flame soared to the sky. Thiasse, the eagle, flying too fast to stop, flew straight into the roaring flames and perished.

There was great rejoicing in Asgard. Idun, changed back once again into a fair lady, gave each of the gods a morsel of the apples of youth. They grew young and beautiful and strong, and were happy once again.

But from then on, the name of Loki became a symbol of evil and dishonor among the dwellers in Asgard.

Baldur The Beautiful

THE TREACHERY OF LOKI

BALDUR was the son of Frigga, the Queen of the Norse gods. Baldur was the most beautiful of the gods, and he was also gentle, good and wise. Wherever he went, people were happy just at the sight of him. He was not only the favorite of his mother, but the favorite of all the other gods.

One night, Baldur dreamed three dreams. Each dream was more sad and terrible than the one before it. In the third of his dreams he found himself in a dark and lonely place. He heard a sad voice cry, "The sun is gone! The spring is gone! Joy is gone! For Baldur, the beautiful, is dead!"

The young god was very much upset. He told his lovely young wife, Nanna, about these sad and terrifying dreams. Nanna ran weeping to Queen Frigga saying, "Oh, mother, this must not come true!" Queen Frigga was deeply frightened. But she spoke soothingly to the young wife and said, "Do not fear, Nanna. Baldur is so dear to all the world, how could there be anything in the world that would hurt him?"

But Queen Frigga was heavy-hearted. The dream had frightened her.

She thought of a plan. "I will travel all over the heavens and all over the earth," she said. "I will make all things promise not to hurt my boy."

First, she went to the gods themselves. She told them of Baldur's dreams. She implored them to promise that none of them would ever harm Baldur. They all promised gladly.

Then Frigga traveled all over the world step by step. From all things, she got the same promise. From the trees and the plants; from the stones and the metals; from earth, air, fire and water; from sun, snow, wind and rain; and from all the diseases that men know—every creature and every thing promised not to harm Baldur.

At last, the weary but joyful Queen returned to Asgard, home of the gods. Frigga brought happy news: there was nothing in the world that would hurt Baldur. And there was great rejoicing in Asgard. All the gods felt relieved. They became quite gay. When someone suggested that they play a game which would prove how wrong the dream was, everyone agreed.

They placed Baldur at one end of the field. He stood there in all his golden beauty, his face glowing with a bright light like that of the sun. And as he stood there, unarmed and smiling, the other gods took turns shooting arrows at him, hurling their spears against him, throwing sticks and stones. It was a jolly game, for every stone fell harmless at Baldur's feet; each arrow and spear turned aside as it reached his body. Baldur stood safe and serene while the missiles piled up around him. Nothing would hurt him.

But among the crowd watching and playing, there was one who did not smile. Loki the crafty one, Loki the evil one, did not laugh and cheer like the others. Loki was filled with jealous anger and malice. Baldur had never done him any harm, yet Loki hated him, for Loki knew full well that no one in the world loved him in the same way they loved Baldur. An evil plan took shape in Loki's mind. While the others were engaged in the happy game, Loki disguised himself as an old woman, and made his way to the place where Queen Frigga was sitting.

"Good day, my lady," he said. "What is all that noise and excitement over yonder in the field?"

"Don't you know?" answered Queen Frigga in surprise. "They are shooting at my son, Baldur. They are proving the promise that every creature and every thing has made, not to injure my beloved son. You see, the promise is being kept."

The old woman pretended to be very much surprised. "Really!" she cried. "Do you mean to say that every single thing in the whole world has promised not to hurt Baldur? It is true that he is a fine fellow, but still that is a remarkable thing. Have you gotten such a promise from absolutely everything in the world?"

"Oh, yes," said Queen Frigga, "everything has promised. Of course, there is one tiny little plant so small and unimportant that I did not even bother to ask."

"And what little plant is that?" said the old woman.

"It is the mistletoe that grows nearby. It is really too harmless to bother with," said Frigga.

Loki hobbled away, but as soon as he saw that no one was noticing him, he picked up his gown and ran as fast as he could to the spot where the little mistletoe grew. Then he took out his knife and cut off a piece of mistletoe. With the same knife, Loki whittled the mistletoe and trimmed it and shaped it until it was a slender arrow. Then he hobbled back to the field where the merry game was still going on. In one corner of the field stood Hod, the blind brother of Baldur. Loki, still in the guise of an old woman, tapped his arm. "Why are you not taking part in the merry game?" she asked. "They all do honor to your brother. Surely you ought to do so, too."

Then Hod touched his sightless eyes. "Ah," he said, "I am blind. How I would rejoice to give honor to my dear brother but I cannot see to aim a weapon."

"You ought to at least throw a little stick," said the old woman. "Here is a little green twig that you can use as a dart. I will guide your arm while you throw it."

Hod smiled with pleasure and stretched forth his arm eagerly. Then Loki placed the arrow of mistletoe in Hod's hand and taking careful aim, hurled it straight at

Baldur's heart. With a cry, Baldur fell forward on the grass. Everyone rushed toward him. They could not understand what had happened. When they saw that Baldur was dead, they knew that it was the end of sunshine and spring and joy in Asgard. The terrible dream had come true!

Then they turned upon Hod ready to tear him to pieces. "What is it! What have I done?" asked the poor blind brother.

"What have you done? You have slain Baldur!" they cried.

"No! No!" cried Hod. "I could never have done such a thing. It was the old woman, the evil old woman, who stood at my elbow and gave me a little twig to throw. She must be a witch."

The gods scattered all over the field to look for the old woman, but she had mysteriously disappeared. Then they noticed that Loki was not amongst them. "It must have been Loki!" they said.

The heartbroken gods placed Baldur on a beautiful ship to send him to Queen Hela, the queen of Death. And weeping and wailing, they sent him on his way. But Queen Frigga sent a message to Queen Hela to find out if there was not some way to win back Baldur from the kingdom of Death.

"I would let him go if I might," Queen Hela said, "but a queen cannot always do as she likes. There is only one way that you can bring Baldur back to life. If everything upon earth will weep for Baldur's death, then he may return. But should even one creature fail to weep, Baldur must remain with me."

The gods sent messages all over the world bidding every creature to weep for Baldur's death. There seemed to be little need for such a message, for already there was weeping and mourning in every part of the world. Even the giants, who were enemies of the gods, wept for Baldur. It began to look as though Baldur might be ransomed from Death.

But when all the messengers returned to Asgard, one of them told how he had found an ugly old giantess in a deep, black cave who refused to weep for Baldur. The messenger had begged her to weep but the giantess had answered, "Baldur is nothing to me. I care not whether he lives or dies." So all the tears of the sorrowing world were useless, because one creature would not weep.

Then the gods knew who the old woman was. It could be no one but Loki. "Loki has done his last evil deed," shouted Thor the Thunderer, as he lifted his mighty hammer. "Come, my brothers, we have wept long enough. It is now time to punish!"

Loki tried to escape by changing himself into a fish, and hiding in a deep river. "They'll never be able to find me here," he said.

But although Odin, the All-Father, had only one eye, he could see everything in the world. He could see through thick mountains and down into the deepest sea. Odin took a net and scooped Loki out of the river. When he grasped

65

Loki's slippery fish body, Loki was changed back into his own shape. There he stood, surrounded by the wrathful gods.

"Kill him! Kill him!" they shouted, as Odin pushed him along the road to Asgard. And on the way to the rainbow bridge which led from Asgard to Midgard, the land of the humans, thousands of men lined the road shouting, "Kill him! Kill him!"

From their caverns in the mountains came the dwarfs. They stood shaking their fists at Loki. The beasts growled and bared their fangs as if they wished to tear Loki into pieces; the birds flew at him trying to peck out his eyes; insects came in clouds to sting him, and serpents darted their fangs at him, ready to poison him with their deadly bite. But Odin decided on an even worse punishment than death. He led Loki down into a damp, dark cave under the ground where sunlight never came. The cave was full of ugly toads and snakes. In this terrible prison chamber, Loki was placed upon three sharp stones. He was bound with thongs of leather; but as soon as the leather bands were fastened to him, they turned into iron bands, so that no one, though he might have the strength of a giant, could ever loosen them. These bands cut deeply into Loki's flesh.

Over his head was hung a venomous serpent. From its mouth poison which burned and stung like fire dropped into Loki's face.

Everybody in the world hated Loki except one. In spite of all his wickedness, Loki's wife, Sigyn, remained faithful to him. She stood by his head and held a bowl to catch the poison which dropped from the serpent's jaw, so that it would not reach Loki's face. But whenever the bowl became full, Sigyn had to take it away to empty it and then the burning, horrible drops of poison fell on Loki's face.

Under the caverns, Loki still lies, struggling to be free. When the poison falls upon his face, he shrieks and struggles so violently that the whole earth trembles. Then people cry, "An earthquake!" and they run away as fast as they can. For Loki, the evil one, though bound, is still dangerous. And bound as he is, Loki will stay imprisoned until the end of the world.

Thor and the Giants

A FAMOUS TRIAL OF STRENGTH

JUST as the ancient Greeks told of their gods and the marvelous things they did, so too did the ancient Norsemen relate wonderful stories about the gods they believed in. According to these stories, the Norse gods dwelt in Asgard, high up in the sky, where they were ruled over by Odin, their king. Ordinary mortals dwelt in Midgard. And there was a race of giants, the enemies of both gods and men, who lived in a region called Jotunheim whose chief city was called Utgard.

Now the Norse gods dearly loved adventure. One day, three of the gods decided to seek danger and excitement by journeying to Jotunheim, the land of the giants.

One of the adventurous three was Thor the Thunderer, Odin's youngest son. He was the strongest of all the gods and possessed a wonderful hammer which destroyed whatever it was hurled against. When Thor hurled his hammer, thunder resounded in the skies.

The second of the three gods was Thor's half-brother, Loki the Red, so called because of the flaming color of his beard. His mother was a giantess, and so Loki was really a half-giant. As such, he was often mischievous and evil. So shrewd and clever was he however, that when he was on his good behavior many of the other gods sought him out as a companion.

The third of the three gods to make the journey was Thialfi the Runner, who could run more swiftly than any creature on the earth or any of the gods.

It was the custom of the gods to travel in disguise when they journeyed from Asgard. So, in their many days of travel, none who saw the three adventurers knew who they were.

As they drew near Jotunheim, the three travelers met an enormous giant, who greeted them in friendly fashion and led them along the road to Utgard.

Soon the city came into view. It was an awesome sight. So high were the walls of Utgard that Thor and his companions could scarcely see the top. They were welcomed with great hospitality by the king. But despite their disguises, Utgard's ruler knew immediately who they were.

"If I do not mistake me," he said with a smile of scorn, "that stripling yonder must be the god Thor. Mayhap he is of greater strength then he looks, but to me he looks like a puny fellow. Tell me, Thor, in what feats of skill and strength do you and your companions deem your-

selves champions?"

The gods from Asgard did not like the giant's tone of mockery, for they were accustomed to great respect.

"The feat that I know," Loki replied angrily, "is to eat faster than anyone else; and I am ready to give proof of my prowess in competition with anyone who will stand up to me."

"That will indeed be a feat," said the giant king. "You shall be tried forthwith."

He ordered one of his men, a giant named Logi, to come forward. Logi and Loki each took a place at opposite ends of a long trough filled with enormous chunks of meat. When the signal was given, Logi began to eat from his end and Loki began to eat from the other end until they met in the middle of the trough. So quickly did the two contestants eat that in a matter of moments the food was all gone. But Loki the god had eaten only the meat, while Logi the giant had eaten the bones and the trough as well! So all the company judged that Loki had lost.

The king of the giants then asked what feat young Thialfi could perform. Thialfi, who was known as the swiftest runner in the world, said he would run a race with anyone who was matched against him.

"That is indeed something to boast of," said the king. "In Midgard or in Asgard you may well be the swiftest runner; but you are now in Utgard where dwell the giants. We shall soon see whether your boast is as vain as I judge it to be."

He arose and led the whole company to a large meadow many miles long, especially laid out for racing. He then called a young giant named Hugi and bade him race against Thialfi.

The signal for the start was given. Thor and Loki watched with bated breath. But although Thialfi flew along as fleet as the wind, he was outdistanced by Hugi who won the race, without even getting out of breath.

The king then spoke scornfully to Thor. "Now, Thor—*mighty* Thor, as you are called in other places—let us hope that you will do better than your companions. I would not like to be disappointed in all of you. Tell me what you would do?"

Thor, burning with shame at the defeat of his party, answered angrily that he would try a drinking match. The king then ordered his cup-bearers to bring in a large drinking horn.

"Good drinkers amongst us can empty this horn at a single draught," he said. "Most of us empty it in two, but even the puniest one amongst us can do it in three. Let us see if you can do it in three draughts."

Thor looked at the horn. It did not seem to be of an extraordinary size, and Thor felt sure that he could empty it easily. He set it to his lips and without drawing breath, pulled long and deeply. But when he set the horn down and looked in it he could scarcely believe his eyes. It seemed as if he had drunk

nothing! Thor took a deep breath, and started his second draught. He drank with mighty gulps, until he thought his heart would burst. But when he put down the horn, it seemed that he had drunk off only a little from the top.

Then Thor was filled with wrath. "This time," he thought, "I will surely drain the cup." He drank and drank until it seemed that there could be nothing left in the horn. Then he set down the horn with an enormous sigh and looked. The liquid had gone down less than half the depth of the horn. Thor had failed!

"I see now plainly," said the king, "that you are even more puny than I thought. But maybe you would try another test?"

"What new trial do you propose?" asked Thor.

"We have a very trifling game here," answered the king. "Our children play it. It consists merely of lifting my cat from the ground."

As the king spoke, a large grey cat sprang out in front of them. Thor immediately stepped forward. Placing his hand under the cat's belly, he tried to lift it from the ground. But the cat, lengthening and lengthening itself, arched its back like a span of a bridge. Thor tugged and tugged but he could not manage to lift more than one of the cat's four feet off the floor.

"O ho!" laughed the king. "My poor little Thor! Even my cat is too strong for you to lift."

69

At this, Thor grew terribly angry. "Let me wrestle against a person, not a cat, and I will show you!" The king of Utgard looked at his men who sat around enjoying themselves hugely.

"I see not one of my warriors here who would not think it was beneath him to wrestle with you," said the king. "However, here is an old woman, my nurse Elli. Let us see how you stand up to her."

"No," answered Thor, "I will not wrestle with a woman."

"Mayhap you are afraid?" taunted the king.

At this, Thor sprang forward, ready for the struggle. Thor grasped the old crone tightly in his iron arms, but she seemed not to mind it at all. The harder Thor pressed her, the stronger she seemed. It was as if she were made of iron. Finally, after a long and violent struggle, Thor began to lose his footing. With a quick turn, the old woman pulled him down upon one knee. She was the winner! In shame and anger, Thor withdrew. His heart was sore, for the giants had shamed the three gods in every test.

Early the next morning, Thor and his companions made ready to leave. The king of the giants accompanied them to the walls of the city. "Tell me truly now, brother Thor," said the giant king, "do you now think you are as mighty a fellow as you thought before you entered our gates? Or do you finally see that

there are folk who are even stronger than you?"

Thor was still angry and ashamed but he had to speak the truth. "My name will be a joke amongst your people," he said. "They will call me Thor the Weakling. I must confess that you have beaten us soundly."

The king was pleased with the humble and honest way in which Thor spoke. "Nay," he answered, "hang not your head in shame. In truth, you have not done so ill as you think. Now I will tell you. By magic alone you were beaten.

"When you came to my city, I was greatly frightened for I knew then as I know now, your great strength. In every contest, you and your fellows were outwitted only by dint of our magic, not by our strength. Loki ate marvelously but Logi who ate with him was none other than Fire; and nothing in the world can devour as rapidly as fire. Thialfi here is a runner as swift as the wind, but Hugi who ran against him is Thought, and who can keep pace with the speed of thought? You, Thor, strove bravely; and truth to tell, I am indeed envious of your great strength and skill. When you drank from the horn (thinking you had done so poorly), in truth you performed a miracle. You knew it not, but the end of the horn was set in the ocean. Your mighty draughts have drained countless rivers dry; and the ocean itself is sunk low in its shores. The cat which you almost lifted—it was no cat, but the great serpent Midgard, whose body encircles the whole world. You raised it so high that he almost touched Heaven. How terrified we giants were when we saw you lift one of his mighty feet off the ground! And as for your wrestling match with old Elli—why, Elli is none other than Age itself. No one ever lived who could overcome age. So grieve not, mighty Thor, for you were beaten by tricks. Now we must part. It is best that we should never meet again. And truly I tell you that never again shall I dare to let you step inside my city. If such a thing should happen, I should overcome you again by magic if that were possible, for I doubt that I could do it any other way."

Then Thor and his companions returned to Asgard, as sure of their strength as they once were, but more humble.

Siegfried

MIME THE BLACKSMITH

Siegfried was born a Prince and grew to be a hero. Though he could fight, and was as strong as a lion, yet he could love too and be as gentle as a child.

The father and mother of the hero lived in a strong castle near the banks of the Rhine. Siegmund, his father, was a rich king; Sieglinde, his mother, a beautiful queen, and dearly did they love their little son Siegfried.

The courtiers and the high-born maidens who dwelt in the castle honored the little Prince, and thought him the fairest child in all the land, as indeed he was.

As he grew older, Siegfried would ride around the country, always attended by King Siegmund's most trusted warriors. One day armed men entered King Siegmund's country and the little Prince was sent away from the castle, lest by some evil chance he should fall into the hands of the foe.

Siegfried was hidden away in the thickets of a great forest, and dwelt there under the care of a blacksmith, named Mime.

Mime was a dwarf, belonging to a strange race of little folk called Nibelungs. The Nibelungs lived for the most part in a dark cavern under the ground.

But Mime had his forge in the forest, and there he trained the young Siegfried to use hammer and axe with great skill. The boy learned so well that in a very short while, seizing the heaviest hammer he could find, he would swing it with a force that splintered the anvil into a thousand pieces.

Siegfried grew up a merry, carefree youth. He loved to break away from the peevish little blacksmith whenever he could and go wandering off into the forest alone, seeking adventure. He enjoyed playing tricks on the dwarf too, and the more frightened Mime became, the more Siegfried would laugh at him and tease him. One day he caught a huge bear, brought it home on a leash, and made it chase Mime into a corner. It was shortly after this painful incident that Mime made up his mind not to endure the boy's pranks any longer. He thought up a scheme to get rid of him.

"We need charcoal for the furnace," he said in his squeaky, whining little voice. "I can't leave the forge, so you will have to go."

Siegfried leaped into the air for joy. The sun was shining, the birds were singing, and he saw himself roaming the deepest part of the forest alone, blow-

ing his silver horn, piping to the birds, and dancing. He did not guess that on that beautiful summer day the evil little dwarf planned to kill him.

Mime was too puny and timid to attack the boy himself, but he had a brother named Regin ready to do anything he was asked. Mime had only to propose that his brother be changed into a terrible dragon and the brother agreed whole-heartedly. Mime had only to say "Seize the boy and devour him!" and Regin's jaws began to gape and belch forth fire. He was immediately transformed into a hideous scaly-tailed monster, so powerful that the trees seemed to tremble and the earth quake

as he scurried off into the forest to hide and await his prey.

Soon the sound of a horn warned the dragon of the youth's approach. Siegfried caught sight of him and stood still in astonishment. He had never seen a dragon before. Could this be one—this strange creature advancing towards him from the shadows, breathing fire? He burst into a peal of boyish laughter, and this so infuriated the dragon that it swept around and swung its great scaly tail, meaning to make a quick end of the impudent boy.

With a bound Siegfried sprang to the monster's back. It reared in anger, and instantly Siegfried's sword was buried in its heart. The boy leaped lightly to the ground as Regin, the dragon, rolled over dead.

Then Siegfried did a curious thing. He had heard Mime and his dwarf companions speak of the magic qualities of dragon's blood. Whoever bathed in it, they said, would never be harmed by the spear or sword-thrust of an enemy. So he undressed and bathed himself in the blood from top to toe—all but one tiny spot. He had not noticed that a linden leaf had fallen on his shoulder, and had left one little spot of skin untouched by the blood. If an enemy's spear should ever pierce his skin at that particular spot on his shoulder, the boy-hero would be wounded just like any ordinary man.

The dragon's blood had another strange power. Whoever tasted it would be given the power to understand the language of birds. Siegfried, having pricked his finger while bathing in the blood, put it to his mouth, tasted blood, and immediately could understand what the birds were saying.

"You are a great hero!" they chirped. "Go seek the ring of fire on the mountain-top. He who can make his way through the flames will find Brunhilde and woo her, the warrior daughter of Odin."

This was just the kind of exploit Siegfried was looking for now that he was free to go where he wanted to. But first he had a duty to perform. The dragon was dead, but the traitor Mime still lived. He must rid the earth of this crea-

ture and his dark evil plotting. He hastened back to the smithy to find the dwarf and make an end of him.

When the deed was accomplished Siegfried left the smithy behind him forever and fared forth in search of a mountain-top ringed with fire.

THE RING OF FIRE

Brunhilde was the favorite daughter of Odin, chief of the gods. She was also the leader of the Valkyries, maidens who carried the souls of brave heroes to Valhalla, their last resting-place.

One day Odin discovered that his daughter had disobeyed his orders. Taking pity on a young handsome warrior doomed to die on the battlefield, she had let him live and had chosen another to be sent to death.

"Brunhilde! Brunhilde!" Odin cried, grief-stricken at his loved daughter's rebellion. "What is this you have done?"

Brunhilde had nothing to say. She bowed her head in submission.

"Your punishment will be severe," her father continued. "I shall banish you to the top of the highest mountain, to remain there alone. You will no longer be a goddess but a human woman who will have to submit to being sought in marriage by men." Then, relenting a little, he went on, "But to protect you from an unworthy marriage I will surround the mountain-top with fierce flames. No one but the bravest hero in the world will dare to pass through such a terrible barrier. I will also touch your eyes with my wand so that you will sleep, and your sleep will last until your hero-husband comes to waken you."

For many years Brunhilde remained sleeping behind her curtains of flame. No hero had succeeded in breaking through that flaming barrier. And the failure of so many brave men only gave Siegfried more self-confidence. A rosy glow colored the sky as he approached the mountain on his good steed Grey-fell. He dug his spurs into the animal's sides. Greyfell raced across the plain and up the mountain slopes, scattering loose stones, rocks, and shrubs that lay in his path. And in a short while a great roaring was heard and a flaming wall rose up before horse and rider, forbidding them to go any farther.

But on they sped, plunging into the heart of the fire, and miraculously the flames parted and let them through without harm.

Siegfried dismounted and walked over to the sleeping figure. He touched an arm, then a shoulder, but could see no sign of life. Then he loosened the warrior-helmet and let it fall back, revealing a face of great beauty framed by shining golden hair. And a moment later Brunhilde, the warrior maiden, opened her eyes. She looked around her at the sun rising in a glory of crimson and gold, at the mountain crags, the bare rock on which she lay. And at last her eyes fell upon Siegfried. In a flash she understood that Odin, her father, had rewarded her, not punished her. For here before her stood the only man she could ever marry—the great hero who had braved the fierce flames to win her love.

Siegfried took her by the hand and raised her to stand beside him.

"Harken," he vowed, earnestly, "while I swear that the sun shall die in the heavens and the day no more be fair if ever I should cease to love thee."

And he slipped an ancient ring upon her finger as a symbol of their betrothal.

There is a Charming Land

By Adam Oehlenschlager

Translated by Robert Hillyer

There is a charming land
Where grow the wide-armed beeches
By the salt eastern Strand.
Old Denmark, so we call
These rolling hills and valleys,
And this is Freia's Hall.

Here sat in days of yore
The warriors in armor,
Well rested from the war.
They scattered all their foes,
And now beneath great barrows
Their weary bones repose.

The land is lovely still,
With blue engirdling ocean
And verdant vale and hill,
Fair women, comely maids,
Strong men and lads are dwelling
In Denmark's island glades.

76

African and Asiatic Tales

The Endless Tale

By James Baldwin

IN THE Far East, many years ago, there was a great King who had no work to do. Every day, and all day long, he sat on soft cushions and listened to story-tellers telling made-up stories. And no matter what the story was about, he never grew tired of hearing it, even though it was very long.

"There is only one fault that I find with your story," he often said to a story-teller, "it is too short."

All the story-tellers in the world were invited to his palace; and some of them told tales that went on and on and on. But no matter how long a story was, the King was always sad when it ended.

At last he sent a message into every city and town and country place, offering a prize to anyone who would tell him an endless tale.

"To the man who will tell me a story which shall last forever," he wrote, "I will give my lovely daughter for his wife; and I will make the man my heir, and he shall be King after me."

But this was not the whole message.

He added a very hard condition: "If any man shall try to tell such a story and *fail*, he shall have his head cut off."

The King's daughter was very pretty, and there were many young men in that country who were willing to do anything to win her. But none of them wanted to lose their heads; so only a few tried for the prize.

One young man invented a story that lasted three months; but at the end of that time, he could think of nothing more. So his head was cut off. His fate was a warning to others, and it was a long time before another story-teller was found who would try for the prize.

But one day a stranger came into the palace.

"Great King," he said, "is it true that you offer a prize to the man who can tell a story that has no end?"

"It is true," said the King.

"And shall this man have your lovely daughter for his wife, and shall he be your heir and become the King after you?"

"Yes, if he succeeds," said the old King. "But if he fails, he shall lose his head."

"Very well, then," said the stranger. "I have a pleasant story about locusts which I should like to relate."

"Tell it," said the King. "I will listen to you."

The story-teller began his tale. This is what he said:

"Once upon a time a certain King seized upon all the corn in his country, and stored it away in a strong granary. But a swarm of locusts came over the land and saw where the grain had been put. After searching for many days they found on the east side of the granary a crack that was just large enough for one locust to pass through at a time. So one locust went in and carried away a grain of corn; then another locust went in and carried away a grain of corn; then another locust went in and carried away a grain of corn."

Day after day, week after week, the strange story-teller kept on saying, "Then another locust went in and carried away a grain of corn."

A month passed; a year passed.

At the end of two years, the King said, "How much longer will the locusts be going in and carrying away corn?"

"O King!" said the story-teller, "they have as yet cleared only one cubit; and there are many thousand cubits in the granary."

"Man, man!" cried the King, "you will drive me mad! I can listen to it no longer. Take my daughter; be my heir; rule my kingdom. But do not let me hear another word about those horrible locusts!"

And so the story-teller married the King's daughter. And he and his bride lived happily in the land for many years. But his father-in-law, the King, did not care to listen to any more stories.

Kassa, the Strong One

By Harold Courlander
and George Herzog

Once among the Mende people in the country known as the Sudan there was a strong young man named Kassa Kena Genanina.

"I am a strong man," he said, "the strongest man alive, and I'm not afraid of anything!"

One day Kassa went hunting in the forest with two other young men named Iri Ba Farra and Congo Li Ba Jelema. Iri and Congo carried guns to hunt with, but Kassa carried a pole of forged iron.

Iri and Congo hunted and hunted, but they found no game. Kassa, who was swift as well as strong, killed twenty large antelopes with his iron pole, and he brought them into the clearing where Iri and Congo waited.

"Here is the meat," Kassa said. "Now who will go into the forest to get firewood?"

But both Iri and Congo were afraid to go into the forest alone, so Kassa said to Iri:

"You stay and guard the meat so that it won't be stolen by the animals of the jungle. Congo and I will get the firewood."

Kassa and Congo went into the forest, and Iri was alone. And while he watched, a huge bird came flying down from the sky and said to him:

"I am hungry. Shall I take you or shall I take the meat?"

The huge bird was frightening, and Iri said: "By all means take the meat!"

The bird took one of the antelopes and flew off with it. When Kassa and Congo came back Iri said:

"While you were gone a huge bird came down and said, 'Shall I take you or the meat?' I said, 'Take the meat!'"

Kassa was scornful.

"You shouldn't have given him an antelope. You should have said, 'Take me!'"

The next day Kassa went again into the forest to get firewood, and this time he took Iri with him and left Congo to guard the meat.

And when they were gone the huge bird came sailing down from the sky

again and said to Congo Li Ba Jelema:

"I am hungry. Shall I take you or the meat?"

Congo was frightened, and he said, "If you're that hungry, then take the meat!"

The bird took one of the antelopes and flew away. When Iri and Kassa returned from the forest Congo told them what had happened.

"The huge bird came back and said, 'Shall I take you or the meat?' and I said, 'Take the meat!'"

Kassa said, "You shouldn't have said that. You should have said, 'Take me.' Tomorrow I shall stay and guard the meat."

So the next day Iri and Congo went together into the forest for firewood, and after they were gone the huge bird sailed down to the clearing and said to Kassa:

"I am hungry. Shall I take you or the meat?"

Kassa sprang up.

"I am Kassa Kena Genanina, the strongest man alive!" he shouted. "You shall take nothing, neither the meat nor me!" He seized his forged iron pole and threw it at the bird. It struck her as she flew, and she fell dead upon the ground.

But a tiny feather came loose and floated downward gently and settled upon Kassa's shoulders. It was heavy. It pushed him to the ground. He lay upon his stomach, and the feather was still on him, and it was so heavy he couldn't move. He struggled to get up, but the feather held him to the earth.

After a long while a woman carrying a child on her back came by, and Kassa said to her:

"Call my comrades from the forest so they can help me!"

She went into the forest and found Iri and Congo, and they came running to where Kassa lay. First Congo tried to lift the feather from Kassa, then Iri tried, but it was too heavy. Then they tried together, but they couldn't budge it.

The woman stood watching them. Finally she bent forward and blew the feather off Kassa's shoulders with her mouth.

Then she picked up the dead bird from the ground and gave it to the child on her back for a toy, and went away.

Guinea Fowl and
Rabbit Get Justice

By Harold Courlander
and George Herzog

Somewhere between the Kong Mountains and the sea, in the country called the Gold Coast, the bird named Guinea Fowl had his farm. It was a good farm. Guinea Fowl worked hard on it, and grew fine yams and bananas. He grew beans and okra, millet and tobacco. His farm always looked green and prosperous. Mostly it was because Guinea Fowl was a hard worker. Not very far away Rabbit had a farm. It wasn't a very good farm because Rabbit never worked too hard. He planted at planting time, but he never hoed his crops or pulled out the weeds that grew there. So when harvest time came along there wasn't very much okra or beans or millet.

One day Rabbit was out walking and he saw Guinea Fowl's farm. It looked so much better than his own that he wished he owned it. He thought it over. He became indignant.

"Why is it that it rains over here on Guinea Fowl's land and not on mine, so that his crops grow and mine don't?" he asked himself. "It's not fair!"

He thought all day. And a wonderful idea came to him.

That night he brought out his wife and his children and marched them to Guinea Fowl's farm, then he marched them back again. He did it again. All night his family went back and forth from their house to Guinea Fowl's farm, until by morning they had made a trail. In the morning they started pulling up Guinea Fowl's vegetables and putting them in baskets.

When Guinea Fowl came to work he saw Rabbit there with his family, pulling up all the fine crops he had planted.

"What are you doing with my yams and okra?" Guinea Fowl said. "And what are you doing on my farm, anyway?"

"*Your* farm?" Rabbit said. "There must be some mistake. It's *my* farm."

"I guess there *is* a mistake. It's my farm. I planted it and I weeded it and I hoed it," Guinea Fowl said. "So I don't see how it can be your farm."

"How could you plant it and weed it and hoe it when I planted it and weeded it and hoed it?" Rabbit said.

Guinea Fowl was very angry.

"You'd better get off my place," he said.

"You'd better get off *my* place," Rabbit said.

"It's absurd," Guinea Fowl said.

"It certainly is," Rabbit said, "when any old Guinea Fowl can come and claim someone else's property."

"It's mine," Guinea Fowl said.

"It's mine," Rabbit said.

"Well, I'll take the case to the chief," Guinea Fowl said.

"It's a good idea," Rabbit said.

So the two of them picked up their hoes and went to the village to the house of the chief.

"This fellow is pulling up my vegetables," Guinea Fowl said, "and he won't get off my farm."

"He's trying to take advantage of me," Rabbit said. "I work and work to grow fine yams and then he comes along and wants to own them."

They argued and argued, while the head man listened. Finally they went out together to look the situation over.

"Where is the trail from your house?" the head man asked Rabbit.

"There," Rabbit said, and pointed out the one he had just made.

"And where is the trail from your house?" the head man asked Guinea Fowl.

"Trail? I never had a trail," Guinea Fowl said.

"Whenever anyone has a farm he has a trail to it from his house," the head man said.

"But whenever I come to work my farm I *fly*," Guinea Fowl said.

The head man thought. He shook his head.

"If a person has a farm he has to have a trail to it," he said after a while. "So the land must belong to Rabbit."

He went away. Rabbit and his family began to pull up more yams. Guinea Fowl went home, feeling very angry.

When Rabbit had a large basket full of vegetables he started off to market with them. But the basket was very heavy. He wasn't used to heavy work, because he was lazy. After he had carried his load a little distance along the road he put it down and rested. And while he sat by the roadside Guinea Fowl came along.

83

"Ah, friend Rabbit, your load is very heavy," Guinea Fowl said sweetly. "Perhaps I can give you a lift with it."

Rabbit was touched. Guinea Fowl wasn't angry any more. He was very friendly.

"Thank you," he said. "You are a real friend to help me with my vegetables."

So Guinea Fowl put the load on his head. He smiled at Rabbit. Then he flapped his wings and went off with the load, not to the market but to his own house.

Rabbit shouted. He ran after Guinea Fowl, but he couldn't catch him. Guinea Fowl soared over the fields and was gone.

Rabbit was angry. He went back to the village to find the head man.

"Guinea Fowl has robbed me!" he shouted. "He flew away with my basket of vegetables!"

The head man sent for Guinea Fowl.

"They were my vegetables I took," Guinea Fowl said.

"They were mine," Rabbit shouted. "I harvested them with my own hands!"

They argued and argued. The head man thought and thought.

"Well," he said at last, "when people carry things a great deal on their heads, after a while the hair gets thin from so much carrying." The people of the village said yes, that always happened.

"Let me see the top of your head," the head man said to Rabbit.

Rabbit showed him. The head man clicked his tongue.

"No," he said to Rabbit, "your hair is thick and long."

He turned to Guinea Fowl.

"Let me see yours," he said, and Guinea Fowl showed him.

Guinea Fowl's head didn't have even a fuzzy feather on it.

"It must belong to you," the head man said, "you are absolutely bald."

"But Guinea Fowl never *had* any feathers on his head!" Rabbit complained. "He was *always* bald!"

"When you carry things on your head the hair becomes thin," the head man said. "So the basket belongs to Guinea Fowl."

They went away. Rabbit prepared another basket of vegetables to take to market. And when he set it down by the side of the road and rested, Guinea Fowl swooped down and took it away. Rabbit prepared another basket, and the same thing happened. It was no use going to the head man any more, because Guinea Fowl's head was so bald.

At last Rabbit got tired of pulling up Guinea Fowl's vegetables for him, and he went back to his own farm to work for himself.

That is why people sometimes say, "The shortest path often goes nowhere."

Talk

by
Harold Courlander and George Herzog

ONCE, not far from the city of Accra on the Gulf of Guinea, a countryman went out to his garden to dig up some yams to take to market. While he was digging, one of the yams said to him:

"Well, at last you're here. You never weeded me, but now you come around with your digging stick. Go away and leave me alone!"

The farmer turned around and looked at his cow in amazement. The cow was chewing her cud and looking at him.

"Did you say something?" he asked.

The cow kept on chewing and said nothing, but the man's dog spoke up.

"It wasn't the cow who spoke to you," the dog said. "It was the yam. The yam says leave him alone."

The man became angry, because his dog had never talked before, and he didn't like his tone besides. So he took his knife and cut a branch from a palm tree to whip his dog. Just then the palm tree said:

"Put that branch down!"

The man was getting very upset about the way things were going, and he started to throw the palm-branch away, but the palm-branch said:

"Man, put me down gently!"

He put the branch down gently on a stone, and the stone said:

"Hey, take that thing off me!"

This was enough, and the frightened farmer started to run for his village. On the way he met a fisherman going the other way with a fish-trap on his head.

"What's the hurry?" the fisherman asked.

"My yam said, 'Leave me alone!' Then the dog said, 'Listen to what the yam says!' When I went to whip the dog with a palm-branch the tree said, 'Put that branch down!' Then the palm-branch said, 'Do it gently!' Then the stone said, 'Take that thing off me!' "

"Is that all?" the man with the fish-trap asked. "Is that so frightening?"

"Well," the man's fish-trap said, "did he take it off the stone?"

"Wah!" the fisherman shouted. He threw the fish-trap on the ground and began to run with the farmer. And on the trail they met a weaver with a bundle of cloth on his head.

"Where are you going in such a rush?" he asked them.

"My yam said, 'Leave me alone!' the farmer said. "The dog said, 'Listen to what the yam says!' The tree said, 'Put that branch down!' The branch said, 'Do it gently!' And the stone said, 'Take that thing off me!' "

"And then," the fisherman continued,

85

"the fish-trap said, 'Did he take it off?' "

"That's nothing to get excited about," the weaver said, "no reason at all."

"Oh yes it is," his bundle of cloth said. "If it happened to you you'd run too!"

"Wah!" the weaver shouted. He threw his bundle on the trail and started running with the other men.

They came panting to the ford in the river and found a man bathing.

"Are you chasing a gazelle?" he asked them.

The first man said breathlessly:

"My yam talked at me, and it said, 'Leave me alone!' And my dog said, 'Listen to your yam!' And when I cut myself a branch the tree said, 'Put that branch down!' And the branch said, 'Do it gently!' And the stone said, 'Take that thing off me!' "

The fisherman panted:

"And my trap said, 'Did he?' "

The weaver wheezed, "And my bundle of cloth said, 'You'd run too!' "

"Is that why you're running?" the man in the river asked.

"Well, wouldn't you run if you were in their position?" the river said.

The man jumped out of the water and began to run with the others. They ran down the main street of the village to the house of the chief. The chief's servants brought his stool out, and he came and sat on it to listen to their complaints. The men began to recite their troubles.

"I went out to the garden to dig yams," the farmer said, waving his arms. "Then everything began to talk! My yam said, 'Leave me alone!' My dog said, 'Pay attention to your yam!' The tree said, 'Put that branch down!' The branch said, 'Do it gently!' And the stone said, 'Take it off me!' "

"And my fish-trap said, 'Well, did he take it off?' " the fisherman said.

"And my cloth said, 'You'd run too!' " the weaver said.

"And the river said the same," the bather said hoarsely, his eyes bulging.

The chief listened to them patiently, but he couldn't refrain from scowling.

"Now this is really a wild story," he said at last. "You'd better all go back to your work before I punish you for disturbing the peace."

So the men went away, and the chief shook his head and mumbled to himself, "Nonsense like that upsets the community."

"Fantastic, isn't it?" his stool said. "Imagine a talking yam!"

The Tiger's Tail

By Harold Courlander

A FARMER was coming home from his rice fields one evening. His mind wandered gently over thoughts of eating, sleeping, and playing his flute. As he walked along the trail he came to a pile of rocks. Protruding through a crack he saw a tail switching back and forth. It was a tiger's tail. It was very large.

The farmer was overcome with panic. He thought of running to the village. But then he realized the tiger was waiting for him to appear around the turn of the trail. So he dropped his sickle and seized the tiger's tail.

There was a struggle. The tiger tried to free himself. He pulled. The farmer pulled. They tugged back and forth. The tiger snarled and clawed. The farmer gasped and perspired, but he clung frantically to the tail.

While the desperate struggle was going on a monk came walking along the trail.

"Oh, Allah has sent you!" the farmer cried. "Take my sickle from the ground and kill this fierce tiger while I hold him!"

The holy man looked at him calmly and said:

"Ah, I cannot. It is against my principles to kill."

"How can you say such a thing!" the farmer said. "If I let go this tail, which sooner or later I must do, the angry animal will turn on me and kill me!"

"I am sorry, brother," the monk said. "But my religion won't permit me to kill any living creature."

"How can you argue this way?" the farmer cried. "If you don't help me you will be the cause of my death. Isn't the life of a man worth as much as the life of a tiger?"

The monk listened thoughtfully and said calmly:

"All around us the things of the jungle kill each other, and for these things I am not responsible. I cannot take a life, it is written so."

The farmer felt his strength leaving him. The tiger's tail was slipping from his tired hands. At last he said:

"Oh, my holy, kind-hearted friend, if

it is so written, it is so written! Do me then one favor. Hold this tiger's tail so that I may kill him!"

The monk looked into the sky and thought.

"Very well, there is nothing written that says I may not hold a tiger's tail."

So he came forward and took hold of the tail.

"Do you have it?" the farmer asked.

"Yes, I have it," the monk replied.

"Do you have it firmly?"

"Yes, I have it firmly."

The farmer released his hold. He wiped the sweat from his face with his head cloth. He picked up his sickle from the ground where he had dropped it. He straightened his clothes and brushed the dust from his hands. Then he started toward the village.

The tiger renewed the tug of war with great energy. The monk clung frantically to the tail. They pulled back and forth desperately.

"Kill him, kill him quickly!" the monk shouted.

The farmer continued toward the village.

"Where are you going? I can't hold on much longer!" the monk cried in alarm. "Kill him with your sickle!"

The farmer turned around placidly. His face was very peaceful.

"Oh, holy and venerable man," he said. "It was good to listen to your sacred words and to hear what is written. I have been moved by your feeling for living things. You have converted me. I now believe as you do. And as it is written, I may not kill any living creature. If you hold on with patience, other men who do not have such high ideals as we do may soon come this way and destroy the tiger for you."

And the farmer bowed and continued his way to the village.

The Blind Men and the Elephant

By John G. Saxe

It was six men of Indostan
  To learning much inclined,
Who went to see the elephant
  (Though all of them were blind),
That each by observation
  Might satisfy his mind.

The first approached the elephant,
  And happening to fall
Against his broad and sturdy side,
  At once began to bawl:
"God bless me! but the elephant
  Is very like a wall!"

The second, feeling of the tusk,
  Cried, "Ho! what have we here
So very round and smooth and sharp?
  To me 'tis mighty clear
This wonder of an elephant
  Is very like a spear!"

The third approached the animal,
  And happening to take
The squirming trunk within his hands,
  Thus boldly up and spake:
"I see," quoth he, "the elephant
  Is very like a snake!"

The fourth reached out his eager hand,
  And felt about the knee,
"What most this wondrous beast is like
  Is mighty plain," quoth he;
" 'Tis clear enough the elephant
  Is very like a tree!"

The fifth, who chanced to touch the ear,
  Said, "E'en the blindest man
Can tell what this resembles most;
  Deny the fact who can,
This marvel of an elephant
  Is very like a fan!"

The sixth no sooner had begun
  About the beast to grope,
Than, seizing on the swinging tail
  That fell within his scope,
"I see," quoth he, "the elephant
  Is very like a rope!"

And so these men of Indostan
  Disputed loud and long,
Each in his own opinion
  Exceeding stiff and strong,
Though each was partly in the right,
  And all were in the wrong!

Why the Dog and the Cat Are Not Friends

A KOREAN FOLK TALE

By Frances Carpenter

"WHY do dogs and cats fight so, Granny?" the little girl asked, looking up from her tray of pine seeds.

"My grandmother used to tell me a story about that," Granny said, "and I'll tell it to you."

And this is the story:

The dog and the cat in my tale lived in a small wine-shop on the bank of a broad river beside a ferry, my children. Old Koo, the shopkeeper, had neither wife nor child. In his little hut he lived by himself except for this dog and this cat. The tame beasts never left his side. While he sold wine in the shop, the dog kept guard at the door and the cat caught mice in the storeroom. When he walked on the river bank, they trotted by his side. When he lay down to sleep upon the warm floor, they crept close to his back. They were good enough friends then, the dog and the cat, but that was before the disaster occurred and the cat behaved so badly.

Old Koo was poor, decent, honest and kind. His shop was not like those where travelers are persuaded to drink wine until they become drunk and roll on the ground. Only one kind of wine was sold, but it was a good wine. Once they had tasted it, Koo's customers came back again and again to fill their long-necked wine bottles.

"Where does Old Koo get so much wine?" the neighbors used to ask one another. "No new jars are ever delivered by bull carts at his door. He makes no wine

90

himself, yet his black jug is never without wine to pour for his customers."

No one knew the answer to the riddle save Old Koo himself, and he told it to no one except his dog and his cat. Years before he opened his wine-shop, Koo had worked on the ferry. One cold rainy night when the last ferry had returned, a strange traveler came to the gate of his hut.

"Honorable Sir," he begged Koo, "give me a drop of good wine to drive out the damp chill."

"My wine jug is almost empty," Koo told the traveler. "I have only a little for my evening drink, but no doubt you need the wine far more than I. I'll share it with you." And he filled up a bowl for this strange, thirsty guest.

The stranger on leaving put into the ferryman's hand a bit of bright golden amber. "Keep this in your wine jug," he said, "and it will always be full."

Now, as Old Koo told his dog and his cat, that traveler must have been a spirit from Heaven, for when Koo lifted the black jug, it was heavy with wine. When he filled his bowl from it, he thought he had never tasted a drink so sweet and so rich. No matter how much he poured, the wine in the jug never grew less.

Here was a treasure indeed. With a jug that never ran dry, he could open a wine-shop. He would no longer have to go back and forth, back and forth, in the ferryboat over the river in all kinds of weather.

All went well until one day when he was serving a traveler, Koo found to his horror that his black jug was empty. He shook it and shook it, but no answering tinkle came from the hard amber charm that should have been inside.

"*Ai-go! Ai-go!*" Koo wailed. "I must unknowingly have poured the amber out into the bottle of one of my customers. *Ai-go!* What shall I do?"

The dog and the cat shared their master's sadness. The dog howled at the moon, and the cat prowled around the shop, sniffing and sniffing under the rice jars and even high up on the rafters. These animals knew the secret of the magic wine jug, for the old man had often talked to them about the stranger's amber charm.

"I am sure I could find the charm," the cat said to the dog, "if I only could catch its amber smell."

"We shall search for it together," the dog suggested. "We shall go through every house in the neighborhood. When you sniff it out, I will run home with it."

So they began their quest. They asked all the cats and dogs they met for news of the lost amber. They prowled about all the houses, but not a trace could they find of their master's magic charm.

"We must try the other side of the river," the dog said at last. "They will not let us ride across on the ferryboat. But when the winter cold comes and the river's stomach is solid, we can safely creep over the ice, like everyone else."

Thus it was that one winter morning the dog and the cat crossed the river to the opposite side. As soon as the owners were not looking, they crept into the houses. The dog sniffed around the courtyards, and the cat even climbed up on the beams under the sloping grass roofs. Day after day, week after week, month after month, they searched and they searched, but with no success.

Spring was at hand. The joyful fish in the river were bumping their backs against the soft ice. At last, one day, high up on the top of a great brassbound chest, the cat smelled the amber. But, *ai*, the welcome perfume came from inside a tightly closed box. What could they do? If they pushed the box off the chest and let it break on the floor, the Master of the House would surely be warned and chase them away.

"We must get help from the rats," the clever dog cried. "They can gnaw a hole in the box for us and get the amber out. In return, we can promise to let them live in peace for ten years." This plan was all against the nature of a cat, but this one loved its master and it consented.

The rats consented, too. It seemed to them almost too good to be true that both the cats and the dogs might leave them alone for ten whole peaceful years. It took the rats many days to gnaw a hole in that box, but at last it was done. The cat tried to get at the amber with its soft paw, but the hole was too small. Finally a young mouse had to be sent in through the wee hole. It succeeded in pulling the amber out with its teeth.

"How pleased our master will be! Now good luck will live again under his roof," the cat and the dog said to each other. In their joy at finding the lost amber charm,

they ran around and around as if they were having fits.

"But how shall we get the amber back to the other side of the river?" the cat cried in dismay. "You know I cannot swim."

"You shall hold the amber safely inside your mouth, Cat," the dog replied wisely. "You shall climb on my back, and I'll swim you over the river."

And so it happened. Clawing the thick shaggy hair of the dog's back, the cat kept its balance until they had almost reached their own bank of the stream. But there, playing along the shore, were a number of children, who burst into laughter when they saw the strange ferryman and his curious passenger. "A cat riding on the back of a dog! Ho! Ho! Ho!" they laughed. "Ha! Ha! Ha! Ho! Ho! Ho! Just look at that." They called to their parents, and they came to laugh, too.

Now the fatihful dog paid no attention to their foolish mirth, but the cat could not help joining them in the fun. It, too, began to laugh, and from its open mouth Old Koo's precious amber charm dropped down upon the river bottom.

The dog shook the cat off his back, he was so angry, and it was a miracle that the creature at last got safely to the shore. In a rage the dog chased the cat, which finally took refuge in the crotch of a tree. There the cat shook the moisture out of its fur. By spitting and spitting, it got rid of the water it had swallowed while in the river. The cat dared not come down out of the tree until the angry dog had gone away.

That, so my grandmother said, is why the dog and the cat are never friends, my dear ones. That is why, too, a cat always spits when a strange dog comes too near. That is why a cat does not like to get its feet wet.

"But what about the amber charm and poor Old Koo?" the little girl asked anxiously.

"It was that dog who finally saved the fortunes of the old wine-shop keeper," Granny explained. "First he tried swimming out into the stream to look for the amber. But it was too deep for him to see the bottom. Then he sat beside the river fishermen, wishing he had a line or a net like theirs that would bring up the golden prize he sought. Suddenly from a fish that had just been pulled out of the water, the dog sniffed amber perfume. Grabbing that fish up in his mouth before the fisherman could stop him, he galloped off home."

"Well done, Dog," said Old Koo. "There is only a little food left under our roof. This fish will make a good meal for you and me." The old man cut open the fish and, to his surprise and delight, the bit of amber rolled out.

"Now I can put my magic charm back into the jug," Koo said to himself. "But there must be at least a little wine in it to start the jug flowing again. While I go out to buy some, I'll just lock the amber up inside my clothes chest."

When Koo came back with the wine and opened the chest, he found that instead of the one suit he had stored in it, there were now two. Where his last string

of cash had been, there were two strings. And he guessed that the secret of this amber charm was that it would double whatever it touched.

With this knowledge Koo became rich beyond telling. And in the gate of his fine new house he cut a doghole for his faithful friend, who had saved him from starving. There, day and night, like our own four-footed gate guard, the fat dog lay watching in peace and well-fed contentment. But all through his life he never again killed a mouse nor made a friend of a cat.

Ghost of the Lagoon

By *Armstrong Sperry*

THE ISLAND of Bora Bora, where Mako lived, is far away in the south Pacific. It is not a large island—you can paddle around it in a single day—but the main body of it rises straight out of the sea, very high into the air, like a castle. Waterfalls trail down the faces of the cliffs. As you look upward, you see wild goats leaping from crag to crag.

Mako had been born on the very edge of the sea, and most of his waking hours were spent in the waters of the lagoon, which was nearly enclosed by the two outstretched arms of the island. He was very clever with his hands; he had made a harpoon that was as straight as an arrow, and tipped with five, pointed, iron spears. He had made a canoe, hollowing it out of a tree. It wasn't a very big canoe—only a little longer than his own height. It had an outrigger, a sort of balancing pole, fastened to one side to keep the boat from tipping over. The canoe was just large enough to hold Mako and his little dog, Afa. They were great companions, these two.

One evening Mako lay stretched at full length on the pandanus mats, listening to Grandfather's voice. Overhead, stars shone in the dark sky. From far off came the thunder of the surf on the reef.

The old man was speaking of Tupa, the ghost of the lagoon. Ever since the boy could remember, he had heard tales of this terrible monster. Frightened fishermen, returning from the reef at midnight, spoke of the ghost. Over the evening fires, old men told endless tales about the monster.

Tupa seemed to think the lagoon of Bora Bora belonged to him. The natives left presents of food for him out on the reef: a dead goat, a chicken, or a pig. The presents always disappeared mysteriously, but everyone felt sure that it was Tupa who carried them away. Still, in spite of all this food, the nets of the fishermen were torn during the night, the fish stolen. What an appetite Tupa seemed to have!

Not many people had ever seen the ghost of the lagoon. Grandfather was one of the few who had.

"What does he really look like, Grandfather?" the boy asked, for the hundredth time.

The old man shook his head solemnly. The light from the cook-fire glistened on his white hair. "Tupa lives in the great caves of the reef. He is longer than this house. There is a sail on his back, not large, but terrible to see, for it burns with a white fire. Once, when I was fishing beyond the reef at night, I saw him come up right under another canoe—"

"What happened then?" Mako asked.

He half rose on one elbow. This was a story he had not heard before.

The old man's voice dropped to a whisper. "Tupa dragged the canoe right under the water—and the water boiled with white flame. The three fishermen in it were never seen again. Fine swimmers they were, too."

Grandfather shook his head. "It is bad fortune even to speak of Tupa. There is evil in his very name."

"But King Opu Nui has offered a reward for his capture," the boy pointed out.

"Thirty acres of fine coconut land, and a sailing canoe as well," said the old man. "But who ever heard of laying hands on a ghost?"

Mako's eyes glistened. "Thirty acres of land and a sailing canoe. How I should love to win that reward!"

Grandfather nodded, but Mako's mother scolded her son for such foolish talk. "Be quiet now, son, and go to sleep. Grandfather has told you that it is bad fortune to speak of Tupa. Alas, how well we have learned that lesson! Your father—" She stopped herself.

"What of my father?" the boy asked quickly. And now he sat up straight on the mats.

"Tell him, Grandfather," his mother whispered.

The old man cleared his throat and poked at the fire. A little shower of sparks whirled up into the darkness.

95

"Your father," he explained gently, "was one of the three fishermen in the canoe that Tupa destroyed." His words fell upon the air like stones dropped into a deep well.

Mako shivered. He brushed back the hair from his damp forehead. Then he squared his shoulders and cried fiercely, "I shall slay Tupa and win the King's reward!" He rose to his knees, his slim body tense, his eyes flashing in the firelight.

"Hush!" his mother said. "Go to sleep now. Enough of such foolish talk. Would you bring trouble upon us all?"

Mako lay down again upon the mats. He rolled over on his side and closed his eyes, but sleep was long in coming.

The palm trees whispered above the dark lagoon, and far out on the reef the sea thundered.

The boy was slow to wake up the next morning. The ghost of Tupa had played through his dreams, making him restless. And so it was almost noon before Mako sat up on the mats and stretched himself. He called Afa, and the boy and his dog ran down to the lagoon for their morning swim.

When they returned to the house, wide awake and hungry, Mako's mother had food ready and waiting.

"These are the last of our bananas," she told him. "I wish you would paddle out to the reef this afternoon and bring back a new bunch."

The boy agreed eagerly. Nothing pleased him more than such an errand, which would take him to a little island on the outer reef, half a mile from shore. It was one of Mako's favorite playgrounds, and there bananas and oranges grew in great plenty.

"Come, Afa," he called, gulping the last mouthful. "We're going on an expedition." He picked up his long-bladed knife and seized his spear. A minute later, he dashed across the white sand, where his canoe was drawn up beyond the water's reach.

Afa barked at his heels. He was all white except for a black spot over each eye. Wherever Mako went, there went Afa also. Now the little dog leaped into the bow of the canoe, his tail wagging with delight. The boy shoved the canoe into the water and climbed aboard. Then picking up his paddle, he thrust it into the water. The canoe shot ahead. Its sharp bow cut through the green water of the lagoon like a knife through cheese. And so clear was the water that Mako could see the coral gardens, forty feet below him, growing in the sand. The shadow of the canoe moved over them.

A school of fish swept by like silver arrows. He saw scarlet rock cod with ruby eyes and the head of a conger eel peering out from a caravan in the coral. The boy thought suddenly of Tupa, ghost of the lagoon. On such a bright day it was hard to believe in ghosts of any sort. The fierce sunlight drove away all thought of them. Perhaps ghosts were only old men's stories, anyway!

Mako's eyes came to rest upon his spear—the spear that he had made with his own hands—the spear that was as straight and true as an arrow. He remembered his vow of the night before. Could a ghost be killed with a spear? Some night, when all the village was sleeping, Mako swore to himself that he would find out! He would paddle out to the reef and challenge Tupa! Perhaps tonight. Why

up near one end were two dark holes that looked like eyes!

Times without number the boy had practiced spearing this make-believe shark, aiming always for the eyes, the most vulnerable spot. So true and straight had his aim become that the spear would

not? He caught his breath at the thought. A shiver ran down his back. His hands were tense on the paddle.

As the canoe drew away from shore, the boy saw the coral reef that, above all others, had always interested him. It was of white coral—a long slim shape that rose slightly above the surface of the water. It looked very much like a shark. There was a ridge on the back that the boy could pretend was a dorsal fin, while

pass right into the eyeholes without even touching the sides of the coral. Mako had named the coral reef "Tupa."

This morning, as he paddled past it, he shook his fist and called, "Ho, Mister Tupa! Just wait till I get my bananas. When I come back I'll make short work of you!"

Afa followed his master's words with a sharp bark. He knew Mako was excited about something.

97

The bow of the canoe touched the sand of the little island where the bananas grew. Afa leaped ashore and ran barking into the jungle, now on this trail, now on that. Clouds of sea birds whirled from their nests into the air with angry cries.

Mako climbed into the shallow water, waded ashore, and pulled his canoe up on the beach. Then, picking up his banana knife, he followed Afa. In the jungle the light was so dense and green that the boy felt as if he were moving under water. Ferns grew higher than his head. The branches of the trees formed a green roof over him. A flock of parakeets fled on swift wings. Somewhere a wild pig crashed through the undergrowth while Afa dashed away in pursuit. Mako paused anxiously. Armed only with his banana knife, he had no desire to meet the wild pig. The pig, it seemed, had no desire to meet him, either.

Then, ahead of him, the boy saw the broad green blades of a banana tree. A bunch of bananas, golden ripe, was growing out of the top.

At the foot of the tree he made a nest of soft leaves for the bunch to fall upon. In this way the fruit wouldn't be crushed. Then with a swift slash of his blade he cut the stem. The bananas fell to the earth with a dull thud. He found two more bunches.

Then he thought, "I might as well get some oranges while I'm here. Those little rusty ones are sweeter than any that grow on Bora Bora."

So he set about making a net out of palm leaves to carry the oranges. As he worked, his swift fingers moving in and out among the strong green leaves, he could hear Afa's excited barks off in the jungle. That was just like Afa, always barking at something: a bird, a fish, a wild pig. He never caught anything, either. Still, no boy ever had a finer companion.

The palm net took longer to make than Mako had realized. By the time it was finished and filled with oranges, the jungle was dark and gloomy. Night comes quickly and without warning in the islands of the tropics.

Mako carried the fruit down to the shore and loaded it into the canoe. Then he whistled to Afa. The dog came bounding out of the bush, wagging his tail.

"Hurry!" Mako scolded. "We won't be home before the dark comes."

The little dog leaped into the bow of the canoe and Mako came aboard. Night seemed to rise up from the surface of the water and swallow them. On the distant shore of Bora Bora, cook-fires were being lighted. The first star twinkled just over the dark mountains. Mako dug his paddle into the water and the canoe leaped ahead.

The dark water was alive with phosphorus. The bow of the canoe seemed to cut through a pale liquid fire. Each dip of the paddle trailed streamers of light. As the canoe approached the coral reef, the boy called, "Ho, Tupa! It's too late tonight to teach you your lesson. But I'll come back tomorrow." The coral shark glistened in the darkness.

And then, suddenly, Mako's breath

caught in his throat. His hands felt weak. Just beyond the fin of the coral Tupa, there was another fin—a huge one. It had never been there before. And—could he believe his eyes? It was moving.

The boy stopped paddling. He dashed his hand across his eyes. Afa began to bark furiously. The great white fin, shaped like a small sail, glowed with phosphorescent light. Then Mako knew. Here was Tupa—the real Tupa—ghost of the lagoon!

His knees felt weak. He tried to cry out, but his voice died in his throat. The great shark was circling slowly around the canoe. With each circle, it moved closer and closer. Now the boy could see the phosphorescent glow of the great shark's sides. As it moved in closer, he saw the yellow eyes, the gill-slits in its throat.

Afa leaped from one side of the canoe to the other. In sudden anger Mako leaned forward to grab the dog and shake him soundly. Afa wriggled out of his grasp, as Mako tried to catch him, and the shift in weight tipped the canoe on one side. The outrigger rose from the water. In another second they would be overboard. The boy threw his weight over quickly to balance the canoe, but with a loud splash Afa fell over into the dark water.

Mako stared after him in dismay. The little dog, instead of swimming back to the canoe, had headed for the distant shore. And there was the great white shark—very near.

"Afa! Afa! Come back! Come quickly!" Mako shouted.

The little dog turned back toward the canoe. He was swimming with all his strength. Mako leaned forward. Could Afa make it? Swiftly the boy seized his spear. Bracing himself, he stood upright. There was no weakness in him now. His dog, his companion, was in danger of instant death.

Afa was swimming desperately to reach the canoe. The white shark had paused in his circling to gather speed for the attack. Mako raised his arm, took aim. In that instant the shark charged. Mako's arm flashed forward. All his strength was behind that thrust. The spear drove straight and true, right into the great shark's eye. Mad with pain and rage, Tupa whipped about, lashing the water in fury. The canoe rocked back and forth. Mako struggled to keep his balance as he drew back the spear by the cord fastened to his wrist.

He bent over to seize Afa and drag him aboard. Then he stood up, not a moment too soon. Once again the shark charged. Once again Mako threw his spear, this time at the other eye. The spear found its mark. Blinded and weak from loss of blood, Tupa rolled to the surface, turned slightly on his side. Was he dead?

Mako knew how clever sharks could be, and he was taking no chances. Scarcely daring to breathe, he paddled toward the still body. He saw the faintest motion of the great tail. The shark was

still alive. The boy knew that one flip of that tail could overturn the canoe and send him and Afa into the water, where Tupa could destroy them.

Swiftly, yet calmly, Mako stood upright and braced himself firmly. Then, murmuring a silent prayer to the Shark God, he threw his spear for the last time. Downward, swift as sound, the spear plunged into a white shoulder.

Peering over the side of the canoe, Mako could see the great fish turn over far below the surface. Then slowly, slowly, the great shark rose to the surface of the lagoon. There he floated, half on one side.

Tupa was dead.

Mako flung back his head and shouted for joy. Hitching a strong line about the shark's tail, the boy began to paddle toward the shore of Bora Bora. The dorsal fin, burning with the white fire of phosphorus, trailed after the canoe.

Men were running down the beaches of Bora Bora, shouting as they leaped into their canoes and put out across the lagoon. Their cries reached the boy's ears across the water.

"It is Tupa—ghost of the lagoon," he heard them shout. "Mako has killed him!"

That night, as the tired boy lay on the pandanus mats listening to the distant thunder of the sea, he heard Grandfather singing a new song. It was the song which would be sung the next day at the feast which King Opu Nui would give in Mako's honor. The boy saw his mother bending over the cook-fire. The stars leaned close, winking like friendly eyes. Grandfather's voice reached him now from a great distance, "Thirty acres of land and a sailing canoe . . ."

The Alligator and
The Jackal

By Marie Frère

A HUNGRY Jackal once went down to the riverside in search of little crabs, bits of fish, and whatever else he could find for his dinner. Now it chanced that in this river there lived a great big Alligator, who, being also very hungry, would have been extremely glad to eat the Jackal.

The Jackal ran up and down, here and there, but for a long time could find nothing to eat. At last, close to where the Alligator was lying among some tall bulrushes under the clear, shallow water, he saw a little crab sidling along as fast as his legs could carry him. The Jackal was so hungry that when he saw this he poked his paw into the water to try to catch the crab, when snap! the old Alligator caught hold of him. "Oh, dear!" thought the Jackal to himself, "what can I do? This great, big Alligator has caught my paw in his mouth, and in another minute he will drag me down by it under the water and kill me. My only chance is to make him think he has made a mistake." So he called out in a cheerful voice, "Clever Alligator, clever Alligator, to catch hold of a bulrush root instead of my paw! I hope you find it very tender." The Alligator, who was so buried among the bulrushes that he could hardly see, thought, on hearing this, "Dear me, how tiresome! I fancied I had caught hold of the Jackal's paw, but there he is, calling out in a cheerful voice. I suppose I must have seized a bulrush root instead, as he says," and he let the Jackal go.

The Jackal ran away as fast as he could, crying, "O wise Alligator, wise Alligator! So you let me go again!" Then the Alligator was very much vexed, but the Jackal had run away too far to be caught. Next day the Jackal returned to the riverside to get his dinner as before. He was very much afraid of the Alligator so he called out, "Whenever I go to look for my dinner, I see the nice little crabs peeping up through the mud. I catch them and eat them. I wish I could see one now."

The Alligator, who was buried in the mud at the bottom of the river, heard every word. So he popped the little point of his snout above it, thinking, "If I just show the tip of my nose, the Jackal will take me for a crab and put in his paw to catch me, and as soon as he does I'll gobble him up."

But no sooner did the Jackal see the little tip of the Alligator's nose than he called out, "Aha, my friend! there you are. No dinner for me in this part of the river, then, I think." And so saying, he ran farther on and fished for his dinner a long way from that place. The Alligator was very angry at missing his prey a second time, and determined not to let him escape again.

So on the following day, when his little tormentor returned to the waterside, the Alligator hid himself close to the bank, in order to catch him if he could. Now the Jackal was rather afraid of going near the river, for he thought, "Perhaps the Alligator will catch me to-day." Yet, being hungry, he did not wish to go without his dinner, so to make all as safe as he could, he cried. "Where are all the little crabs gone? There is not one here and I am so hungry. Generally, even when they are under water, one can see them going bubble, bubble, bubble, and all the little bubbles go pop! pop! pop!"

On hearing this the Alligator. who was buried in the mud under the river bank, thought, "I will pretend to be a little crab." And he began to blow, "Puff, puff, puff! Bubble, bubble, bubble!" and all the great bubbles rushed to the surface of the river and burst there, and the waters eddied round and round like a whirlpool.

There was such a commotion when the huge monster began to blow bubbles in this way that the Jackal saw very well who must be there, and he ran away as fast as he could, saying, "Thank you, kind Alligator, thank you, thank you! Indeed, I would not have come here had I known you were so close."

This enraged the Alligator extremely. It made him quite cross to think of being so often deceived by a little Jackal, and he said to himself, "I will be taken in no more. Next time I will be very cunning." So for a long time he waited

and waited for the Jackal to return to the riverside. But the Jackal did not come, for he had thought to himself, "If matters go on in this way, I shall some day be caught and eaten by the wicked old Alligator. I had better content myself with living on wild figs." And he went no more near the river, but stayed in the jungles and ate wild figs, and roots which he dug up with his paws.

When the Alligator found this out, he determined to try and catch the Jackal on land. The ground under the largest of the wild fig-trees was covered with the fallen fruit. So he collected a quantity of it together, and, burying himself under the great heap, waited for the Jackal to appear. But no sooner did the cunning little animal see this great heap of wild figs all collected together than he thought, "That looks very like my friend the Alligator." And to discover if it were so or not, he called out, "The juicy little wild figs I love to eat always tumble down from the tree, and roll here and there as the wind drives them, but this great heap of figs is quite still. These cannot be good figs. I will not eat any of them." "Ho, ho!" thought the Alligator, "is that all? How suspicious this Jackal is! I will make the figs roll about a little, and then, he will doubtless come and eat them."

So the great beast shook himself, and all the heap of little figs went roll, roll, roll—some a mile this way, some a mile that, farther than they had ever rolled

before or than the most blustering wind could have driven them.

Seeing this, the Jackal scampered away, saying "I am so much obliged to you, Alligator, for letting me know you are there, for indeed I should hardly have guessed it. You were so buried under that heap of figs." The Alligator, hearing this, was so angry that he ran after the Jackal, but the latter ran away very, very fast, too quickly to be caught.

Then the Alligator said to himself, "I will not allow that little wretch to make fun of me another time and then run away out of reach. I will show him that I can be more cunning than he fancies." And early the next morning he crawled as fast as he could to the Jackal's den (which was a hole in the side of a hill) and crept into it, and hid himself, waiting for the Jackal, who was out, to return home. But when the Jackal got near the place, he looked about him and thought, "Dear me! the ground looks as if some heavy creature had been walking over it, and here are great clods of earth knocked down from each side of the door of my den, as if a very big animal had been trying to squeeze himself through it. I certainly will not go inside until I know that all is safe there." So he called out: "Little house, pretty house, my sweet little house, why do you not give an answer when I call? If I come, and all is safe and right, you always call out to me. Is anything wrong, that you do not speak?"

Then the Alligator, who was inside,

thought, "If that is the case I had better call out, that he may fancy all is right in his house." And in as gentle a voice as he could, he said, "Sweet little Jackal."

At hearing these words the Jackal felt quite frightened, and thought to himself, "So the dreadful old Alligator is there. I must try to kill him if I can, for if I do not he will certainly catch and kill me some day." He therefore answered, "Thank you, my dear little house. I like to hear your pretty voice. I am coming in a minute, but first I must collect firewood to cook my dinner." And he ran as fast as he could, and dragged all the dry branches and bits of stick he could find close up to the mouth of the den. Meantime, the Alligator inside kept as quiet as a mouse, but he could not help laughing a little to himself as he thought, "So I have deceived this tiresome little Jackal at last. In a few minutes he will run in here, and then won't I snap him up!"

When the Jackal had gathered together all the sticks he could find and put them around the mouth of his den, he set them on fire and pushed them as far inside as possible. There was such a quantity of them that they soon blazed up into a great fire, and the smoke and flames filled the den. They smothered the wicked old Alligator and burned him to death, while the little Jackal ran up and down outside dancing for joy and singing:

"How do you like my house, my friend? Is it nice and warm? Ding-dong! ding-dong! The Alligator is dying! ding-dong, ding-dong! He will trouble me no more. I have defeated my enemy! Ring-a-ting! ding-a-ting! ding-ding-dong!"

The Wonderful Mallet

An Old Japanese Tale

ONCE upon a time there were two brothers. The elder was an honest and good man, but he was very poor, while the younger, who was dishonest and stingy, had managed to pile up a large fortune. The name of the elder was Kané, and that of the younger was Chô.

Now, one day Kané went to Chô's house, and begged for the loan of some seed-rice and some silkworms' eggs, for he was in want of both.

Chô had plenty of good rice and excellent silkworms' eggs, but he was such a miser that he did not want to lend them. At the same time, he felt ashamed to refuse his brother's request, so he gave him some worm-eaten musty rice and some dead eggs, which he felt sure would never hatch.

Kané, never suspecting that his brother would play him such a shabby trick, put plenty of mulberry leaves with the eggs, to be food for the silkworms when they should appear. Appear they did, and throve and grew wonderfully, much better than those of the stingy brother, who was angry and jealous when he heard of it.

Going to Kané's house one day, and finding his brother was out, Chô took a knife and killed all the silkworms, cutting each poor little creature in two.

Then he went home without having been seen by anybody.

When Kané came home he was dismayed to find his silkworms in this state, but he did not suspect who had done him such a bad turn. He tried feeding them with mulberry leaves as before. The silkworms came to life again, and doubled their number, for now each half had become a living worm. They grew and throve, and the silk they spun was twice as much as Kané had expected. So now he began to prosper.

The envious Chô, seeing this, cut all his own silkworms in half, but, alas! they did not come to life again, so he lost a great deal of money, and became more jealous than ever of his brother.

Kané also planted the rice-seed which he had borrowed from his brother, and it sprang up, and grew far better than Chô's had done.

The rice ripened well, and Kané was just ready to cut and harvest it when a flight of thousands upon thousands of swallows came and began to devour it. Kané was much astonished, and shouted and made as much noise as he could in order to drive them away. They flew away, indeed, but came back immediately, so that he kept driving them away, and they kept flying back again.

At last he pursued them into a distant field, where he lost sight of them. He was by this time so hot and tired that he sat down to rest. Little by little his eyes closed, his head dropped, and he fell fast asleep.

Then he dreamed that a merry band of children came into the field, laughing and shouting. They sat down upon the ground in a ring, and one who seemed the eldest, a boy of fourteen or fifteen, came close to the bank on which he lay asleep, and, raising a big stone near his head, drew from under it a small wooden mallet.

Then in his dream Kané saw this big boy stand in the middle of the ring with the mallet in his hand, and ask the children each in turn, "What would you like the mallet to bring you?"

The first child answered, "A kite." The big boy shook the mallet, upon which appeared immediately a fine kite with tail and string all complete.

The next cried, "A battledore."

Out sprang a splendid battledore and a shower of shuttlecocks.

Then a little girl shyly whispered, "A doll."

The mallet was shaken, and there stood a beautifully-dressed doll.

"I should like all the fairy-tale books that have ever been written in the whole world," said a bright-eyed intelligent maiden, and no sooner had she spoken than piles upon piles of beautiful books appeared.

And so at last the wishes of all the children were granted, and they stayed a long time in the field with the things the mallet had given them. At last they got tired, and prepared to go home; but first the big boy carefully hid the mallet under the stone from whence he had taken it. Then all the children went away.

Presently Kané awoke, and gradually remembered his dream. In preparing to rise he turned around, and there, close to where his head had lain, was the big stone he had seen in his dream. "How strange!" he thought, expecting he hardly knew what. He raised the stone, and there lay the mallet!

He took it home with him, and, following the example of the children he had seen in his dream, shook it, at the same time calling out, "Gold" or "Rice," "Silk" or "Saké." Whatever he called for flew immediately out of the mallet, so that he could have everything he wanted, and as much of it as he liked.

Kané being now a rich and prosperous man, Chô was of course jealous of him, and determined to find a magic mallet which would do as much for him. He came, therefore, to Kané and borrowed seed-rice, which he planted and tended with care, being impatient for it to grow and ripen soon.

It grew well and ripened soon, and now Chô watched daily for the swallows to appear. And, to be sure, one day a flight of swallows came and began to eat up the rice.

Chô was delighted at this, and drove them away, pursuing them to the distant field where Kané had followed them before. There he lay down, intending to go to sleep as his brother had done, but the more he tried to go to sleep the wider awake he seemed.

Presently the band of children came skipping and jumping, so he shut his eyes and pretended to be asleep, but all the time he watched anxiously to see what the children would do. They sat down in a ring, as before, and the big boy came close to Chô's head and lifted the stone. He put down his hand to lift the mallet, but no mallet was there.

One of the children said, "Perhaps that lazy old farmer has taken our mallet." So the big boy laid hold of Chô's nose, which was rather long, and gave it a good pinch, and all the other children ran up and pinched and pulled his nose, and the nose itself got longer and longer. First it hung down to his

chin, then over his chest, next down to his knees, and at last to his very feet.

It was in vain that Chô protested his innocence; the children pinched and pummeled him to their hearts' content, then capered around him, shouting and laughing, and making game of him, and so at last went away.

Now Chô was left alone, a sad and angry man. Holding his long nose painfully in both hands, he slowly took his way toward his brother Kané's house. Here he related all that had happened to him from the very day when he had behaved so badly about the seed-rice and silkworms' eggs. He humbly begged his brother to pardon him, and, if possible, do something to restore his unfortunate nose to its proper size.

The kind-hearted Kané pitied him, and said: "You have been dishonest, mean, selfish and envious. That is why you have got this punishment. If you promise to behave better for the future, I will try to see what can be done."

So saying, he took the mallet and rubbed Chô's nose with it gently, and the nose gradually became shorter and shorter until at last it came back to its proper shape and size. But ever after, if at any time Chô felt inclined to be selfish and dishonest, as he did now and then, his nose began to smart and burn, and he fancied he felt it beginning to grow. So great was his horror of having a long nose again that these symptoms never failed to bring him back to good behavior.

Stories from
the Arabian Nights

Once there was a Sultan of Persia who, on discovering that his wife was in love with one of his slaves, ordered her to be killed. Then, to guard against such outrage in the future, he announced that he would marry a new wife every evening and have her killed the next morning.

Now, the Sultan's Grand Vizier, whose duty it was to lead these unfortunate ladies to his master, had two beautiful daughters, Scheherazade and Dinarzade.

One day, to her father's horror, Scheherazade asked him whether she could be the Sultan's next wife. "But, my dear girl," exclaimed her father, "he would kill you tomorrow morning!"

"I have a plan," replied Scheherazade, "that would prevent that cruel plan of his. Do let me try, father."

Unconvinced but persuaded, he at last consented.

Forthwith Scheherazade spoke to her sister, saying, "Dinarzade dear, before I go to the Sultan tonight, I am going to ask him to let you stay overnight in the palace too. If he agrees, I want you to wake me early tomorrow morning and say, 'I have not been able to sleep, my sister. Would you tell me one of those delightful stories you know?'"

And so it came to pass.

"Will your Majesty permit me to grant my sister's request?" Scheherazade asked the Sultan. And moved by the pleading eyes of his lovely bride, he agreed.

So, directing her words to the Sultan, Scheherazade began telling the first of the fabulous tales she continued telling him for the next thousand and one nights!

Some of her most famous stories are retold in the pages that follow.

The Three Wishes

A Sultan in ancient India had three sons, Hassan, Ali, and Ahmed, who were all in love with their cousin, the lovely Princess Nouronnihar.

"I wish to gather curiosities for my museum," the Sultan said to them. "Whoever brings me the rarest curiosity will have my niece in marriage."

The three Princes left together early one morning. That evening they rested at an inn. They agreed to separate, and to meet, after a year, at this same inn.

Prince Hassan, the oldest brother, traveled by caravan to the city of Bisnagar. There he met a merchant who offered to sell him a small carpet for forty purses of gold.

"Why so much?" asked Prince Hassan.

"This is a wishing carpet," explained the merchant. "Whoever sits on it, and wishes himself anywhere, will instantly be taken thither."

To test the carpet-seller's story, the Prince wished himself in his room at the inn. Instantly he found himself there. Prince Hassan readily gave the carpet-seller forty purses of gold, and made him a handsome present besides.

Prince Ali, the second son, traveled to the city of Shiraz in Persia. He met a merchant with a plain ivory tube which he was trying to sell for forty purses of gold.

"Why so much?" asked Prince Ali.

"It is a magic tube. If you look through it, you will at once behold any one you wish to see," replied the merchant.

Prince Ali placed the tube to his eye, and wished to see the Sultan, his father. Immediately he saw him on his throne. Then he wished to see the Princess Nouronnihar, and he saw her, too, as beautiful as ever.

Prince Ali gladly paid the price, and gave the man a handsome present as well.

Prince Ahmed, the youngest son, made his journey to Samarkand in Central Asia. He came upon a merchant selling what appeared to be a common imitation apple for forty purses of gold.

Prince Ahmed asked the merchant, "What is there about this apple that makes you put so high a price on it?"

"Sir," he responded, "this apple is a treasure. It can cure sick people even if they are dying."

Another merchant, overhearing this, said, "Sir, a friend of mine is deathly ill. Let us test the apple on him."

The merchant led them to the bedside of his sick friend. The apple-seller held the apple to the dying man's nose, and in a few moments he got up, quite recovered.

For forty purses of gold, and a gift besides, Prince Ahmed got the wonderful apple.

A year after their departure, the three brothers met at the inn where they had last dined together. Each was eager to boast of his purchase.

First, Prince Hassan showed his magic carpet, upon which he had returned from Bisnagar.

Then Prince Ali showed his ivory tube. Prince Hassan put it to his eye in his anxiety to see the Princess Nouronnihar. But what he saw filled him with grief.

"Alas, my brothers!" he cried, "our dear Princess is dying. I see her motionless on her bed, with all her women in tears."

Prince Ali looked through the tube, and passed it sadly to Prince Ahmed, who said: "Alas, it is true. She is dying. But I can save her life. Let us return immediately to the palace by the wishing carpet."

In a flash they were beside the Princess. As soon as Prince Ahmed held the magic apple to her nose, she opened her eyes and sat up.

The three Princes then went to pay their respects to the Sultan their father.

The Sultan listened thoughtfully to his sons as they presented their gifts. At last he said, "The Princess owes her life to Prince Ahmed's apple. But it was Prince Ali's tube which warned you of her danger, and Prince Hassan's carpet which brought you all hither in the nick of time. I shall have to let Nouronnihar decide for herself which of you she shall marry."

The lovely Princess, who had been in love with Prince Ahmed all along, chose him to be her husband. "After all," she said, "were it not for his magic apple, neither the wishing carpet nor the seeing-tube could have saved my life."

So they were married, and lived together in joy and happiness for the rest of their lives.

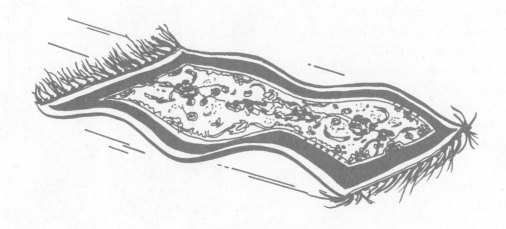

Aladdin and The Wonderful Lamp

FAR AWAY on the other side of the world, in one of the great wealthy cities of China, there once lived a poor tailor called Mustapha. He had a wife whom he loved dearly and an only son whose name was Aladdin.

But, sad to say, although the tailor was good and industrious, his son was so idle and bad that his father and mother did not know what to do with him. All day long he played in the streets with other idle boys, and when he grew big enough to learn a trade he said he did not mean to work at all. His poor father was very much troubled, and ordered Aladdin to come to the workshop to learn to be a tailor, but Aladdin only laughed, and ran away so swiftly that neither his father nor his mother could catch him.

"Alas," said Mustapha sadly, "I can do nothing with this idle boy."

And he grew so sad about it, that at last he fell ill and died.

Then the poor widow was obliged to sell the little workshop, and try to make enough money for herself and Aladdin by spinning.

Now it happened that one day when Aladdin was playing as usual with the idle street boys, a tall dark old man stood watching him, and when the game was finished he made a sign to Aladdin to come to him.

"What is thy name, my boy?" asked this old man, who, though he appeared so kind, was really an African magician.

"My name is Aladdin," answered the

112

boy, wondering who this stranger could be.

"And what is thy father's name?" asked the magician.

"My father was Mustapha the tailor, but he has been dead a long time now," answered Aladdin.

"Alas!" cried the wicked old magician, pretending to weep, "he was my brother, and thou must be my nephew. I am thy long-lost uncle!" and he threw his arms round Aladdin's neck and embraced him. "Tell thy dear mother that I will come and see her this very day," he cried, "and give her this small present." And he placed in Aladdin's hands five gold pieces.

Aladdin ran home in great haste to tell his mother the story of the long-lost uncle.

"It must be a mistake," she said, "thou hast no uncle."

But when she saw the gold she began to think that this stranger must be a relation, and so she prepared a grand supper to welcome him.

They had not long to wait before the African magician appeared, bringing with him all sorts of fruits and delicious sweets for dessert.

"Tell me about my poor brother," he said, as he embraced Aladdin and his mother. "Show me exactly where he used to sit."

The widow pointed to a seat on the sofa, and the magician knelt down and began to kiss the place and weep over it.

The poor widow was quite touched, and began to believe that this really must be her husband's brother, especially when he began to show the kindest interest in Aladdin.

"What is thy trade?" he asked the boy.

"Alas," said the widow, "he will do nothing but play in the streets."

Aladdin hung his head with shame as his uncle gravely shook his head.

"He must begin work at once," he said. "How would it please thee to have a shop of thine own? I could buy one for thee, and stock it with silks and rich stuffs."

Aladdin danced with joy at the very idea, and next day set out with his supposed uncle, who bought him a splendid suit of clothes, and took him all over the city to show him the sights.

The day after, the magician again took Aladdin out with him, but this time they went outside the city, through beautiful gardens, into the open country. They walked so far that at any other time Aladdin might have grown tired, but the magician gave him a cake and some delicious fruit and told him such wonderful tales that he scarcely noticed how far they had gone. At last they came to a deep valley between two mountains, and there the magician paused.

"Stop!" he cried. "This is the very place I am in search of. Gather some sticks to make a fire."

Aladdin quickly did as he was bid, and had soon gathered together a great heap of dry sticks. The magician then set fire to them, and the heap blazed up merrily. With great care the old man now sprinkled some curious-looking powder on the flames, and muttered strange words. In an instant the earth beneath their feet trembled, and they heard a rumbling like distant thunder. Then the ground opened in front of them, and showed a great square slab of stone with a ring in it.

By this time Aladdin was so frightened that he turned to run home as fast as he could, but the magician caught him, and gave him a blow that felled him to the earth.

"Why dost thou strike me, Uncle?" sobbed Aladdin.

"Do as I bid thee," said the magician, "and then thou shalt be well treated. Dost thou see that stone? Beneath it is a treasure which I will share with thee. Only obey me, and it will soon be ours."

As soon as Aladdin heard of the treasure, he jumped up and forgot all his fears. He seized the ring as the magician directed, and easily pulled up the stone.

"Now," said the old man, "look in and thou wilt see stone steps leading downwards. Thou shalt descend those steps until thou comest to three great halls. Pass through them, but take care to wrap thy coat well round thee so that thou touch nothing, for if thou dost, thou wilt die instantly. When thou hast passed through the halls thou wilt come into a garden of fruit trees. Go through it until thou seest a niche with a lighted lamp in it. Put the light out, pour forth the oil, and bring the lamp to me."

So saying the magician placed a magic ring upon Aladdin's finger to guard him, and bade the boy begin his search.

Aladdin did exactly as he was told and found everything just as the magician had said. He went through the halls and the garden until he came to the lamp, and when he had poured out the oil and placed the lamp carefully inside his coat, he began to look about him.

He had never seen such a lovely garden before, even in his dreams. The fruits that hung upon the trees were of every color in the rainbow. Some were clear and shining like crystal, some sparkled with a crimson light and others were green, blue, violet, and orange, while the leaves that shaded them were silver and gold. Aladdin did not guess that these fruits were precious stones, diamonds, rubies, emeralds, and sapphires, but they looked so pretty that he filled all his pockets with them as he passed back through the garden.

The magician was eagerly peering down the stone steps when Aladdin began to climb up.

"Give me the lamp," he cried, stretching his hand for it.

"Wait until I get out," answered Aladdin, "then I will give it thee."

"Hand it up to me at once," screamed the old man angrily.

"Not till I am safely out," repeated Aladdin.

Then the magician stamped with rage.

He rushed to the fire, threw on it some more of the curious powder, and uttered the same strange words as before. Instantly the stone slipped back into its place, the earth closed over it, and Aladdin was left in darkness.

This showed indeed that the wicked old man was not Aladdin's uncle. By his magic arts in Africa he had found out all about the lamp, which was a wonderful treasure, as you will see. But he knew that he could not get it himself, that another hand must fetch it to him. That was the reason he had fixed upon Aladdin to help him. He had meant, as soon as the lamp was safely in his hand, to kill the boy.

As his plan had failed he went back to Africa, and was not seen again for a long, long time.

But there was poor Aladdin, shut up underground, with no way of getting out! He tried to find his way back to the great halls and the beautiful garden of shining fruits, but the walls had closed up, and there was no escape that way either. For two days the poor boy sat crying and moaning in his despair, and just as he had made up his mind that he must die, he clasped his hands together, and in doing so rubbed the ring which the magician had put upon his finger.

In an instant a huge figure rose out of the earth and stood before him.

"What is thy will, my master," it said. "I am the Slave of the Ring, and must obey him who wears the ring."

"Whoever or whatever you are," cried Aladdin, "take me out of this dreadful place."

Scarcely had he said these words when the earth opened, and the next moment Aladdin found himself standing at his mother's door. He was so weak for want of food, and his joy at seeing his mother was so great, that he fainted away. But when he came to himself he promised to tell her all that had happened.

"First give me something to eat," he cried, "for I am dying of hunger."

"Alas!" said his mother, "I have nothing in the house except a little cotton, which I will go out and sell."

"Stop a moment," cried Aladdin, "rather let us sell this old lamp which I have brought back with me."

Now the lamp looked so old and dirty that Aladdin's mother began to rub it, wishing to brighten it a little that it might fetch a higher price.

But no sooner had she given it the first rub than a huge dark figure slowly rose from the floor like a wreath of smoke until it reached the ceiling, towering above them.

"What is thy will?" it asked. "I am the Slave of the Lamp, and must do the bidding of whoever holds the Lamp."

The moment the figure began to rise from the ground Aladdin's mother was so terrified that she fainted away, but Aladdin managed to snatch the lamp from her, although he could scarcely hold it in his own shaking hand.

"Fetch me something to eat," he said in a trembling voice, for the terrible genie was glaring down upon him.

The Slave of the Lamp disappeared in a cloud of smoke, but in an instant he was back again, bringing with him a most delicious breakfast, served upon plates and dishes of pure gold.

By this time Aladdin's mother had recovered, but she was almost too frightened to eat, and begged Aladdin to sell the lamp at once, for she was sure it had something to do with evil spirits. But Aladdin only laughed at her fears, and said he meant to make use of the magic lamp and wonderful ring, now that he knew their worth.

As soon as they again wanted money they sold the golden plates and dishes, and when these were all gone Aladdin ordered the genie to bring more, and so they lived in comfort for several years.

Now Aladdin had heard a great deal about the beauty of the Sultan's daughter, and he began to long so greatly to see her that he could not rest. He thought of a great many ways of getting to see her, but they all seemed impossible, for the Princess never went out without a veil, which covered her entirely. At last, however, he managed to enter the palace and hide himself behind a door, peeping through a chink when the Princess passed to go to her bath.

The moment Aladdin's eyes rested upon the beautiful Princess he loved her with all his heart, for she was as fair as the dawn of a summer morning.

"Mother," he cried when he reached

home, "I have seen the Princess, and I have made up my mind to marry her. Thou shalt go at once to the Sultan, and beg him to give me his daughter."

Aladdin's mother stared at her son, and then began to laugh at such a wild idea. She was almost afraid that Aladdin must be mad, but he gave her no peace until she did as he wished.

So the next day she very unwillingly set out for the palace, carrying the magic fruit wrapped up in a napkin to present to the Sultan. There were many other people offering their petitions that day, and the poor woman was so frightened that she dared not go forward. No one paid any attention to her as she stood there patiently holding her bundle. For a whole week she had gone every day to the palace, before the Sultan noticed her.

"Who is that poor woman who comes every day carrying a white bundle?" he asked.

Then the Grand Vizier ordered that she should be brought forward, and she came bowing herself to the ground.

She was almost too terrified to speak, but when the Sultan spoke so kindly to her, she took courage and told him of Aladdin's love for the Princess, and of his bold request. "He sends you this gift," she continued, and opening the bundle she presented the magic fruit.

A cry of wonder went up from all those who stood around, for never had they beheld such exquisite jewels before. They shone and sparkled with a thousand lights and colors, and dazzled the eyes that gazed upon them.

The Sultan was astounded, and spoke to the Grand Vizier apart.

"Surely it is fit that I should give my daughter to one who can present such a wondrous gift!" he said. He sent Aladdin's mother home satisfied that her request had been granted.

After three months she again presented herself before the Sultan, and reminded him of his promise that the Princess should wed her son.

"I always abide by my royal word," said the Sultan. "But he who marries my daughter must first send me forty golden basins filled to the brim with precious stones. These basins must be carried by forty black slaves, each led by a white slave dressed as befits the servants of the Sultan."

Aladdin's mother returned home in great distress when she heard this, and told Aladdin what the Sultan had said.

"Alas, my son," she cried, "thy hopes are ended."

"Not so, mother," answered Aladdin. "The Sultan shall not have long to wait for his answer."

Then he rubbed the magic lamp, and when the genie appeared, he bade him provide the forty golden basins filled with jewels, and all the slaves which the Sultan demanded.

Now when this splendid procession passed through the streets on its way to the palace, all the people came out to see the sight, and stood amazed at the golden basins filled with sparkling gems

carried on the heads of the slaves. And when the palace was reached, and the slaves presented the jewels to the Sultan, he was so surprised and delighted that he was more than willing that Aladdin should marry the Princess at once.

"Go, fetch thy son," he said to Aladdin's mother, who was waiting near. "Tell him that this day he shall wed my daughter."

But when Aladdin heard the news he refused to hasten at once to the palace, as his mother advised. First he called the genie, and told him to bring a scented bath, and a robe worked in gold, such as a King might wear. After this he called for forty slaves to attend him, and six to walk before his mother, and a horse more beautiful than the Sultan's, and lastly, for ten thousand pieces of gold put up in ten purses.

When all these things were ready, and Aladdin was dressed in his royal robe, he set out for the palace. As he rode along on his beautiful horse, attended by his forty slaves, he scattered the golden pieces out of the ten purses among the crowd, and all the people shouted with joy and delight. No one knew that this was the idle boy who used to play about the streets. They thought he was some great foreign Prince.

Thus Aladdin arrived at the palace in great state, and when the Sultan had embraced him, he ordered that the wedding feast should be prepared at once, and that the marriage should take place that day.

"Not so, your Majesty," said Aladdin. "I will not marry the Princess until I have built a palace fit for the daughter of the Sultan."

Then he returned home, and once more called up the Slave of the Lamp.

"Build me the fairest palace ever beheld by mortal eye," ordered Aladdin. "Let it be built of marble and jasper and precious stones. In the midst I would have a great hall, whose walls shall be of gold and silver, lighted by four-and-twenty windows. These windows shall all be set with diamonds, rubies, and other precious stones. But one shall be left unfinished. There must also be stables with horses, and slaves to serve in the palace. Begone, and do thy work quickly."

And lo! in the morning when Aladdin looked out, there stood the most wonderful palace that ever was built. Its marble walls were flushed a delicate pink in the morning light, and the jewels flashed from every window.

Then Aladdin and his mother set off for the Sultan's palace, and the wedding took place that day. The Princess loved Aladdin as soon as she saw him, and great were the rejoicings throughout the city.

The next day Aladdin invited the Sultan to visit the new palace, and when they entered the great hall, whose walls were of gold and silver and whose windows were set with jewels, the Sultan was filled with admiration and astonishment.

"It is the wonder of the world," he cried. "Never before have mortal eyes beheld such a beautiful palace. One thing alone surpises me. Why is one window left unfinished?"

"Your Majesty," answered Aladdin, "this has been done with a purpose, for I wished that thine own royal hand should have the honor of putting the finishing touch to my palace."

The Sultan was so pleased when he heard this that he sent at once for all the court jewelers and ordered them to finish the window exactly like the rest.

The court jewelers worked for many days, and then sent to tell the Sultan that they had used up all the jewels they possessed, and still the window was not half finished. The Sultan commanded that his own jewels should be given to complete the work. Even when these were used the window was not finished.

Then Aladdin ordered the jewelers to stop their work, and to take back all the Sultan's jewels as well as their own. And that night he called up the Slave of the Lamp once more, and bade him finish the window. This was done before the morning, and great was the surprise of the Sultan and all his workmen.

Now Aladdin did not grow proud of his great riches but was gentle and courteous to all, and kind to the poor, so that the people loved him dearly. He fought and won many battles for the Sultan, and was the greatest favorite in the land.

But far away in Africa there was trouble brewing for Aladdin. The wicked old magician who had pretended to be Aladdin's uncle found out by his magic powers that the boy had not perished when he left him underground, but had somehow managed to escape and become rich and powerful.

"He must have discovered the secret of the lamp," shrieked the magician, tearing his hair with rage. "I will not rest day or night until I have found some way of taking it from him."

So he journeyed from Africa to China, and when he came to the city where Aladdin lived and saw the wonderful palace, he nearly choked with fury to see its splendor. He disguised himself as a merchant, and bought a number of copper lamps, and with these he went from street to street, crying, "New lamps for old."

As soon as the people heard his cry, they crowded around him, laughing and jeering, for they thought he must be mad to make such an offer.

Now it happened that Aladdin was out hunting, and the Princess sat alone in the hall of the jeweled windows. When, therefore, she heard the noise that was going on in the streets outside, she called to her slaves to ask what it meant.

Presently one of the slaves came back, laughing so much that she could hardly speak.

"It is a curious old man who offers to give new lamps for old," she cried. "Did any one ever hear of such a strange way of trading?"

The Princess laughed too, and pointed to an old lamp which hung in a niche close by.

"There is an old enough lamp," she said. "Take it and see if the old man will really give a new one for it."

The slave took it down and ran out to the street once more, and when the magician saw that it was indeed what he wanted, he seized the Magic Lamp with both his hands.

"Choose any lamp you like," he said showing the slave several of bright new copper. He did not care now what happened. She might have all the new lamps if she wanted them.

Then he went a little way outside the city, and when he was quite alone he took out the Magic Lamp and rubbed it gently. Immediately the genie stood before him and asked what was his will.

"I order thee to carry off the palace of Aladdin, with the Princess inside, and set it down in a lonely spot in Africa."

And in an instant the palace, with every one in it, disappeared, and when the Sultan happened to look out of his window, there was no longer a palace to be seen.

"This must be enchantment," he cried.

Then he ordered his men to set out and bring Aladdin to him in chains.

The officers met Aladdin as he was returning from the hunt. They immediately seized him, loaded him with chains, and carried him off to the Sultan. But as he was borne along, the people gathered around him, for they loved him dearly, and vowed that no harm should befall him.

The Sultan was beside himself with rage when he saw Aladdin, and gave orders that his head should be cut off at once. But the people had begun to crowd into the palace, and they were so fierce and threatening that he dared not do as he wished. The people insisted that he order the chains to be taken off, and Aladdin to be set free.

As soon as Aladdin was allowed to speak he asked why all this was done to him.

"Wretch!" exclaimed the Sultan, "Come hither, and I will show thee."

Then he led Aladdin to the window and showed him the empty space where his palace had once stood.

"Think not that I care for thy vanished palace," said the Sultan. "But where is the Princess, my daughter?"

So astonished was Aladdin that for some time he could only stand speechless, staring at the place where his palace ought to have been.

At last he turned to the Sultan.

"Your Majesty," he said, "grant me grace for one month, and if by that time I have not brought back thy daughter to thee, then put me to death as I deserve."

So Aladdin was set free, and for three days he went about like a madman, asking every one he met where his palace was. But no one could tell him. Then he went to the river to drown himself. But as he knelt on the bank and clasped his hands to say his prayers before throwing himself in, he once more rubbed the Magic Ring. Instantly the Slave of the Ring stood before him.

"What is thy will, O master?" it asked.

"Bring back my Princess and my palace," cried Aladdin, "and save my life."

"That I cannot do," said the Slave of the Ring. "Only the Slave of the Lamp has power to bring back thy palace."

"Then take me to the place where my palace now stands," said Aladdin, "and put me down beneath the window of the Princess."

And almost before Aladdin had done speaking he found himself in Africa, beneath the windows of his own palace.

He was so weary that he lay down and fell fast asleep. When day dawned, he was awakened by the song of birds, and as he looked around him his courage returned. He was now sure that all his misfortunes must have been caused by the loss of the Magic Lamp, and he determined to find out as soon as possible who had stolen it.

That same morning inside the palace, the Princess awoke feeling happier than she had felt since she had been carried off. The sun was shining brightly and the birds were singing gaily when she went to the window to greet the opening day. And whom should she see standing beneath her window but Aladdin!

With a cry of joy she threw open the casement and the sound made Aladdin look up. It was not long before he made his way to her through a secret door and held her in his arms.

"Tell me, my Princess," said Aladdin, when they had embraced many times, "what has become of the old lamp which hung in a niche of the great hall?"

"Alas, my husband," answered the Princess, "I fear my carelessness has been the cause of all our misfortunes."

Then she told him how the wicked old magician had pretended to be a merchant, and had offered new lamps for old, and how he had thus managed to secure the Magic Lamp.

"He has it still," she added, "for I know that he carries it always, hidden in his robe."

"Princess," said Aladdin, "I must recover this lamp, and thou shalt help me. Tonight when the magician dines with thee, dress thyself in thy costliest robes, and be kind and gracious to him. Then bid him fetch some of the wines of Africa, and while he is gone, I will tell thee what thou shalt do."

So that night the Princess put on her most beautiful robes and looked so lovely and was so kind that when the magician came in he could scarcely believe his eyes. For she had been sad and angry ever since he had carried her off.

"I believe now that Aladdin must be dead," she said, "and I have made up my mind to mourn no longer. Let us begin our feast. But see! I grow weary of these wines of China. Fetch me instead the wine of thine own country."

Now Aladdin had meanwhile prepared a powder which he directed the Princess to place in her own wine-cup. And when the magician returned she was to offer him this cup in token of friendship.

She followed Aladdin's instructions. The magician drank up the African wine eagerly, and scarcely had he done so than he dropped down dead.

Then Aladdin came out of the next room where he had hidden himself, and searched the magician's robes until he found the Magic Lamp. He rubbed it joyfully, and when the genie appeared, ordered that the palace should be carried back to China, and set down in its own place.

The following morning, when the Sultan rose early, for he was too sad to take much rest, he went to the window to gaze on the place where Aladdin's palace had once stood. He rubbed his eyes, and stared in bewilderment.

"This must be a dream," he cried, for there stood the palace in all its beauty, looking fairer than ever in the morning light.

Not a moment did the Sultan lose. He rode over to the palace at once, and when he had embraced Aladdin and his daughter, they told him the whole story of the African magician. Then Aladdin showed him the body of the wicked man, and there was peace between them once more.

But there was still trouble in store for Aladdin. The African magician had a young brother who also dealt in magic, and who was, if possible, even more wicked than his elder brother.

Bent on revenge, this younger brother started for China, determined to punish Aladdin and steal the Magic Lamp for himself. As soon as he arrived he went in secret to the cell of a holy woman called Fatima, and obliged her to give him her robe and veil as a disguise. Then to keep the secret safe he killed the poor woman.

Dressed in the robe and veil, the wicked magician walked through the streets near Aladdin's palace, and all the people as he passed by knelt and kissed his robe, for they thought he was indeed the holy woman.

As soon as the Princess heard that Fatima was passing by in the street, she sent word for her to be brought into the hall. She treated the supposed holy woman with great respect and kindness, for she had often longed to see her.

"Is not this a fine hall?" she asked, as they sat together in the hall of the jeweled windows.

"It is indeed most beautiful," answered the magician, who kept his veil carefully down. "But to my mind there is one thing wanting. If only thou couldst have a roc's egg hung in the dome it would be perfect."

As soon as the Princess heard these words she became discontented and miserable, and when Aladdin came in, she looked so sad that he at once asked what was the matter.

"I can never be happy until I have a roc's egg hanging from the dome of the great hall," she answered.

"In that case thou shalt soon be happy," said Aladdin gaily, and taking down the lamp, he summoned the genie.

But when the Slave of the Lamp heard the order his face grew terrible with rage, and his eyes gleamed like burning coals.

"Vile wretch!" he shrieked. "Have I not given thee all thy wishes, and now dost thou ask me to kill my master, and hang him as an ornament in thy palace? Thou deservest truly to die. But I know that the request cometh not from thine own heart, but from that wicked magician who pretends to be a holy woman."

With these words the genie vanished, and Aladdin went at once to the room where the Princess was awaiting him.

"I have a headache," he said. "Call the holy woman, that she may place her hand upon my forehead and ease the pain."

But the moment the false Fatima appeared Aladdin sprang up and plunged his dagger into that evil heart.

"What hast thou done?" cried the Princess. "Alas! Thou hast slain the holy woman."

"This is no holy woman," answered Aladdin, "but an evil magician whose purpose was to destroy us both."

So Aladdin was saved from the wicked design of the two magicians, and there was no one left to disturb his peace. He and the Princess lived together in great happiness for many years, and when the Sultan died they succeeded to the throne, and ruled both wisely and well. And so there was great peace throughout the land.

—*Adapted by Amy Steedman*

124

Sindbad The Sailor

A poor porter, named Sindbad, one day sat down to rest beside a large house in Bagdad. The sound of sweet music and melodious voices that came through the open doors delighted him.

A grand feast was going on inside. Sindbad inquired who lived in this fine house and learned that the house belonged to another Sindbad—the famous Sindbad the Sailor.

The poor porter had often heard of the wealth of this great sailor, and now, comparing his own sad lot with the easy life of the rich man at whose gate he sat, he could not help crying out, "What has *this* Sindbad done to deserve such happiness? And what have I done that I should be so wretched?"

Now this complaint was heard by those within the house, and presently a slave came out to take Sindbad before his master.

The poor porter was quite dazzled by the richness of the banqueting-hall, and bowed humbly to the gaily-dressed guests. The great Sindbad received him very kindly, and made him sit down beside him, saying, "My friend and namesake, I heard your complaint just now, and I do not blame you. Yet you make a mistake if you imagine that I reached my present happiness without much suffering and trouble. If my guests are willing, I will tell you the story of my seven voyages, and from that you will see that what I say is the truth."

The guests were ready enough to listen to the story of the great sailor's adventures, and Sindbad began the tale of his first voyage:

"When my father died he left me a good fortune. I lived extravagantly for a while, and then discovered that my money was all gone. I had to start thinking what to do. And the result of my thinking was that I sold all my houses and furniture and bought merchandise I could sell at a profit. I threw in my lot with some merchants, and, having fitted out a trading vessel, we set sail, calling at various islands to buy and sell our goods.

"One day three of us landed on a small island. But no sooner had we made a fire to cook our food than the island began to tremble and quake most horribly. Then we saw that what we had taken for an island was really the back of a huge whale. In terror we made a wild dash for our ship. Before I could get away, however, the monster dived into the sea, tossing me into the waves, and by the time I rose to the surface I found that the ship had sailed away, for the captain thought I had been drowned. I clung to a piece of floating wood which I managed to seize, and, after struggling

125

with the waves for hours, I was at last flung upon the shores of an island.

"I rested for a while, and, after eating some wild fruits, began exploring the island. Soon I came to a plain, where I found a very handsome horse feeding. While I was admiring his beauty, a man came up and asked what I was doing there. I told him my story, and he led me to a cave, where a number of other men were resting. They gave me some food, and, while I ate, they told me they were grooms to the great King Mihrage who ruled over the island. They were now going to his palace with the fine horse I had seen.

"Next day they set off for the capital, taking me with them. King Mihrage received me very kindly, and invited me to stay with him as long as I pleased. I saw many curious things in that island and learned much from the merchants and Indians there.

"Ships from all parts often came to the harbor, and one day, as I stood watching a merchant vessel unloading some bales of merchandise, I saw, to my surprise, that these goods were marked with my own name.

"I went on board, and, finding that the captain was indeed the one with whom I had set sail, I made up my mind to return with him.

"I took some of my best merchandise as a gift to King Mihrage, and having thanked him for his kindness, I set sail once more.

"We traded at the various islands we passed, and at last arrived safely at Balsora. I made my way at once to Bagdad with the large sum of money I had got for my wares. There I built a fine house, gave money to the poor, and settled down to enjoy my good fortune."

Sindbad halted his story here, and, giving a hundred sequins to the porter, invited him to come back next day and hear more of his adventures.

Next day another feast was held, and, as soon as it was over the host began the story of his second voyage:

"I soon grew tired of an idle life, and went to sea again with another party of merchants.

"One day we landed on a desert island. After wandering about for a time, I felt tired and lay down in a quiet spot to sleep. When I awoke, I found, to my dismay, that the ship had sailed without me. I was alone.

"At first I was full of despair, but after a while I began to look about me. I soon noticed a huge white object lying a little distance off, and, making my way up to it, I found it was as smooth as ivory. As I stood wondering what it could be, the sky suddenly grew dark. To my surprise, I found that this darkness was the shadow of a monster bird flying down toward me. I had often heard sailors talk of a giant bird called the roc, and I decided this must be one, and that the huge white object beside me was its egg.

"I saw in this bird a means of escape

126

and thanked God for his mercy. When the bird reached the ground I tied myself with my turban to one of her legs, which was as thick as the trunk of a tree. And when she flew away next morning, she carried me with her. She rose to a great height, and then came down so suddenly that I fainted.

"When I again opened my eyes, I had just time to free myself from the roc before she flew away again.

"I now saw that I had been left in a deep valley, entirely shut in on every side by such high rocky mountains that it was impossible to climb them. The valley was strewn with dazzling diamonds of the largest size, and, as I had nothing better to do, I filled my pockets with them.

"To my horror, at one end of the valley I saw a swarm of dreadful serpents. Observing, however, that they came out only at night, I wandered about seeking a way of escape until night came, when I shut myself in a cave for safety.

"Next day, I was surprised to see pieces of raw meat being thrown down into the valley, and I soon understood what this meant. A party of merchants on the rocks above, not being able to get down into the valley, had found that they could obtain the diamonds by means of a clever trick. They threw pieces of raw meat down, and these fell upon the sharp points of the diamonds, which stuck into them. So, when eagles carried the meat to their nests at the top of the rocks, they carried with it a

number of diamonds. The merchants then frightened the eagles off their nests, and picked the diamonds from the meat.

"When I had watched this for a while I realized that here was my means of escape.

"I tied a large piece of raw meat to my back by means of my turban, and lay down flat on my face. Presently one of the largest eagles caught me up by the piece of meat on my back, and flew away with me to its nest above.

"You may guess how surprised the merchants were to find me there. I told them my story and, as they were returning home next day, I went with them. After many adventures, I arrived in Bagdad. Having made a huge fortune, I gave large gifts to the poor, and began to live in splendid style."

Sindbad, having ended this story, gave the porter another hundred sequins, and invited him to come again

next day to hear about his third voyage.

You may be sure that the porter did not forget to come, and when the guests had all feasted, Sindbad went on with his story:

"It was not long before I set sail once again, with another party of merchants, to seek adventure and treasure. One day we were caught in a terrible storm, and took shelter in the harbor of the first island we reached. No sooner had we entered this harbor than a swarm of frightful savages came swimming toward us and climbed into the ship. They were so fierce and came in such numbers that we could not fight them back. They made us go on shore and left us there, taking our ship with them.

"We wandered about the island, seeking food. Coming to a huge palace that seemed to be empty, we entered, and found ourselves in a large hall, into which there suddenly came a dreadful black giant with but one eye in the middle of his forehead. He had fearful long teeth and nails like an eagle's claws, and he was so frightful to look at that we all fell down and lay on the floor like dead men.

"When we opened our eyes again, the ogre suddenly seized the fattest of our number and killed him. Thrusting a spit through him, he roasted and ate his prey. He then lay down and fell asleep.

"Full of terror, we wandered about the island all next day, seeking some means of escape, but finding none. And when evening came the ogre appeared again and made his supper off another of my companions.

"This went on for several days, until at last I suggested that we should try to escape by sea. We found plenty of wood on the shore and we made rafts. And when these were ready, we returned to the palace for the last time.

"The ogre came as usual, and, having eaten another of our party for his supper, lay down and fell asleep. Those of us who were left then seized the spits and, making them red-hot in the fire, thrust them into the giant's great eye and blinded him. We then ran down to the shore and, jumping on to rafts, pushed our craft out to sea.

"But we had not gone far when the giant appeared with his wife who was as large as himself. They both threw great stones at us and sank all the rafts except the one I was on with two companions. Having managed to get out to sea, we were at last thrown upon another island, and here we were attacked by a most fearful serpent, which swallowed both my companions. I escaped however, and, rushing down to the shore, was overjoyed to see a ship not very far away.

"I managed to attract the notice of the captain, who sent a boat to take me to the ship. And I found, to my surprise, that he was the captain with whom I had sailed on my second voyage, when I was left on the desert island. He was delighted to see me again, and showed me my own bales of goods, still untouched.

"After trading with him for some time, I arrived safely in Bagdad once more, with riches so great that I knew not their value. I gave alms to the poor and rejoiced to be once more among my friends and relatives, living merrily and forgetting the horrors I had endured."

When Sindbad had finished this story, he gave his namesake another hundred sequins. And next day he began the story of his fourth voyage:

"My love of adventure soon took me on board another merchant ship. We had not been long at sea, however, when we were caught in a sudden gale, and our ship was soon dashed to pieces on a rock. I and a few others were cast ashore on a strange land.

"Here we were seized by some cannibals, who took us to their huts. I soon found out that they meant to eat us as soon as we grew fat enough, and for this reason I ate scarcely any of the food they gave us. Seeing that I remained very thin, they left me alone, and after a while I managed to escape.

"After wandering about for eight days, I met with some friendly people. They took me to their King, who received me very kindly and made me live at his court. We became very intimate.

"One day the King told me that he wished me to marry a lady of his court. I dared not disobey his command for fear of offending him, so I was married at once. My wife, however, very soon died, and then I found out that it was the custom in that country for the living husband to be buried with the dead wife.

"My wife, dressed in her most gorgeous robes and jewels, was first put into a large cave. I was lowered into the cave too, and given seven small loaves to keep me alive for a while. The top of the cave was then covered over, and I was left to my fate. I made my loaves last as many days as I could. When I had eaten the last morsel I prepared to die. Just then, however, I heard something moving in the cave and a sound like an animal panting. Following this sound as best I could, I came to a passage that had evidently been made by some animal. I followed it and came out at the seashore.

"Delighted at this chance of escape, I returned to the cave and gathered together as many of the rich clothes and jewels as I could find in the dark.

"Having brought my treasures out, and made them up into bales, I waited on the shore until a ship should pass. A merchant vessel soon came by, and, hear-

ing my cries, the captain stopped and took me on board. This ship was going to my own country, and so, after trading my goods, I again arrived in Bagdad with great riches."

Sindbad stopped here, and, giving the porter another purse of a hundred sequins, invited him to come the following day to hear the story of his fifth voyage. The guest did not fail to come, and Sindbad went on with his story:

"In spite of all the dangers I had gone through, I very soon went off to sea again, and this time I sailed in a ship of my own, joined by some merchant friends.

"We made a long voyage. The first place we stopped at was a desert island, where we found a roc's egg as large as the one I had seen before. It was just ready to be hatched, and my companions, in spite of my warnings, broke open the shell with their axes, dragged the young roc out and roasted and ate it.

"No sooner had they finished their feast than the two parent rocs appeared in the sky, flying toward us. They were in a frightful rage when they found their young one gone, and, as we rushed on board our ship, they flew after us, dropping great stones from their huge claws with such force that the vessel broke into a thousand pieces. I alone escaped drowning. Only with a great effort did I at last manage to reach dry land.

"Next day, as I walked about under some trees, I came across a wild-look-

ing old man, who asked me to carry him over a stream.

"I lifted him to my back. But no sooner had I done so than the wretched old creature clasped his legs firmly around my neck and, sitting astride my shoulders, ordered me to carry him up and down. I was obliged to carry him in

this manner all day, nor would he let me go when night came, but kept his arms tightly clasped around my neck while I slept.

"Next day, and for many days after that, he made me carry him again, and I saw that the wicked old creature meant to kill me in time. But at last I thought out a plan of escape. I squeezed some grape-juice into an empty gourd-shell one day, and, coming to it some days later, I found that it had turned into a very good wine. I drank some of it. Seeing that it refreshed me, the old man asked for some. I gave him the shell at once, and was glad to find that the wine made him lively and careless.

"Presently, to my great joy, he loosened his hold of me, so that I was able to shake him off my back, and quickly seizing a large stone, I crushed the life out of the tiresome old wretch. I then hurried down to the beach, where I met with some sailors who took me on board their ship. When I told them my story, they said I had had a very narrow escape, since I had fallen into the clutches of the famous Old Man of the Sea, who never let his victims go till he had strangled them.

"We soon landed on another island, and there I did such a fine trade in cocoanuts that at last I could give up trading and go home again. I therefore took a ship to Bagdad, where I was glad to settle down to an easy life once more."

Having finished this story, Sindbad sent the porter away with another hundred sequins, and next day he began the story of the sixth voyage.

"I had been at home only a year when I made up my mind to go to sea again. This time I took a longer voyage than I had ever taken before. We met with such stormy weather that our ship was driven out of her way altogether and dashed to pieces on a rocky shore.

"The cliffs there rose up into a steep mountain, impossible to climb, and the fearful current that had brought us would have kept us from sailing away even if we had had a boat. So we divided our store of food equally amongst us, and I spent my time wandering about. I found many treasures that had been cast ashore from wrecks, and in one place I saw a strange river which flowed into a cave.

"My companions died off one by one, until at last I was left alone. Then I made up my mind to try to escape by means of the strange underground river, which I felt must surely have an outlet on the other side of the mountain. I soon made a strong raft. Then, having loaded it with the treasures I had found, I guided it into the cave, and for days floated in utter darkness, soon falling into a half-fainting state.

"When I once more opened my eyes, I found myself lying in a meadow, with a number of Negroes standing about me. I went with them to the capital of Serendib, as that island was called, and there they presented me to their King, who received me with great honor.

"After spending some happy months there, I asked to be allowed to return to my own land, and the King ordered a ship to be got ready for me, and gave me many fine gifts. He also gave me a letter and a handsome present for my sovereign lord, the Caliph Haroun Alraschid.

"When I arrived at Bagdad, I presented the King's letter and gifts to the Caliph, who was delighted to receive them, and sent me away with a handsome present."

Sindbad stopped here, gave the porter his usual hundred sequins, and next day he began the story of his seventh and last voyage:

"As I was now growing old, I made up my mind not to go to sea any more. But one day the Caliph sent for me, and begged me so hard to take a return letter and gift from him to the King of Serendib that I could not well refuse.

"I arrived safely in Serendib, and, having presented the Caliph's letter and gift to the King, I set sail homeward. We had not been at sea long, however, when our ship was seized by fierce pirates, who afterward sold us as slaves in a strange country.

"I was bought by a rich merchant who treated me kindly. Finding that I could shoot well with a bow and arrow, he took me into a forest, and told me to shoot elephants for him. I climbed into a tall tree, and shot at the great animals as they tramped the woods below me, and every day I managed to kill an elephant for my master.

"But one day, to my dismay, one of the largest elephants rooted up the tree on which I was sitting. Then, followed by the rest of the herd, he carried me to what was evidently their burying-place, for the ground was covered with bones and tusks. I made up my mind that the elephants had brought me there to show me that I could get as much ivory as I wanted without killing any more of them.

"I told my master of the great treasure of ivory, and he was so delighted that he said I should be a slave no longer. He ordered a ship to be got ready to take me back to my own land, loading it with ivory tusks for me.

"I traded my ivory at various places, and when I once more arrived safely in Bagdad I brought with me more riches than I had ever owned before.

"Having told the Caliph the story of my adventures, I returned home, to settle down and enjoy my vast riches in peace and comfort."

When Sindbad had finished his story, he said to the porter, "You have now heard, my friend, of the many dangers and sufferings I have gone through. Do you not think I deserve to spend the rest of my life in ease and enjoyment?"

"Ah, yes, my Lord!" answered the porter, humbly kissing Sindbad's hand. "My own poor troubles are as nothing, and I hope you may long live to enjoy the riches you have gained at such a cost."

Sindbad was so pleased with this reply that, giving the man yet another hundred sequins, he begged him to give up his work as a porter and come to feast with him every day.

So Sindbad the porter became a rich and happy man, and all the rest of his life had good cause to remember the kindness of Sindbad the Sailor.

An Old Song

by Marie Syrkin

In the blossom-land Japan
Somewhere thus an old song ran:

Said a warrior to a smith
"Hammer me a sword forthwith.
Make the blade
Light as wind on water laid.
Make it long
As the wheat at harvest-song.
Supple, swift
As a snake, without rift,
Full of lightnings, thousand-eyed!
Smooth as silken cloth and thin
As the web that spiders spin.
And merciless as pain, and cold."

"On the hilt what shall be told?"

"On the sword's hilt, my good man,"
Said the warrior of Japan,
"Trace for me
A running lake, a flock of sheep
And one who sings her child to sleep."

The Barber's Fifth Brother

Here are two stories about the brothers
of an Arabian barber:

My fifth brother was called Alnaschar. As long as our father lived my fifth brother was very lazy. Instead of working he used to beg, and lived upon what he got. The old man, our father, at his death, left seven hundred dirhens. We divided this sum equally, so that each of us had a hundred for his share. Alnaschar, who had never before possessed so much money, was much perplexed to know what he should do with it. He consulted a long time with himself, and at last resolved to lay it out in glassware, which he bought of a wholesaler dealer. He put it all in an open basket, and sat with it before him, and his back against a wall, in a place where he might sell it. In this posture, with his eyes fixed on his basket, he began to meditate in the following manner:

"This basket cost me a hundred dirhens, which is all I have in the world. I shall make two hundred of them by selling my glass. Of these two hundred, which I will again lay out in glassware, I shall make four hundred. And going on thus, I shall at last make four thousand dirhens; of four thousand I shall easily make eight thousand; and when I come to ten thousand, I will leave off selling glass and turn jeweler. I will trade in diamonds, pearls, and all sorts of precious stones, then when I am as rich as I want to be, I will buy a fine mansion, a great estate, slaves, asses, and horses. Nor will I stop there, for I will, by the favor of heaven, go on till I get one hundred thousand dirhens, and when I have amassed so much I will send to demand the grand vizier's daughter in marriage.

"I will clothe myself like a prince, and, mounted upon a fine horse, with a saddle of fine gold, with housings of cloth of gold, finely embroidered with diamonds and pearls, I will ride through the city, attended by slaves before and behind. I will go to the vizier's palace in view of all the people, great and small, who will show me the most profound respect. When I alight at the foot of the vizier's staircase, my own people will be ranged right and left. And the grand vizier, receiving me as his son-in-law, will give me his right hand, and set me above him, to do me the more honor."

My brother was so full of these dazzling visions that he quite forgot where he was, and unfortunately gave such a push to his basket and glasses that they were knocked over and broken into a thousand pieces.

The Barber's Sixth Brother

THE BARMECIDE'S FEAST

My brother Shacabac, O Commander of the Faithful, was once a rich man, but he became so poor that he was reduced to beggary. One day he went forth as usual to seek alms, and on his way he beheld a handsome house, with servants standing at the door, commanding and forbidding. So he came up to the doorkeepers and begged them to give him something.

"Enter," said one of them, "and thou shalt get whatever thou hast need of from our master himself."

Thus encouraged, my brother entered the palace and found himself in a magnificent hall, paved with marble and hung with curtains. At the upper end of a room which opened into this hall sat an old man with a long white beard. Seeing my brother, the Barmecide rose, greeted him kindly, and asked him what he could do to serve him. My brother replied that he was sorely in need of food.

"What!" cried the old man, "art thou actually hungry? Thou shalt eat with me. I will have food brought in at once. Ho, boy! bring us water that we may wash our hands, and order supper immediately."

Shacabac was about to express his gratitude for this friendly reception, when the old man began to rub his hands together as if he were washing them. No boy appeared, nor was there either basin or water, yet my brother felt that he must do as his host did, for the sake of courtesy.

"Come," said the Barmecide, "thou art surely famished." And though nothing had been brought in, he pretended to eat as if food had been set before him.

"Eat, my friend," he went on. "There is no need to feel shame, for I myself have known what it is to be hungry."

So my brother made all the motions of eating and drinking, while his host called for dish after dish, which did not appear. "Ho, boy!" he would cry, "bring us mutton and barley broth, unless my

136

guest prefers some of the goose with the sweet sauce. Come, taste of these chickens stuffed with pistachio nuts. Hast thou ever tasted any like them?"

"Never," protested my brother, who was fainting with hunger. "Never have I eaten anything so delicious," and he pretended to feast heartily on the invisible dainties.

Then the Barmecide named other dishes, and my brother did not fail to praise them warmly, until at length he declared he could eat no more.

"But," cried the Barmecide, "thou hast had no sweets! Try one of these delicious fritters before the sirup runs out of it." And he went on urging upon his guest all manner of fruits and sweetmeats.

At last Shacabac became weary of the jest and said to himself, "I will make him sorry for having fooled me thus." Accordingly, when the boy was ordered to bring in wine my brother said, "O my Master, I must drink no wine with thee. Surely it is forbidden."

"Keep me company in a single glass," said the Barmecide, and my brother bowed low as if he would drink to the health of his host. But even as the old man lifted the invisible glass a second time to his lips my brother struck him such a blow that the room rang with it.

"What does this mean?" cried the Barmecide, trembling with rage.

"O my Lord," said my brother, "thou hast given me too much of that rare old wine. See, it has taken away my wits, and has made me behave like a madman."

Then the Barmecide laughed very heartily and said, "Long have I made game of men, but thou art the first I have seen who could endure this trick. Now, therefore, I pardon thee for thy rudeness, and thou shalt eat with me in good earnest."

So saying, he clapped his hands, and the servants brought in a delicious supper, including all the good things the Barmecide had pretended to offer his guest. My brother continued to make himself so agreeable to his host that he became his close friend and companion, and they lived together for a period of twenty years.

The Story Of The Fisherman

ONCE upon a time there was an aged fisherman, so poor that he could barely obtain food for himself, his wife, and his three children. He went out early every morning to fish, and he had imposed a rule upon himself never to cast his nets more than four times a day.

On one occasion he set out before daybreak. He reached the seashore and cast his nets. In drawing them to land three times in succession, he felt sure, from their resistance and weight, that he had a fine haul of fish. Instead, he found on the first haul only the carcass of an ass, on the second, a large pannier filled with sand and mud, and on the third, a large quantity of heavy stones, shells, and filth. It is impossible to describe his disappointment and despair.

The day now began to break, and having, like a good Mussulman, finished his prayers, he cast his nets for the fourth time. Again he supposed he had caught a great quantity of fish, as he drew them in with as much difficulty as before. He nevertheless found none. But what he did draw up was a heavy vase of yellow copper, fastened with lead and sealed. "I will sell this to a metal-caster," said he joyfully, "and with the money I shall get for it I will purchase a measure of corn."

He examined the vase on all sides, shook it, and could hear nothing. But the impression of the seal on the lead made him think the vase could not be empty. It might, he thought, even be filled with something valuable. In order to find out, he took his knife, and got the vase open. He turned it upside down, and was much surprised to find nothing come out. He then set it down before him, and while he was attentively observing it, there issued from it so thick a smoke that he was obliged to step back a few paces. This smoke, by degrees, rose almost to the clouds, and spread itself in a thick fog over both the water and the shore.

The fisherman, as may easily be imagined, was a good deal surprised at such a strange sight.

When the smoke had all come out of the vase, it again collected itself and became a solid body, taking the shape of a genie of gigantic size. The genie, looking at the fisherman, exclaimed, "Humble thyself before me, or I will kill thee!"

"And for what reason, pray, will you kill me?" answered the fisherman. "Have you already forgotten that I have set you at liberty?"

"I remember it very well," returned he, "but that shall not prevent my destroying thee. I will grant thee only one favor."

"And pray what is that?" said the fisherman.

"It is," replied the genie, "to permit thee to choose the manner of thy death. I can treat thee no otherwise, and to convince thee of it, hear my history:

"I am one of those spirits who rebelled against the King of the Genii. He commanded me to acknowledge his authority, and submit to his laws. I haughtily refused. In order therefore to punish me, he enclosed me in this copper vase, and, to prevent me from forcing my way out, he put upon the leaden cover the impression of his seal, on which his name is engraved. This done, he gave the vase to one of those genii who obeyed him, and ordered him to cast me into the sea.

"During the first century of my captivity, I swore that if anyone delivered me before the first hundred years were passed I would make him rich. During the second century, I swore that if any released me I would discover to him all the treasures of the earth. During the third, I promised to make my deliverer a most powerful monarch, and to grant him each day any three requests he chose to make. These centuries passed away without any deliverance. Enraged at last at being so long a prisoner, I swore that I would, without mercy, kill the man who should release me, no matter who he was."

The fisherman was in great distress at finding him thus resolved on his death.

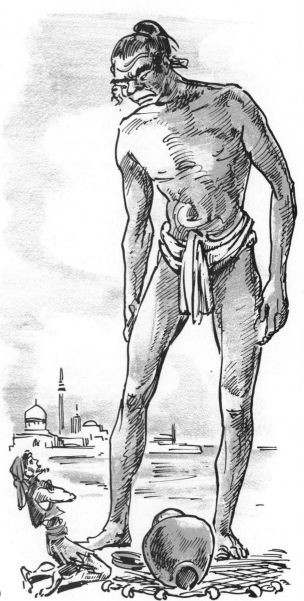

"Alas!" he cried, "have pity on me! Remember what I have done for thee!"

Necessity is the mother of invention, and the fisherman thought of a stratagem. "Since, then, I cannot escape death," said he, "I submit to the will of God, but before I choose what sort of death, I conjure you by the great name which is graven upon the seal to answer me truly a question I am going to put to you."

The genie trembled at this, but he said to the fisherman, "Ask what thou wilt, and make haste."

"Dare you, then, swear by that great name that you really were in that vase? This vase is not large enough to contain one of your feet. How, then, can it hold your whole body?"

"I swear to thee, notwithstanding," replied the genie, "that I was there just as thou seest me! Wilt thou not believe me after the solemn oath I have taken?"

"No, truly," added the fisherman, "I should not believe you unless I were to see you inside that vase."

Immediately the form of the genie began to change in to smoke, and extended itself, as before, over both the shore and the sea. Then, collecting itself, it began to enter the vase, and continued to do so at a slow and regular speed, till nothing remained outside.

The fisherman immediately took the leaden cover and put it on the vase. "Genie!" he cried, "it is now your turn to ask pardon. I shall throw you again into the sea. I will build, opposite the very spot where you are cast, a house upon the shore, in which I will live, to warn all fishermen that come and throw their nets not to fish up so evil a genie as thou art, who makest an oath to kill the man who shall set thee at liberty."

The genie tried every argument to move the fisherman's pity, but in vain. "You are too treacherous for me to trust you," returned the fisherman. "I should deserve to lose my life if I put myself in your power a second time."

And so Scheherazade went on until she had told tales to the Sultan for a thousand-and-one nights. The Sultan could not but admire the wit and charm his wife displayed as she related one after the other these stories of days long gone by. His temper was softened, and his prejudice against women removed.

"I confess, lovely Scheherazade," he said on the morning of the one-thousand-and-second day, "that you have appeased my anger. I renounce the law I had imposed on myself. You shall hereafter be my *only* consort, and I will have you known as the deliverer of the many damsels I had intended to sacrifice to my anger."

The fair Scheherazade threw herself at his feet in the utmost gratitude and joy.

Her father, the Grand Vizier, was the first to learn the good news and be relieved of his terrible and constant anxiety. It was then instantly carried to the city, the towns, and the provinces, and gained for the Sultan and the lovely Scheherazade, his consort, the blessings of all the people of Persia.

Old Favorites from the Old Country

Bruce and the Spider

A LONG time ago, there lived a King of Scotland named Robert Bruce. He was a greatly troubled man because his country was at war with England, and the English were winning. In battle after battle they drove back the Scottish army until at last the King himself had to retreat to the mountains to save his life.

Wandering desperately through the mountain forests, cold and hungry and exhausted, at last the King found a miserable little wooden hut empty and deserted. Glad of any kind of shelter, he lay down on the floor of the hut in deep despair.

"There is no use in going on," he thought. "The enemy has thrown back our armies six times. We can never repulse them. I have failed my people. I might as well give up."

At that moment the King noticed a little gray spider spinning a long thread from one of the rafters. The spider swung along on the thread in an effort to attach the other end to another rafter so he could start spinning his web. But the thread broke and the spider fell to the floor of the hut.

A little dazed perhaps, but with no hesitation at all, the spider climbed up the wall and began spinning again. He kept patiently at it until the thread was long enough. Then he again swung himself to the end of it and tried once more to attach it to the rafter across the corner. But again the thread broke and again the spider fell to the floor.

And once more he climbed up and began again.

Six times the spider's thread broke. Six times he fell to the ground. Six times he began again. Six times he failed.

Robert Bruce, the King of Scotland, watched in fascination. He became so absorbed in the little spider's efforts that for a time he forgot his own troubles.

The spider did not give up even when he failed for the sixth time. He just tried again, and this time, on the seventh try, he was successful. The end of the thread held! The spider attached it to the far rafter and began spinning his web.

Robert Bruce arose and bowed low to the tiny gray insect. "O little spider!" he cried. "You have taught me a wonderful lesson in persistence. You were not ready to give up, as I was. No matter how often you failed, you were always willing to try again. Perhaps I too shall win if I keep on trying."

And so, though he was still cold and hungry and weary, he was no longer disheartened. Watching the spider had given him new strength and courage. He buckled on his sword, gathered together his scattered armies, and, with the example of the courageous spider to inspire him, King Robert Bruce led his men, on the seventh try, to victory.

King Alfred and the Cakes

Many years ago England was ruled by a wise and good King named Alfred. King Alfred's people loved him and were very loyal to him. But many of them were poor—so poor that they had to work hard all day long just to get enough to eat. What they had to eat wasn't much either. Mostly it was just what they could raise in their fields or pick from the trees and bushes.

It made King Alfred sad to think of how poor his people were. But he was even more troubled because his country had many enemies and he often had to lead his men into war.

The worst enemy the English had in those days were the Danes. Today the Danes are a civilized and peace-loving people. But in those long-ago times they were bold and warlike. They wanted to take England away from the English so they could live there themselves.

Great battalions of them sailed across the sea in Viking ships and engaged the English in a bloody war. Led by their noble King the English fought bravely to defend their country from the invaders. But the Danes were stronger in force and greater in numbers. In battle after battle they defeated the English until at last they had to retreat. King Alfred himself fled into the forest. He had to remain hidden to save his life.

Alfred was a courageous man and a conscientious one. His one thought was to gather his armies together again and repulse the enemy. But he knew he must remain in hiding for the time being or the Danes would be sure to kill him, and then there would be no one to lead his scattered men.

Weary and discouraged he wandered through the woods trying to think out a plan of battle. On and on he tramped through the thicket of trees and marshes until, just as it was getting dark, he came to a little hut.

A woodcutter and his wife lived there. You could see that they were poor and hard-working people. When Alfred knocked at their door, they thought he was just an ordinary soldier. They had no idea that this man, so shabby and battle-stained, was their King. In those days, of course, there were no newsreels or television sets or even newspapers, so people who had never seen the King in person had no way of knowing what he looked like.

"Come in, stranger," said the woodcutter hospitably. "I must go out into the fields again to work until nightfall. But you are welcome to rest by our hearth and my wife will give you something to eat."

A little fire was burning in the fireplace and Alfred was grateful to be able to warm himself at it and to rest his weary bones.

The woodcutter's wife was busily shaping some coarse meal into cakes and putting them on the hearth where they would cook slowly. The cakes were all they had for their supper. She felt very sorry for the unhappy man sitting there. He was so ragged and seemed so tired and hungry. She was glad there would be an extra hotcake for him.

Would you mind doing something for me?" she asked. "I must go out to milk the cow and get some water from the spring. While I am gone, will you watch these cakes for me? Just turn them once and see that they don't burn."

"Gladly," replied the stranger.

Alfred watched the pale cakes darken to a nice golden brown. But as the fire flickered before his tired eyes his mind wandered back again to his troubles. How could he get his armies together again? What could he do to defeat those fierce Danes, to get them to leave his land and let his people dwell in peace? He forgot where he was. He forgot his hunger and his weariness. He forgot the cakes.

Suddenly the door of the hut flew open and the woodcutter's wife rushed in with a pail of water. The smell of something burning choked her. The air was thick with smoke. The cakes were burned to cinders.

"Look what you have done, you lazy beggar!" she shouted at Alfred. "You were willing enough to let us share our supper with you, but you couldn't be trusted to do a little thing like turning the cakes and seeing that they didn't burn!" She poured the pail of water on the smoking hearth. "Now we haven't any supper at all!" she wailed.

Before Alfred had time to say a word, a tall man came bursting into the hut. Alfred recognized him as one of his soldiers.

"Your Majesty!" exclaimed the man kneeling before the King, "We have

been searching for you everywhere. It is a blessed miracle that I have found you here. I bring you good tidings. Our armies are once more gathered together and waiting for you to lead them against the Danes. We find they are no longer as powerful as we thought. I beseech you, Your Majesty, come!"

"*Majesty!*" echoed the woodcutter's wife in an awed whisper. "Majesty!" She twisted the corner of her apron in confusion and embarrassment. "If I had had any idea that you were the King— Oh, Your Royal Highness, can I ever hope to be forgiven?"

The King's smile was very kind. "It is *I* who must ask *you* to forgive *me*," he said bowing courteously. "I do apologize for having been so careless about the cakes. But you see I was thinking about how I could save our country."

"Your Majesty, Your Majesty," was all the poor flustered woman could say.

The King buckled on his sword and, forgetting his hunger and his fatigue, strode out of the hut.

He met his army and once more led his men into battle against the Danes. And this time the English conquered them so decisively that they retreated across the sea to their homes in Denmark never to try such tactics again.

The King did not forget the woodcutter and his wife who had so generously offered to share what they had with a ragged stranger who came footsore and weary to their hut. After the war was over he made the woodcutter the Chief Forester in the royal forests and saw to it that he and his wife had nourishing meals and a good house to live in for the rest of their lives.

The Discontented Village

By Rose Dobbs

THERE WAS once a village that had every reason to be the happiest in the world but was in fact the saddest. It was situated in a pleasant valley with protecting mountains all around. It had fertile fields, industrious workers, and a prosperous market-place. But it was not happy because there lived in it not one contented inhabitant. Each person believed himself weighed down with troubles like an old nag with bones. And what is more, each believed *his* troubles were heavier than any of his neighbor's. If you saw a little group of people standing together and sidled over to hear what they were talking about, you would find yourself listening not to good talk about the weather, or crops, or the price of cheese, or the arrival of a new baby. No—you would hear nothing but talk about trouble.

"Ah me," like as not one would be saying, "was there ever a more unfortunate man than I? Things are so bad with me that trouble has moved right into my house and is now a steady boarder."

"What do you know about trouble?" his neighbor answers. "Trouble is so familiar with me, he calls me by name."

"Have you heard?" a third chimes in. "Trouble is calling *me* brother."

It is said where there is smoke, there must be fire. Perhaps there is good reason for such talk? Let us see.

Here is the miller—a fine man, sole owner of a busy mill, completely free and master of himself. He earns more than one pretty penny and no one to tell him what to do with it. But is he happy? No. Why not? Because he has no wife.

"The baker, now," sighs the miller. "The baker is a happy man. When he comes home at the end of the day his place is neat and his supper hot upon the table. What does he know of having to shift for himself? What does he know of trouble?"

And the baker—is he happy? No. And why not? Because he has no child.

"What is the use of putting up with the restrictions of married life," mumbles the baker, "if there is no child to look after a man in his old age? It is an unfair world. Here I have none and the carpenter has six."

And the carpenter—is he happy? No. And why not? Because he has too many children. All day long the carpenter complains: "By my hammer and nails, is there a curse on me? Other men's children grow like weeds and are soon farm hands and wage earners. But mine, now, they stay on all fours for ever and the cradle never empty. Ah me, does any man have such troubles as I?"

And what about the people whose children are grown—are they happy? No.

147

And why not? Listen, and you shall hear.

Here is the tailor with a good steady son, a dreamer and scholar. "Of what use are dreamers and scholars?" moans the tailor. "The world is too busy for dreaming and too much learning leads but to destruction. Now why, if only one child was given me, could it not have been a strong, ambitious lad like the tinker's or a pretty girl like the widow's—a girl who will marry well and keep her mother in comfort?"

But the tinker is unhappy because his strong, ambitious lad is ever off adventuring, and the widow is unhappy because her pretty daughter will have none of the rich farmer's son but is casting soft glances in the direction of the scholar. And so the tinker and the widow complain too.

"Children seldom grow up good and steady and obedient," they both wail. "Children are best when they're in the cradle. Yes, the carpenter with his little ones, and the baker and the miller with no children at all—there are happy men."

And the carpenter and the baker and the miller? We have already heard them.

And so it went. The people who worked envied those who loafed and those who loafed envied those who worked and made money. And the young longed for the irresponsibilities of old age and the old wept for their lost youth. And if they didn't have any immediate reason for being unhappy, you can be sure that they looked hard enough until they found one.

So day by day this discontent grew, and the moans and groans and mumbles and grumbles rose like a great thick fog. And one day the fog hid the sun. So busy were the people at first with their troubles that they paid no attention, but when many sunless hours went by, it occurred to them that here was trouble indeed, touching all of them.

"Truly we are an unhappy folk," they now cried, all together. "Even the sun won't shine on us."

Out of the gloom one day came a trav-

eler. It had been murky for so long that no one expected any visitors, and the first the villagers knew of his approach was the sound of a merry voice singing gaily:

Heigh ho,
Life is jolly.
Content is wisdom,
Complaint is folly.

The people gathered in the main street to see who it was that subscribed to such an outlandish theory. And presently there emerged out of the gloom a tall figure. It was a man, not old, not young; not well dressed, not shabby; not loaded with provisions, yet not entirely bereft, for the small bundle slung over his shoulder seemed comfortably full. He stopped in front of the people and put down his bundle.

"Greetings," he said. "Forgive me, my friends, for not giving you the good of the morning or the evening, for by my life, how is a man to tell in this gloom if it be day or night here?"

"The sun has deserted the world," said one of the villagers. "And," he added severely, "small cause for singing, I should say."

The stranger smiled. "The sun is shining warm and bright somewhere, I warrant. When this fog lifts, you will see."

The villager regarded him suspiciously. This cheerful comment was not to his liking. "Who are you?" he asked bluntly.

"I?" The stranger shrugged his shoulders. "I am no one and every one. I am a homeless wanderer but own the earth."

"Poor man," said another villager.

"Trouble has addled your brain."

"Trouble?" said the stranger. "Now that is a word I do not know."

The people crowded round him and examined him closely.

"Are you ill?" they asked in amazement. "How can you say you know not trouble with no hearth or fire or chick or child to call your own? Wandering over the face of the earth, and walking without rest. That does not make for any foolish philosophy of contentment. That makes for trouble. Trouble in the form of weary legs."

"Ah well," said the stranger, "there is no ill but somewhere a cure exists for it.

And as for weary legs, the best cure is to take the weight off them."

And down he sat, under a tree.

The villagers gathered around him open-mouthed. And the stranger calmly sat there. Finally the miller said, "Well, now, since you are so much-traveled, perhaps in your wanderings you have heard of a cure for fog?"

"Perhaps," said the stranger. He rose, turned his long nose up, then down, then this way, then that. He sniffed like a dog. Then he stuck out his tongue, tasted the fog, and made a wry face. "This is no ordinary fog," he said, "for, unpleasant as it is, fog is still nothing but vapor, and vapor is nothing but water which neither smells nor tastes bad. Still this looks like fog, and it feels like fog. It must be some special kind, caused by something most disagreeable. If I knew the cause, I might know the cure."

"We do not know the cause," said the baker. "The sun suddenly left us. I remember it was some time ago. I was thinking of how unhappy I was when—"

"Yes," interrupted the carpenter. "I was thinking of how little reason others have for unhappiness, compared to me, when—"

The tailor interrupted the carpenter and the tinker interrupted the tailor and soon everyone was shouting.

And as they shouted the fog grew thicker and thicker.

"Stop!" cried the stranger. "It needs no Solomon to see what is wrong here. Well. Well. There is no ill but somewhere a cure exists for it. Yes, even for this ill."

"And what might the cure be?" asked the widow, eagerly.

"Simple," said the stranger, "if you will listen carefully and follow instructions."

All the people solemnly and silently nodded their heads.

The stranger sat down again.

"Now then," he said, "let's see: you must string up a stout line from one end of the market-place to the other. Then you must each go home and put your troubles into a sack—"

"No sack in the world is large enough to contain mine," cried the carpenter.

"Nor mine," sighed the widow.

"Nor mine," wailed the tailor.

"Nor mine," cried they all.

The stranger frowned. "Well, then, if you will not listen and will not obey—" He began to rise once more.

And the fog grew thicker and thicker.

"Stay!" cried the people. "We will manage somehow. Let us hear the cure."

The stranger sat back once more.

"Then you must each go home and put your troubles into a sack," he said again, "and bring the sacks down to the market-place and hang them up on the line. Then you must step back—a good way back—and wait until I give you the signal. At the signal each of you may rush forward and take any sack he wishes off the line. For the fog will not lift until you stop complaining."

The people were entranced. Their eyes gleamed and thoughts rushed through their heads like scurrying mice. No doubt you have already guessed what these thoughts were. Each person saw himself quickly getting rid of his troubles by grabbing his neighbor's sack. And each hugged the wicked thought close to himself, for fear his neighbor might catch it.

The stranger leaned back against the tree and peering through the gloom watched the villagers string up the line. Then they made for their homes and presently he saw them again—a long line of people—each lugging a sack. They reached the market-place and with much panting hung the sacks up on the line.

Then they drew back—a good way back—and stood or sat in little groups.

151

The stranger did not move. Every eye was fastened on him, but he gave no sign.

And so they waited. Still no sign.

And still they waited. And still no sign. Finally the people took their eyes off the stranger and fixed them upon the line of sacks. Each person heaved a mighty sigh as he looked at his own sack and compared it with his neighbor's, for of course to each one his own sack loomed largest and heaviest. They looked again at the stranger. Still no sign. So they turned back to the sacks. And they gazed and they gazed, and as they gazed they began to think, and as they thought their musing took an unusual turn.

The carpenter's eyes had been darting from the sack of the tailor to the sack of the tinker; from the sack of the tinker to the sack of the widow. Presently he fixed his gaze on the widow's sack. The carpenter sits up with a start. Is it possible? Can that be the widow's sack dragging on the ground, while his, the carpenter's, swings gaily and lightly above? The carpenter recalls it is many weeks since the village has seen ribbon or flounce of the widow's pretty daughter. The girl went off to her aunt vowing she would not return until the scholar was made welcome in the widow's home. Poor widow. Poor lonely woman. Into the carpenter's ears comes the joyous sound of his little children's jolly voices, and into the carpenter's heart comes the proud knowledge that disobedience is unknown in his home. But for how long?

"Ah me," thinks the carpenter, "how short a while are children little; how short a time do they obey us; how quickly are they grown up and become wilful and independent; how apt to go off and leave the home empty and the parents lonely and sorrowful." For the first time in his life, the carpenter remembers gratefully the extreme youth of his own children. He turns in pity to the widow, but the widow's eyes are glued on the carpenter's sack . . . A terror grips the carpenter.

The tailor's gaze is fixed on the tinker's sack. Suddenly he sits up with a start. Is it possible? Can the tinker's sack be bigger than his? Into the tailor's mind flashes the rumors he has been hearing of war. He sees the tinker's strong, ambitious son march off. His own son, the frail scholar and dreamer, stays behind. Will the tinker ever see his son again? The tailor's heart almost stops beating. Into his mind comes a thought: When the world is weary of hate and destruction and sick over the loss of the young and the strong, it will turn to the comfort which the dreamers will bring and the healing the scholars will send. For dreams are ever made of hope, and from learning comes understanding, and in understanding lies man's salvation. The tailor's eyes grow moist. He looks in compassion at the tinker. But the tinker's gaze is fixed upon the tailor's sack . . . A sudden terror grips the tailor.

The miller had been keeping one eye on the stranger and one on the baker's sack. But when he turned both his eyes on the baker's sack, he sat up with a start. Was it possible? Could it be that the baker's sack was larger than his? The miller stares and thinks. It occurs to him

152

153

that he never sees the baker in the tavern of an evening. "That wife of his," the men say, "she won't let him enjoy a glass of ale with us. Poor man, he cannot call his soul his own." The miller thinks and stares. "Everyone knows," he recalls his cronies saying, "that the tongue of the baker's wife is tied in the middle and wags from both ends. Poor man, he knows not one peaceful moment." The miller looks with sympathy at the baker. But the baker had decided that little children mean small troubles, and big children mean large troubles, and a wife means trouble all the time. So he does not meet the miller's sympathetic look. His eyes are riveted on the miller's sack . . . A sudden terror grips the miller.

And so it happened that as each one of the villagers turned greedy eyes on some one else's sack, it was only to see that the sack he coveted was always bigger and heavier than his own. And gradually each pair of eyes came to rest on its own sack and each heart beat impatiently for the signal. And as the people's hearts filled with thoughts of pity and compassion and sympathy and gratitude—and content—the fog began to lift. The air became sweet and cool and clear. A full moon sailed the sky, lighting up the whole market-place. Like a silver ship, the moon followed her starry course and eventually disappeared in the west. In the east a faint glow appeared behind the mountains. The glow turned pink and gold and orange, and when the happy face of the sun just peeped over the mountains, the stranger rose and stretched himself.

The people were overjoyed to see the sun. And now they noticed too that the fog had gone. They breathed deeply of the sweet, cool, clear air. Oh never again would they pollute it with complaints.

But the sign. Would it never be given? They turned anxiously to the stranger. He picked up his bundle, slung it slowly over his shoulder, and called out: "Go!"

Off like a shot went each of the villagers. And straight as an arrow did each one head for his very own sack.

How light each felt to its owner as he took it off the line. And how happy was each man to have his own sack once more.

They turned to thank the stranger—but there was no one under the tree. The soft morning breeze brought them back the echo of a song:

> *Heigh ho,*
> *Life is jolly.*
> *Content is wisdom,*
> *Complaint is folly.*

154

A Dream of Paradise

CHANINA BEN DOSA—that is, Chanina, the son of Dosa—was a famous Rabbi who lived in Palestine about two thousand years ago. He was poor like most Rabbis of that day, but his wants were few and he did not complain.

His wife did not much mind being poor either, though as time went on her burden grew heavier. Gentle and loving as she was she was proud, too. Like her husband, she would not accept help from their friends, so the efforts they had to make to conceal their poverty grew more and more of a burden.

One day she asked Chanina, "Shall we always be as poor as this? I could bear it better if I could see some end to it." Chanina tried to comfort her but he had no suggestion to offer.

"You are always praying to God for others," his wife went on, sadly, "Why don't you ever ask something for ourselves?"

"What could I ask? I do not understand," replied Chanina.

"Ask God to give us some of the good things He has stored up for the righteous in Paradise. Ask Him to let us enjoy only a little here on earth."

Chanina was touched by the words of his patient wife and also by her thin, pinched cheeks, so he did as she asked.

He prayed long and earnestly, with his face to the wall.

Immediately there was a rush of sound at the window. Chanina hurried to see what was happening.

"A miracle!" he cried. "Look what the Lord has sent us." His wife followed him and saw him reach out for a bright shining object.

"What is it?" she cried in great excitement.

"The golden leg of a beautiful golden table," replied Chanina in hushed tones. "There was a hand out there holding it. The hand vanished as I reached out and caught the offering."

"Oh!" cried his wife joyfully. "How heavy it is! We can sell it for a great sum of money and live comfortably for the rest of our lives."

Chanina nodded, but looked thoughtful.

"And what will be our fortune in the hereafter?" he wondered.

"My good and dear Chanina," said his wife, "let us live happily now and keep God's law. He will not let us suffer if we show that we love Him and serve Him."

"Very well," agreed Chanina.

But that night it was his wife who was disturbed. She had had a strange dream.

In it she seemed to have reached Paradise. She was surrounded by good and faithful men and women of all nations who had done God's will upon earth. Each one sat at a little golden table. And each table stood firmly upon three legs.

She looked around for Chanina, and when at last she saw him he too was sitting at a little golden table. But his table had only two legs, and it was so unsteady that nothing would stand upright upon it, not even for a moment.

In a great fright she awoke and called to her husband.

"Oh, what a bad dream I've had," she explained. "Hold me close while I tell you the great wrong we have done."

"My sweet wife," said Chanina. "It was but a dream. You will forget it."

"No, no!" she sobbed. And she told him about her dream of Paradise.

"I see," said her husband. "In Paradise everyone will be sitting at their golden tables, while we, simply because we were dissatisfied with our lot on earth, sit forever at a rickety table."

"Yes. So you must pray to God again, dearest husband, and ask Him to take back the golden table leg He gave us. We must not sacrifice the peace and contentment of eternity to a little ease in this life."

Rabbi Chanina smiled happily. He hurried toward the wall and made another prayer to God, as his wife wished. Then he went to the window and his wife brought him the golden table leg. He took it from her and placed it in the mysterious hand that again had appeared outside the window.

There was great peace and happiness in the hearts of the Rabbi and his wife. They could not forgo the pleasure of telling their friends the wonderful story.

"A miracle! A two-fold miracle!" their friends exclaimed, rejoicing. "God has bestowed gifts without stint in the past. But we have never before known Him to be so generous as to take one back."

—Adapted from
BABYLONIAN TALMUD, TA'ANITH, 25A

The Cap That Mother Made

THIS is a story about a little boy named Anders. For his birthday his mother had given him a present, a cap that she had knitted for him. A prettier cap you never did see! It was almost all red except for a small part in the middle which was green because there hadn't been enough red wool to finish it. The tassel was a deep ocean blue.

Anders was very proud of his new cap. His mother and father told him he looked very fine in it. His brothers and sisters walked all around him to see the cap from all sides. They, too, said the cap was most becoming and that Anders looked quite splendid in it.

Caps, of course, are for out-of-doors. So Anders put his on, stuck his hands in his pockets, and went out for a walk. He wanted everyone to see how fine he looked in his new cap.

The first person he met was a farmer. The farmer was walking beside a wagonload of wood. When he saw Anders with his new cap of red, green, and blue, he stopped and bowed deeply. "A boy with such a fine cap might like to ride on my wagon," he said. But Anders thanked him and kept right on walking. He held his head higher. How proud he was of that new cap!

The next person he met was Lars, the tanner's boy. Lars was such a big boy that he wore high boots and carried a bright new jack-knife. He stared and stared at Anders and his splendid new cap, and came up close to feel it.

"I like your cap. Will you give it to me in exchange for my new jack-knife?" asked the big boy.

Now Anders had never had a jack-knife, and this one was bright and shiny. Anders also knew that as soon as a boy owns a knife he is almost grown up. But still, even for this fine jack-knife, or for all the jack-knives in the world, Anders would not give up the red, green, and blue cap his mother had made him.

"I'm sorry, Lars," he said, "but I cannot give you my new cap." So he said goodby and off he trotted down the road.

Soon he met a little old lady. When she saw Anders' beautiful cap of red, green, and blue, she curtsied deeply to the little boy, spreading her skirts very wide. "Little boy," she said, "you certainly look fine enough to go to the king's ball!"

Anders smiled happily. "I think I *will* go there. With this fine cap on my head, I may as well pay a visit to the king." And off he started for the king's palace.

But at the palace gate stood two soldiers wearing shining helmets and carrying muskets over their shoulders.

"Where are you going, young fellow?" asked one of the soldiers. Anders smiled cheerfully and answered, "I'm going to the king's ball."

"But you have no uniform," said the soldier, "and no one can go to the king's ball without a uniform."

"My cap is surely as fine as any uniform," thought Anders. He felt sad, though, for he saw that the soldiers did not agree with him.

Just then, the princess came running across the courtyard. She was dressed in a gown of white satin, with bows of golden ribbon. When she saw Anders and the soldiers at the gate, she stopped to find what the commotion was about.

"What is wrong? Why won't you let this little boy come to the ball?" asked the princess.

"He's not wearing a uniform," one of the soldiers answered, "and nobody may enter the ballroom without a uniform."

"Oh," said the princess, "but he's wearing such a very fine cap. That will do just as well as a uniform. He shall come to the ball with me."

So the princess took Anders' hand and they walked together up the broad marble steps to the king's palace. Down the long halls and into the ballroom they went. Ladies wearing splendid silks and satins and gentlemen wearing gleaming gold braided uniforms stood talking with one another. As Anders and the princess passed by, they bowed very low, for they thought, "Surely he must be a prince with that fine red cap."

At one end of the ballroom a long table was set with golden cups and golden plates in long rows. Piles of tarts and cakes were heaped up on silver platters. There were baskets of delicious fruits, and all sorts of candies and goodies. The princess seated herself on a golden chair at the end of the table, and she told Anders to sit beside her.

"But you cannot eat with your cap on your head," said the princess and she started to reach for the cap.

Anders was too quick for her. "Oh yes, I can eat just as well with it on," he said, and he held on to it with both hands. Without the cap on his head, he knew nobody would any longer believe he was a prince. Besides, how could he let his fine cap be taken away? He might never get it back again.

"If I give you a kiss, will you give me your cap?" asked the princess.

The princess was very beautiful, and Anders would have liked to be kissed by her. But he just could not give up the cap that mother made. So Anders shook his head gently.

Now the princess filled his pockets with cakes and goodies. She slipped her

158

own golden necklace around his neck, and bent down and kissed him.

"Won't you give me your cap now?" coaxed the princess. Anders only moved farther back in his chair and did not take his hands from his head.

At this moment the doors of the ballroom opened, and the king himself entered. He wore a purple velvet robe with a border of ermine fur. On his head was a golden crown set with jewels. Behind him, carrying his mantle, walked gentlemen in gold-braided uniforms and hats.

The king smiled when he saw Anders next to the princess on the golden chair.

"That is a very fine cap you have, young man!" said the king.

"Yes, it is," replied Anders proudly. "My mother made it for me, but everyone wants to get it away from me."

"Surely you would like to change caps with me," said the king, and he raised the heavy golden crown from his head. He held it out to Anders with one hand, and reached for Anders' red cap with the other.

Anders did not say a word. Quick as a flash, he jumped out of his chair and dashed across the ballroom. Like an arrow he darted through the long halls. He skipped down the marble steps and out into the yard, and slipped through the palace gates.

He ran so fast that the cakes and goodies tumbled out of his pockets, but Anders did not stop to pick them up. And he did not stop when the golden necklace that the princess had given him became unfastened and fell off his neck.

But he had his cap! He still had his cap! He held on to it with both hands, and ran and ran till at last he was home.

As soon as he caught his breath, Anders told his mother and his father and his brothers and sisters all that had happened to him during the day. He told them how everyone had admired his fine red cap and how everyone had tried to get it away.

The whole family listened eagerly. When Anders had finished, his big brother said, "You were very foolish, Anders, not to take the golden crown! Just think, you could buy anything if you were king—a jack-knife, high boots—even a velvet cap with a long feather—much nicer than your knitted cap!"

At that Anders became very angry, and his blue eyes flashed. "I was *not* foolish," he cried. "Not all the king's money would buy me a finer cap than the one mother made me!"

Then Anders ran to his mother. She hugged him close and gave him a kiss. He knew that mother's cap was the very finest cap in all the world.

The Stone in the Road

THERE was once a very rich man who lived in a beautiful castle near a village. He loved the people who lived in the village and tried to help them. He planted beautiful trees near their houses, and had picnics for their children, and every Christmas he gave them a tree.

But the people did not like to work. They were unhappy because they, too, were not rich like their friend.

One day the rich man got up very early in the morning, and put a large stone in the road that led past his home. Then he hid himself behind the hedge, and waited to see what would happen.

By and by a poor man came along driving a cow. He scolded because the stone lay in his path, but he didn't pick it up. He walked around it and went on.

Then a farmer came on his way to the mill. He complained because the stone was there, but he, too, merely drove around it and went on his way.

So the day passed. Every one who came by complained because the stone lay in the road, but nobody touched it.

At last, just at nightfall, the miller's boy came past. He was a hard-working fellow, and he was very tired, because he had been busy since dawn at the mill.

But he said to himself, "It is almost dark. Somebody may fall over this stone in the night and perhaps be badly hurt. I will move it out of the way."

So he tugged at the heavy stone. It was hard to move, but he pulled and pushed and lifted until at last he moved it from its place. To his surprise he found a bag lying beneath it.

He lifted the bag. It was heavy, for it was filled with gold. Upon it was written "This gold belongs to the one who moves the stone."

The miller's boy went home feeling very happy indeed, and the rich man went home to his castle. He was glad that some people are willing to do hard things, and he was glad the miller's boy had been rewarded for his good work.

160

The Lion-Makers

Translated by Arthur W. Ryder

In A certain town were four Brahmins, that is to say, four very educated men. They were great friends. Three of them were famous scholars, but they had no common sense. The fourth had never been able to learn anything at all. He had nothing *but* common sense.

One day the four friends met to talk things over.

"What is the use of knowing a lot," said they, "and being very smart, if one does not travel, win the favor of kings, and make a lot of money? Whatever we do, let us all travel."

So they set out. But when they had gone a little way, the eldest of them said,

"One of us, the fourth, is a stupid fellow. He has nothing but sense. Now nobody gains the favorable attention of kings just by having common sense. One must be a scholar too. Therefore, I don't think we ought to share our earnings with him. Let him turn back and go home."

Then the second Brahmin turned to the man of sense and said, "You know this is true. Please go home."

But the third said, "No, no. This is no way to behave, for we have been friends and played together since we were little boys. Come along, my good friend. You shall have a share of the money we earn."

To this the others at last agreed and

161

they continued on their journey. Soon they came to a forest and there in front of them lay the bones of a dead lion.

Then one of the educated men said, "Here is a good chance to show how much we know. Here lies some kind of creature, dead. Let us bring it to life by means of all we have learned."

The first Brahmin said, "I know how to put together the skeleton."

The second said, "I can give it skin, flesh, and blood."

The third said, "I can give it life."

So the first put together all the bones. The second gave it skin, flesh, and blood. But while the third was busy breathing life into it, the fourth, the man of common sense, spoke up.

"My worthy and learned friends," he said, "common sense would tell us that this creature is a lion. I would not advise you to bring it to life. If you do, he will surely eat every one of us."

The Brahmins were very angry. "You simpleton!" they said. "Are you trying to tell us that you know more than we do?"

"I only know what my common sense tells me," said the fourth Brahmin. "However, if you insist on going ahead, just wait until I climb this convenient tree."

After the fourth Brahmin climbed up the tree, the lion was brought to life. He rose up, opened wide his jaws, and ate up all three scholars.

But the man of sense, after the lion had gone off, climbed down from the tree and went home.

—From *Tales of the Panchatantra*

The Dutch Boy and the Dike

PIETER was a small boy who lived, a long time ago, with his mother and father in Holland. Like most Dutch people, they lived in a spotlessly clean white cottage, and there was a big field of red and yellow tulips right next to their own neat flower garden.

Pieter loved his home and the tulips, and he loved looking beyond them to the slowly-turning windmills that dotted the landscape, and beyond the windmills to the sea.

It has always been easy to see the sea from anywhere near the shore in Holland because the land there is lower than the ocean. Indeed the waves would easily engulf the land but for the strong high walls, called dikes, which keep the water out. It is the job of many men in Holland to watch these walls and to repair them instantly if a hole appears. Even little children are taught to watch the dikes for they know how quickly a small hole can become a big one and how dangerous it would be if the water came pouring in.

One day Pieter went to see his grandmother who lived several miles out in the country. He had enjoyed his visit very much and it was almost sunset when he started for home.

Hurrying along the top of the dike—for he wanted to be home in time for supper —he noticed that the water seemed very high. But it had been raining for many days and it was natural that the sea should be swollen.

Suddenly Pieter heard the sound of water trickling. He scrambled down the side of the dike to look for the hole he feared might be there. It didn't take him long to find the hole. It was a very small one but water was already gushing through it. Pieter thought of running home as fast as he could. He was hungry and tired. But he knew what a leak in the dike could mean. He looked around to see if he could find someone to call. But there was no one in sight.

It was getting dark and Pieter was lonely and frightened. But he did what he knew he had to do: He put his finger in the dike to keep the water from coming through.

"I can't stay here all night," he thought to himself in terror. But he didn't know what to do. His finger grew stiff; so he tried another finger and then another. Each time he changed fingers, water poured through the dike. Finally he put in his thumb because it was his biggest finger, and he didn't dare take it out even for a minute.

His whole hand grew cold and numb and he wondered how he could stand the pain if no one came. But he knew he would have to stand it; if he took his finger away the water would rush in faster and faster making the hole so large

that there would be no plugging it up any more. And he knew that then the water would swell to a roaring flood which could engulf the whole countryside.

Keeping his thumb in the hole became harder and harder as night descended dark and cold. Every now and then Pieter called loudly "Help! Help!" But only the echo of his own words answered him.

Pieter began to sob. Then he had a cheering thought. "Mother will miss me," he said to himself, "and will come looking for me soon."

But she didn't come. When her little boy didn't come home at supper-time, she thought he had stayed at his grandmother's. And of course his grandmother thought he was safely at home.

Pieter was stiff with cold, hungry, and so weary that his whole body ached to fall asleep. But he knew he must keep his position until someone came to relieve him no matter how painful it might be. He couldn't let the roaring waters rush in and flood his beloved country. So he stayed all night, suffering miserably. But he would never give up no matter how miserable he was.

It wasn't until early next morning that Pieter heard someone walking along the road. It was a man on his way to work. Relief at last!

"Help!" cried Pieter in as loud a voice as he had left after his long night's vigil.

The man stopped. The pitiful cry for help had turned to a moan. Where was it coming from? The man looked over the edge of the dike and saw the boy clinging to the side of the great wall.

"Help! Help!" repeated Pieter feebly. "There's a leak in the dike and I've been plugging it up."

The man jumped down to where Pieter lay cramped and faint.

"What on earth!" the man exclaimed, for he did not see how there could actually be a leak in the tall strong dikes that had protected the low lands of Holland for so many years against the sea. Much less could he understand how, if there *was* a leak, one small boy could have stopped it. But he soon saw that that was exactly what had happened.

By this time other men and women were passing by on their way to work, and Pieter's rescuer shouted to them for help as he lifted the shivering boy in his arms and wrapped him, for warmth, in his overcoat.

In no time at all men and women came running to the spot, and, working feverishly with their tools, they soon repaired the hole in the dike which Pieter's thumb had been filling for all of that long lonely frightening night.

By this time more and more people had arrived and some of them carried Pieter, on their shoulders, home to his mother. They all soon knew of the heroic thing he had done and they set up a great cheer, shouting, "Make way for the brave boy who saved our country from the sea! All praise to the hero of Holland!"

Pieter had indeed done a heroic thing. And how proud his mother was of him when she heard the story of what her boy had done! But as Pieter snuggled down under the blankets of his bed and ate hungrily of the big bowl of hot soup his mother brought him, he murmured just before he fell asleep, "I would do it again if I had to. I am glad I could do something, especially if it was something really helpful, for my country—the country I love so much."

King Canute and His Courtiers

ONCE upon a time in a far country of the North, there ruled over the people of many lands a great and wise King named Canute.

He lived in a palace among rich surroundings and he had many courtiers to do his bidding. These courtiers were forever flattering him and telling him he was the greatest king and the mightiest man in the world.

"Nothing in the world will ever disobey you, O mighty King," they would say, or "No enemy will ever dare to defy our all-powerful King."

But King Canute was a truly wise man. He knew that no man on earth, no matter how mighty, was "all-powerful," and besides he grew tired of hearing all this silly praise over and over again.

One day when the King and some of his courtiers were on the shore of a seaport town, one of them said, with his usual sickening flattery, "O King, your power will last forever. Nothing can ever disobey you. There is nothing on earth that will not do your bidding."

Sick and tired of foolish speeches like this, King Canute decided to teach his courtiers a lesson. So he bade one of them to carry him, in his chair of state, down to the very edge of the shore where the waves of the ocean were lapping at the sandy beach.

There King Canute sat gazing out at the sea while his courtiers wondered what he was going to do. One by one they sang the King's praises in their usual exaggerated words: "You are the greatest man in the world; nothing dares disobey you," and so on.

"Will the sea obey me?" asked the King gazing down at the incoming waves that were even now approaching his feet.

"Merely command it, O King," said the foolish courtiers, "and it will obey you."

Then King Canute rose up, and with a look of pity for the servile courtiers he stretched out his hand toward the sea and called in a mighty voice, "I command you, ocean, to come no farther! Stop your rolling, you waves! Do not dare to come nearer me or to touch my feet!"

But the waves came in steadily just as they always had. They swelled higher and higher; they came farther and farther in on the shore and were already wetting not only the King's feet but the hem of his robe.

The courtiers were alarmed, not understanding what the King was trying to do. But the King turned to them saying, "My men, may you and all the people on earth learn from what you have seen that no earthly man is all-powerful. There is only One King who is worthy to be called All-Powerful, only One who rules

the heaven and the earth and all that in them is. Only the Almighty can command. His is the only law that all men and all nature must obey."

And with these words King Canute removed his golden crown vowing never to wear it again. It hangs today, we are told, in one of the churches of King Canute's country, and beneath it, for all who would praise man above God, is a small metal plate. On it you may read these words: "Here, in the year of our Lord 1032, King Canute taught his courtiers the lesson of humility."

The Poor Count's Christmas

By Frank R. Stockton

MANY years ago there lived a noble Count who was one of the kindest men in the world. Every day in the year he gave to the poor, but at Christmas time his goodness shone brightest. He had even vowed that, as far as he was able to make them so, every child he knew should be happy on Christmas Day.

Early every Christmas morning each boy and girl in the neighborhood came to the castle of Count Cormo, and there the Count and Countess welcomed them all, and through the whole day there were games and festive merry-making and good things to eat and fun of every kind, and besides all this there was a great Christmas tree, with a present on it for each of the eager, happy youngsters who stood around it.

But although the good Count had a castle and rich lands, he gave away so much money that he became poorer and poorer, so that at last he and his wife found it hard to get the clothes and food they needed.

But this made no difference at Christmas time. The Count managed so the children could still have their Christmas presents. Year by year he had sold for this purpose some of the beautiful things which the castle contained, so that now there was scarcely enough furniture left for himself and the Countess.

One night, about a week before Christmas, they sat in the great hall before a fire smaller and poorer than the fires which burned on the hearth of most of the cottagers in the surrounding country, for the cottagers could go into the woods and pick up sticks and twigs, whereas the Count had sold all his forests, so that he could not cut wood, and he had only one old man for outdoor work, and he had already picked up all the fallen branches near the castle.

"Well, one thing is certain," said the Countess Cormo, as she drew her chair nearer to the little pile of burning sticks, "We cannot have the children here at Christmas this year."

"Why not?" asked the Count.

"Because we have nothing to give them," she said. "We have nothing for them to eat, nothing to put on the tree, and no money to buy anything. What would be the good of their coming when we have nothing at all for them?"

"But we must have something," said the Count. "Think of all the years we have had these Christmas gatherings, think how hard it would be, both for us and the little ones, to give them up now when we are growing old. We may not be with the children another year. There are still several days before Christmas; I can sell something tomorrow, and

168

we can have the tree and everything prepared in time. There will not be so much to eat as usual, and the presents will be smaller, but it will be our good old Christmas just the same."

"I should like very much to know what you are going to sell," said the Countess. "I thought we had already parted with everything we could possibly spare."

"Not quite," said the Count. "There is our old family bedstead. It is very large; it is made of the most valuable woods, and it is inlaid with gold and silver. It will surely bring a good price."

"And what are we going to sleep on, I'd like to know?" cried the Countess.

"Oh, we can get along very well," said the Count. "There is a small bedstead which you can have, and I will sleep on the floor."

"On the floor, at your age!" exclaimed the Countess. "It will be the death of you! But if you have made up your mind, I suppose there is no use in my saying anything more about it."

"Not the least in the world," replied her husband, with a smile.

The morning of the next day there came through the forest, not very far from Count Cormo's castle, a jolly Giant called Feldar. As he strode along he appeared to be talking to the forefinger of his left hand, which he held up before him. He was not, however, talking to his forefinger, but to a little fairy called Tillette, who was sitting on it, chatting away in a very lively manner.

"Where are you going?" said the Fairy to the Giant.

"My old uncle is dead, and I am going to see if he has left me any money!"

"All right," said the Fairy, "but if you get any money you ought to do something for poor Count Cormo."

"Count Cormo? Why, I thought he was rich!"

"No, he *was*, but he has given everything away. Yesterday when I went there, he and his wife had just finished their dinner, and were sitting before the fireplace. I saw no fire in it. They were busy talking, and so I did not disturb them, but just climbed up on the table to see what I could find to eat. You haven't any idea what a miserable meal they must have had. Of course, there was enough left for me, for I need only a few crumbs, but everything was so hard and stale that I could scarcely eat it. I don't see how

169

they can live in that way. But after the meal, when I heard them talking, I found out how poor they really are. They were talking about the Christmas tree, and although they are so poor, they are going to do just the same this year."

"I don't see how they can," said the Giant.

"The Count is going to sell his big bedstead," said the Fairy.

"It ought to be stopped," said the Giant. "He shouldn't be allowed to do such a thing."

"Indeed he shouldn't," the Fairy said. Before very long they came to a great castle where a warden stood the gate.

"Ho, warden!" said the Giant. "So my uncle is dead!"

"Dead a month," said the warden, "and his property divided among his heirs."

"That is not so," roared the Giant. "I am one of his heirs, and I haven't got anything."

"I don't know anything about it," said the warden. "I was told to give that message to everyone who came."

"Who told you to give it?" cried the Giant.

"My master, Katofan, who is the old Giant's heir, and owns the castle."

"What, my cousin Katofan!" exclaimed the Giant. "What impudence! He's only a ninth cousin by marriage. Where is he? I want to see him."

"I don't think he is well enough to see anybody today," said the warden.

"Open that gate!" the Giant roared.

The warden turned pale, and opened the gate as wide as it would go, while the Giant, with the Fairy still on his finger, walked boldly in.

In a large inner hall, sitting before a great fire, they saw a Giant so tall and thin that he looked as if he had been made of fishing-poles. He turned uneasily in his chair when he saw his cousin.

"Well, Katofan, I'd like to know what all this means! How did you come to be heir to this castle?"

"Because it came to me from my dear good old uncle," said Katofan.

"Well," said Feldar, stretching himself up high, "I am one of the heirs, and I want my share. Who does the dividing business? Do you do it yourself?"

"Oh, no!" said Katofan. "I am not well enough for that. I cannot go about much. But I will send for my dividing agent. He will see that you get your share."

He rang a bell, and a small man appeared. When the Fairy saw him she could not help laughing, for he had a bushy head of hair, which was black as ink on one side, and white as milk on the other.

"Flipkrak," said Katofan, "here's another heir that we overlooked. I wish you would take him, and let him choose something that he would like to have."

"Certainly," said Flipkrak. "This way, good sir," and he went out of a side door, followed closely by Feldar.

The young Giant walked through several of the vast rooms of the castle. "I see you have a lot of fine furniture here," he said to Flipkrak, "and I need furniture. I will mark some of it with this piece of chalk, and you can send it to me."

"Oh yes, good sir," cried Flipkrak.

Feldar took a piece of chalk from his pocket, and marked enough furniture to furnish a castle.

"This kind of chalk will not rub off," he said, "and I've put the marks where they won't show. But don't overlook any of them. Now, where are your money-vaults?"

"Oh, good sir!" cried Flipkrak, "you can't go there—I mean we haven't any money-vaults!"

"Give me the key," said Feldar.

"Oh, good sir!" cried Flipkrak, shaking with terror, "I must not let that go out of my keeping—I mean I haven't it."

The Giant made no answer, but taking Flipkrak by the heels, he held him upside down in the air, and shook him. A big key dropped from his pocket.

When he reached the money-vault, Feldar easily opened the door and walked in. Great bags of gold and silver were piled up around the walls. Feldar took out his piece of chalk, and marked about a dozen bags which held the gold coin.

"Oh, that's right, good sir," cried Flipkrak, feeling a little better. "We can send them to you after you go away."

"What is in those small bags on that shelf?" asked Feldar.

"Those are diamonds, good sir," said Flipkrak. "You can mark some of them.

"I will mark one," said the Giant to the Fairy, who was now nestled in his shirt-sleeve, "and that I will give to you."

"All right, good sir," said Flipkrak. "We will send them to you—very soon"

"Oh, you needn't trouble yourself about that," said Feldar; "I will take them along with me." And so saying, he put the bag of diamonds in one of his coat-pockets, and began to pile the bags of money on his shoulders.

Flipkrak yelled and howled, but it was of no use. Feldar loaded himself with his bags, and walked off, without even looking at Flipkrak, who was almost crazy at seeing so much of his master's treasure boldly taken away from him.

Feldar stopped for a moment in the great hall, where Katofan was still sitting before the fire.

"I've taken my share of the money," he said, "and I've marked a lot of furniture and things which I want you to send me, in a week. Do you understand?"

The thin Giant gave one look at the piles of bags on Feldar's shoulders and fainted away. He had more money left than he could possibly use, but he could not bear to lose the least bit of the wealth he had seized upon.

"What in the world are you going to do with all that money?" the Fairy asked.

"I am going to give one bag of it to Count Cormo, so that he can give the children a Christmas tree, and the rest I shall carry to my own castle on Shattered Crag."

"You can't do it like that," said the Fairy. "The Count is very proud, and he would say that *you* were giving the Christmas feast and not he. I wish you would let me manage this for you; I'll do the thinking, and you can do the working. It's easy for me to think."

"And it's just as easy for me to work,"

said Feldar, with hearty good will.

The day before Christmas poor Count Cormo sat in his castle hall, before a hearth where there was no fire. He had sold his family bedstead, but he had received very little money for it. People said such old bedsteads were not worth much, even if they were inlaid with precious metals. So he had been able to prepare only a small tree, on which he had hung the cheapest kind of presents, and his feast was very plain and simple. The Countess, indeed, was afraid the things would not go around, for their old servant told them he had heard there would be more children at the castle the next day than had ever been there before. She was in favor of giving up the whole affair and sending the children home as soon as they came.

"What is the use of having them here," said the Countess, "when we have so little to give them? They will get more at home; and then if they don't come we shall have the things for ourselves."

"No, no, my dear," said the Count. "This may be the last time we shall have the children with us, for I do not see how we can live much longer in this sorrowful condition, but the dear boys and girls must come tomorrow. I should not wish to die knowing that we had missed a Christmas. We must do the best we can

with what we have, and I am sure we can make the children happy if we try. And now let us go to bed, so as to be up early tomorrow."

The Countess sighed. There was only one little bedstead, and the poor Count had to sleep on the floor.

Christmas Day dawned bright, clear, and sparkling. The Count was in good spirits.

Very soon he heard the sound of many merry voices, and his eyes began to twinkle.

"They are coming!" he cried, and throwing open the door of the castle he

went to meet his little guests. But when he saw them he started back.

"What do you think?" he exclaimed to the Countess. "There is a long procession of them, and they are headed by a Giant—the young Giant Feldar! Who ever heard of such a thing as a Giant coming to a children's party! He will eat up everything in a few mouthfuls!"

"You might as well let him do it!" said the Countess. "There won't be enough for the others, anyway. There seem to be hundreds of them; and if there isn't a band of music striking up!"

Sure enough, quite a procession was approaching the castle. First came the Giant Feldar, with Tillette, the little Fairy, on his finger; then four or five musicians; and after them a long line of children, all dressed in their best clothes, and marching two by two.

"Merry Christmas!" shouted the Giant, as soon as he saw Count Cormo, and then all the children shouted "Merry Christmas!" until the castle courtyard echoed with the cheerful greeting, while the band played loudly and merrily.

"Come in, my dears," cried the Count to the children. "I am glad to see you. As for you, good Giant, I feel my door is not quite large enough. But perhaps you can stoop and squeeze yourself in."

"Count Cormo!" cried the Fairy, from the Giant's finger. "I have a plan."

"If it isn't a dear little Fairy!" the Count exclaimed. "Why, certainly, if you have a plan to propose, I shall be happy to hear it."

"Well then," said Tillette, "suppose we go first into the great hall. That is so large it will hold us all, and we can have a grand dance."

"I am afraid the great hall would be very uncomfortable," said the Count. "No one has lived in it for many years, and everything must be covered with dust and cobwebs."

"But it would be so nice to march around that great hall with the music and everything. I don't believe there's any dust," replied the Fairy.

"Well, then," said the Count, "as you have set your heart on it, we'll go."

So the Count and Countess took their places in the procession, at the head of the line of children and just behind the musicians. Then they all marched across the great courtyard to the old wing of the castle, and when they had reached the doors of the great hall, the Giant swung them open, and everybody entered.

Never were there two such astonished people as the Count and Countess!

Right in the middle of the hall stood a great Christmas tree, which the Giant had brought in on his shoulders from the woods. On the wide-spreading branches of this tall tree were hung hundreds of presents and sparkling ornaments.

"What does this mean?" gasped the Count. "Whose tree is this?"

"It is yours! It is yours!" cried the children in a merry chorus which made the old walls ring. "It is your Christmas tree, and we, who love you, give it to you!"

The Count looked around from one to another of the children, but did not say

173

a word. His heart was too full for him to speak. Then the Giant put the Fairy on his shirt frill, and, stooping down, took up the Count and Countess, one in each hand, holding them gently, but very firmly, and carried them around the tree, raising them up and down, so that they could see all the presents, even those at the very top.

Everything was labeled—not with the name of the person they were for, for they were all for the Count and Countess, but with the names of those who gave them.

Presently the Count began to read out every name aloud, and each time a child's name was called, all the other children would clap and cheer. There were a good many small bags, which looked as if they were very heavy, hanging here and there, and these were all marked, "From Feldar," while some beautiful clusters of diamonds, which glittered in the sunlight that poured in through the windows, were labeled, "From Tillette."

It took a long time to look at all the presents, which were rather different from the things generally seen on Christmas trees, for the great branches and boughs held every kind of useful and ornamental article that the Count and Countess needed. Many of these were old family treasures which they once had owned, but had been obliged to sell to keep up their Christmas festivals.

The Count and his wife were more and more delighted as they were carried around the tree, but at last this happy festivity was over, and the Giant put them down upon the floor.

"Now for a dance!" cried the Fairy in her clear little voice. The band began to play gay music, and all the children danced around the tree.

The Count and Countess, with the Giant and Fairy, stood aside, while this happy play was going on, enjoying it almost as much as the children. When the children tired of dancing the Count thought the party ought to have something to eat, but his heart failed him when he remembered how little he had to offer.

He need not have troubled his mind about that! As soon as the dance was done, the Giant stepped to a door which led to another apartment, and throwing it open, he cried:

"Enter the banquet hall! This is the feast the children are giving to the good Count Cormo and his wife. He has feasted them often and often, and made them happy, for many a Christmas. It is their turn now."

Everybody trooped through the door, the children gently pushing the Count and Countess before them. The room was truly a banquet hall. A long table was covered with delicious goodies to eat, and on smaller tables were more and more and more. Here and there, on the long table, were enormous cakes, great bowls of jelly, and vast pies. Everybody knew these were for the Giant.

The Count and Countess took their places at the head and foot of the table. All the children gathered around and everybody had a splendid appetite. Just in the center of the table there was a little table about three inches high, on which there were little morsels of dainties. At this table, on a little chair, the Fairy Til-lette sat, where she could see everything, and she enjoyed herself as much as anybody.

When the feast was over, they all went into the great hall, where they had dances and games and singing, and there never was a merrier company.

When evening approached, the Count stood up and made a little speech. He tried to tell the children how good he thought they were, and how happy they

had made him. He did not say much, but they all understood him. When he had finished, there was a silence over the whole room. The children looked at one another, some of them smiled, and then, all together, they cried:

"The Giant and the Fairy did it all. He gave us the money, and she told us what to buy."

"Oh, pshaw!" said the young Giant, his face turning very red. "I thought nothing was to be said about that."

Now all the children came up, and each in turn bade the Count and Countess farewell, and then, headed by the Giant's band of music, and singing merrily, they marched away to their homes.

But Count Cormo would not let the Giant and the Fairy go away so soon. He made them come with him to the dwelling part of the castle, and there, after a little squeezing and stooping by the Giant at the door, they all sat around the hearth, on which a fine fire was blazing.

"I don't know what to say, my dear

175

Feldar," said the Count, "and I can never repay you——"

"Oh, yes, dear Count," the Fairy broke in, "you can repay him. You can adopt him. You have no children and you are getting old. He has no parents, he is rich, and you can show him how to do good with his great wealth. He could come and live in the old wing of the castle where the rooms are so large. The furniture he has inherited could be sent here, and you all could be so happy together! Will you take him?"

The Count's eyes filled with tears.

"Would you like us to adopt you?" he said to Feldar.

"Indeed I should," was the reply. Then the young Giant kneeled on the floor, and the Count got up on a table, and put his hands on the young Giant's head, and adopted him.

"Now you ought to adopt Tillette," said Feldar, after he had kissed the Count and Countess and sat down again by the fire.

"No," said Tillette, "I cannot be adopted. But I will often come to see you, and we shall be happy together, and the children will have a splendid Christmas festival every year."

"As long as we live," said the Count and Countess.

"As long as I live," said Feldar.

When the Count and Countess went up to their room that night, they found the family bedstead, all cleaned and polished, with its gold and silver ornaments sparkling like new.

"What a happy Christmas I have had!" said good Count Cormo.

"May you have many more, my dear," said the Countess.

—Adapted

THE TWENTY-FOURTH OF DECEMBER

THE clock ticks slowly, slowly in the hall,
And slow, slow, slower still the long hours crawl;
It seems as though this long, long day
Would never, never pass away.
The clock ticks endlessly—tick-tock upon the wall . . .
I wonder now if Christmas Day
Will ever really dawn at all!

The Last Class

(A Young Alsatian's Story)

I WAS very late going to school that morning, and I was very much afraid I should be scolded, especially as Monsieur Hamel had told us that he would question us on the participles, and I did not know a word of them. For a moment I thought of shirking the class, and going off across country.

The weather was so hot and clear. You could hear the blackbirds whistling on the edge of the wood, and in the meadow behind the saw-mill the Prussians were at their drill. These things were much more attractive than the rules of participles. But I had the strength to resist them, and I ran very quickly toward the school.

Passing the townhall I saw that there was a group of people by the little notice-board.

As I ran across the square, the blacksmith, who was there with his apprentice, reading the notice, shouted to me: "Don't hurry so, little one; you will always get fast enough to that school of yours!"

I thought he was laughing at me, and, out of breath, I went into Monsieur Hamel's little courtyard. Usually, at the beginning of a class, a great noise could be heard there, desks opening and shutting, lessons being repeated all together at the top of the voice, with stopped ears, to learn them the better, and the master's big ruler tapping on the tables for "A little silence."

I counted on all this fuss to let me reach my seat unnoticed; but on this particular day all was quiet, as on a Sunday morning. Through the open window I saw my schoolfellows already in their places, and Monsieur Hamel walking to and fro with his terrible iron ruler under his arm. I had to open the door and enter in a great calm. You may think how I blushed and trembled.

But nothing happened. Monsieur Hamel looked at me without anger, and said, very gently, "Go quickly to your place, my little Franz; we were going to begin without you."

I stepped over the bench, and sat down at once at my desk. Only then, I noticed that our teacher was wearing his beautiful green frock-coat, his fine frilled shirt-front, and the embroidered black cap that he put on only on inspection days, or for prize-givings. There was something unusual and solemn, too, about the whole class.

But what surprised me most was to see at the end of the room, on the benches that were usually empty, the men of the village, seated and silent like

ourselves—the old mayor, the old post-man, and others besides. They all seemed sad; and one had brought an old dog-eared spelling-book that he held wide open on his knees, his big spectacles laid across the page.

While I was wondering at all this, Monsieur Hamel said, in the same grave and gentle voice with which he had received me, "My children, this is the last of your classes that I shall take. The order has come from Berlin that in the future nothing but German shall be taught in the schools of Alsace and Lorraine . . . The new teacher comes to-morrow. To-day's is your last lesson in French. I beg you to be very attentive."

These few words horrified me. Ah! that was what they had posted up at the town-hall.

My last lesson in French! And I, who scarcely knew how to write! I should never learn!

How I longed now to have once more all the time I had lost! The lessons shirked for bird-nesting, or sliding on the frozen river! My books that so lately I found dull, and heavy to carry—my grammar, my history—seemed now old friends from whom I should find it hard to part.

The idea that Monsieur Hamel was going away, that I should not see him again, made me forget punishments and blows with the ruler. Poor man! It was in honor of this last lesson that he had put on his fine Sunday clothes, and I understood now why the old men of the village had come to sit at the back of the room. It was a way of thanking our teacher for his forty years of good service, and of paying their respects to the departing fatherland.

It was my turn to recite. What would I not have given to be able to say from end to end that famous rule of the participles, in a loud voice, without a mistake; but I got muddled, and dared not lift my head.

My master spoke, "I shall not scold you, little Franz, you are sufficiently punished. That is how it is. Every day one says to one's self, 'I have plenty of time. I will learn to-morrow.' And then you see what happens. . . . Ah, the great misfortune of our Alsace has been always to put off learning till to-morrow. Now, these people have the right to say to us, 'What! you pretend to be French, and you do not know how to read or write your own language!'

"In all that, my poor Franz, you are not alone to blame. Have I nothing to regret? Have I not often made you water my garden instead of working? And when I wished to go trout-fishing, did I scruple to give you a holiday?"

And then, passing from one thing to another, Monsieur Hamel began to talk to us of the French language, saying that it was the most beautiful language in the world; that we ought to keep it among us, and never forget it, because, when a nation falls into slavery, so long as it clings close to its language, it holds the key of its prison.

Then he took a grammar and read us our lesson. I was surprised to see how well I understood. Everything he said seemed easy to me. I think, too, that I had never listened so well, and that he had never put so much thought into his explanations. One would have said that the poor man wished to give us all his knowledge before he left us, to get it into our heads at a single blow.

When the lesson was done we went on to writing. For that day, Monsieur Hamel had prepared new copies for us, on which were written, in a fine round hand: *France, Alsace, France, Alsace*. It was strange to see how we all worked, and in what silence. There was nothing to be heard but the scratching of the pens on the paper. On the roof of the schoolhouse pigeons were gently cooing, and I said to myself as I heard them, "Will they make them sing in German, them too?"

From time to time, when I looked up from my page, I saw Monsieur Hamel motionless in his chair, gazing at the objects about him, as if he wished to carry away with him in his mind's eye the whole of his little schoolhouse.

Think! For forty years he had been there in the same place, with his court-yard in front of him and his class just the same. Only the benches and desks had been polished with the rubbings of use. The walnut trees in the yard had grown, and the hop he had planted himself now climbed around the window and up to the roof.

How heart-breaking it must have been for the poor man to be leaving all these things, and to hear his sister packing their boxes in the room overhead. For they were to go next day, to leave the country forever. Still he had the courage to go on with our lesson to the end. After the writing we had our his-

179

tory class. I shall not forget that last lesson.

Suddenly the church clock struck twelve. At the same moment the bugles of the Prussians coming back from drill sounded under our windows. Monsieur Hamel rose, very pale, from his chair. I had never thought him so tall. "My friends," he said, "my friends . . . I . . . I . . ." But something stifled him. He could not finish his sentence

Then he turned to the blackboard, took a piece of chalk, and, pressing on it with all his strength, wrote as large as he could:

Long live France

He stayed there, leaning his head against the wall, and, without speaking, signed to us with his hand—"That will do. Dismiss."

Breathes There The Man With Soul So Dead

By Sir Walter Scott

Breathes there the man with soul so dead
Who never to himself hath said,
This is my own, my native land!
Whose heart hath ne'er within him burned,
As home his footsteps he hath turned
From wandering on a foreign strand?
If such there breathe, go, mark him well;
For him no minstrel raptures swell;
High though his titles, proud his name,
Boundless his wealth as wish can claim,
Despite those titles, power, and pelf,
The wretch, concentred all in self,
Living, shall forfeit fair renown,
And, doubly dying, shall go down
To the vile dust from whence he sprung,
Unwept, unhonored, and unsung.

(From The Lay of the Last Minstrel)

Master of All Masters

By Joseph Jacobs

A GIRL once went to the fair to hire herself for a servant. At last a funny-looking old gentleman engaged her, and took her home to his house. When she got there, he told her that he had something to teach her, for that in his house he had his own names for things.

He said to her: "What will you call me?"

"Master or Mister, or whatever you please, sir," says she.

He said: "You must call me 'Master of all Masters.' And what would you call this?" pointing to his bed.

"Bed or couch, or what you please, sir."

"No, that's my 'barnacle.' And what do you call these?" said he, pointing to his pantaloons.

"Breeches, or what you please, sir."

"You must call them 'squibs and crackers.' And what would you call her?" pointing to the cat.

"Cat or kit, or what you please, sir."

"You must call her 'white-faced sim-miny.' And this, now," showing the fire, "what would you call this?"

"Fire or flame, or what you please, sir."

"You must call it 'hot cockalorum.' And what, this?" he went on, pointing to the water.

"Water or wet, or whatever you please, sir."

"No, 'pondalorum' is its name. And what do you call all this?" asked he, as he pointed to the house.

"House or cottage, or whatever you please, sir."

"You must call it 'high topper mountain.'"

That very night the servant woke her master up in a fright and said: "Master of all Masters, get out of your barnacle and put on your squibs and crackers. For white-faced simminy has got a spark of hot cockalorum on its tail, and unless you get some pondalorum, high topper mountain will be all on hot cockalorum." . . . That's all.

The Arrow and the Apple

THE STORY OF WILLIAM TELL

ABOUT six hundred years ago the people of the little mountainous country of Switzerland were ruled by the Emperor of Austria who sent a tyrant named Gessler to be their Governor. Then came hard and bitter times for the Swiss. Gessler wanted to gain the Emperor's favor and so he ruled with an iron hand.

He imposed heavy fines and long prison terms for the slightest disobedience. He seemed to be able to do whatever he wished. But there was one thing he could not do. He could not make these proud people bow down to him.

He was angry at this and determined to find a new way to make them feel his power.

One morning the market-place of the town of Altdorf was buzzing with excitement. Down the street Austrian soldiers came marching. One soldier carried a long pole and another a red cap with a feather fastened on it.

As the townspeople gazed, the soldier placed the red cap on top of the pole. Then the pole was planted firmly in the ground.

"Now what can that mean?" whispered the baker to his neighbor, as he brushed some flour off his apron.

"You may be sure it will bring us no good," answered the neighbor, a clock-maker. "Some scheme of Gessler's, no doubt, to make things even harder for us."

"How could things be harder?" asked a farmer's wife. "Only a few days ago my husband was ploughing our field with our oxen when some of Gessler's men came and took them away. My husband tried to drive the soldiers off for he knew we'd starve if we couldn't work our fields. Now he's in prison because he tried to drive Gessler's men away. I don't know if I shall ever see him again. What is to become of our children?" And the woman began to weep.

"The Austrian rule becomes harder every day," whispered the clock-maker. "We have heard Gessler's spies reported to him on the meeting of Swiss patriots, those men who swore to free our country or die."

"And now," said the baker, speaking softly behind his hand, "Gessler says he'll track down every man who took that oath. No one is safe."

The townspeople did not have to wonder much longer about the cap on the pole. A herald, handsomely dressed in the colors of the Austrian Emperor, stepped out and marched to the foot of the pole. He blew his long brass trumpet and proclaimed, "See ye this cap here set up? It is the emblem of Austria. All who pass beneath it must bow down before it. Should any fail to do this, he shall be made to suffer death or lifelong imprisonment. Hear ye! Hear ye!"

This was a new insult to the people. "This is the crafty Gessler's plan to find out who is loyal to the Austrians and who is not," they muttered.

The people hated the tyrant, but they were afraid of him; so most of them bowed to the cap when it was impossible not to pass the pole.

On the day the Governor's cap was put on the pole, there came toward the market-place a tall, strong man named William Tell. He had with him his young son, Walter. William Tell was celebrated for his skill as an archer and he had sworn to help his countrymen win their freedom even if it should cost him his life. His great crossbow hung from his sturdy shoulder.

Tell was going to Altdorf on an errand for his wife and Walter was happy to go to Altdorf with his father. The boy chattered all the way down the mountain path, asking questions about everything.

But when the two came within sight of the slender spire of the Altdorf church, William Tell wondered at the strange silence that had fallen on the usually humming market-place.

Before his friends could warn him, Tell walked right past the pole and the cap.

At once guards who had been hiding behind the bell-tower seized him. "Are you blind? Don't you see that cap on the pole?" they yelled. They pointed their spears at Tell and demanded, in the name of the Emperor, that he bow to the cap.

"This is not the Emperor's command," cried Tell. "It is Gessler's folly and tyranny! Let me go!"

"Bow to that cap, you knave, or I'll run you through with this," shouted one of the soldiers lowering his great spear.

"Why should I bow to the cap?" asked Tell, his voice shaking with rage. "If the Emperor himself were here, I would bow to him in reverence. But to a cap—never!" He tried to tear himself away from the soldiers. Little Walter stood near, frightened.

Suddenly a guard blew a bugle. Other soldiers streamed in from the streets. Hearing angry voices, the townspeople began to gather. Soon there was a crowd. Everyone shouted at once and the noise and confusion grew.

Then above all the shouting was heard the tramp of horses' hoofs and the clang of swords and armor. Mounted on a fine black steed and surrounded by his followers, Gessler himself rode across the square to where William Tell was standing. His face was cruel. The crowd scattered as the mounted men galloped into the market-place.

Gessler wore a fine embroidered tunic

and over it a suit of shining chain armor. His helmet glittered in the sun and at his side he wore a broadsword in a heavy scabbard. He looked haughtily down at the tall bowman dressed in his rough leather jerkin and patched shoes.

"What is this rioting?" he demanded.

"My lord," said a soldier, "this scoundrel refuses to bow to the cap, as your lordship commanded.

"Who dares disobey my orders?" asked Gessler, his face growing darker.

"It is William Tell, my lord," answered the soldier.

"Tell?" said Gessler, turning in his saddle and looking down again at Tell who stood holding Walter by the hand.

"Oh, so he is too fine to bow before the cap of Austria, is he? Bow, I say, or you will be killed!" warned Gessler.

Tell remained silent, but his eyes blazed. Walter trembled but held himself proudly like his father.

"So you have no tongue now. Speak, or you'll be sorry, Tell," Gessler shouted.

Now William Tell was really angry. His voice rang out. "I will not bow before a cap. I bow only to wise men, to the man of God, and to the good Lord Himself. I will not bend my knee before a cap of rags and feathers."

Gessler's face became white with fury. But suddenly his eyes glinted slyly. He had long heard of Tell's skill with crossbow and arrow. He glanced sharply at Walter.

"Who is that boy that clings to you, Tell?" asked Gessler.

"My son," answered Tell pressing the boy's hand.

"I have heard you are a great shot with the crossbow, Tell," said Gessler scornfully. "Let us see how good you really are! If you can shoot an apple from your son's head at one hundred paces, you shall go free. But—if you harm the boy, or miss the apple, you will *both* die!"

Tell turned pale. "You cannot mean that, Gessler. This boy is innocent. I'll do anything rather than that."

A wave of pity and rage swept through the market-place. Men trembled and mothers clutched their children to them.

"You will shoot an apple off your boy's head," repeated Gessler. "I want to see that wonderful skill of yours. I command you to do it at once."

"I will die first," said Tell.

"Very well," said Gessler. "But don't think you will save your boy that way. He shall die with you. Shoot or both of you die."

"Would you have me kill my own son?" pleaded Tell.

"But I thought you were a great bowman, Tell," replied Gessler. "I see you are just a cowardly wind-bag!"

At these stinging words, Walter shouted, "Father, I am not afraid. I'll stand as quiet as a rock. You *will* hit the apple, Father. I am not afraid!"

"Tie the boy to that tree," ordered Gessler pointing to a lime-tree at some distance from the center of the square.

Two soldiers seized Walter and bound

184

him fast to the tree. He stood up against the trunk straight and quiet. Then, when the apple was brought, Gessler rode up to him, and, bending from the saddle, placed it on Walter's head.

"Clear a path there," shouted Gessler. The soldiers charged among the townsfolk, scattering them right and left. When the path had been cleared, two soldiers, starting from the tree where Walter stood, measured off a hundred paces and halted.

"One hundred paces, my lord," they said turning to Gessler.

Gessler rode to the spot and called, "Come, Tell, you shall shoot from here." The soldiers freed Tell from their grasp. Tell slipped his bow from his shoulder and raised it. He placed the arrow. Then, without moving, he looked at his son tied to the tree.

The crowd stood in breathless silence. A mist swam before Tell's eyes. His arm trembled, and his bow dropped to his side. He could not shoot. The sight of his boy standing so quietly against the tree unnerved him.

He groaned. "My lord," he said to Gessler, "have pity. I cannot do this to a trusting child. Please spare my son."

"So it is 'my lord' at last, Tell! See the strong bowman tremble like a woman. Where is your boasted skill with the bow, Tell?" Gessler jeered.

185

Then from far away under the lime-tree Walter called, "Shoot, Father, I am not afraid. You cannot miss."

Walter's voice brought back his father's courage. Tell took another arrow from his quiver and slipped it into his belt.

Once more he raised his bow. He sighted the apple on his son's head. Gessler watched with piercing eyes. Tell pulled back the bowstring. Many of the townspeople were on their knees now, silently praying. The arrow sang through the air straight and true. A second later Walter felt the apple on his head split and fall to the ground. The arrow buried itself in the gnarled trunk of the tree and swung there.

A great shout of triumph and relief rose from the crowd. "Tell is a hero, a great hero!" They swarmed about the bowman. A man sprang forward and cut the rope that bound Walter to the tree. Another picked up the apple and ran with it to Gessler.

But Tell stood motionless, his bow still in his hand, his eyes staring as if still trying to follow the arrow's path.

"He has really done it!" exclaimed Gessler. "Right through the center, too."

Walter ran to his father and threw his arms about him. "I knew you could do it! I was not a bit afraid," he cried.

Suddenly Tell came to life. He took Walter in his arms and held him close. "You are safe, my son," was all he could say.

Gessler, meanwhile, sat on his horse with a cruel smile on his face. "Tell," he said grudgingly, "you *are* a fine shot. But what was that second arrow for, the one you slipped into your belt?"

William Tell, the honest mountaineer, answered simply, "The second arrow was for you if I had killed my son!"

That night, at a signal, the patriots fell with bows and arrows, spears and battle axes, upon their enemies, Gessler and his henchmen. William Tell led the attack. There began the struggle that finally made Switzerland free.

To this day, Switzerland remembers and loves William Tell. And in Altdorf stands a huge statue of the heroic mountaineer who refused to bow to tyranny.

The Bell of Atri

By James Baldwin

ATRI is the name of a little town in Italy. It is a very old town, nestling half-way up the side of a steep hill.

A long time ago, the King of Atri bought a fine large bell, and had it hung at the top of a tower in the market place. A long rope that reached almost to the ground was fastened to the bell. The smallest child could ring the bell by pulling on this rope.

"It is the bell of justice," said the King.

When at last the bell was in place, the people of Atri had a great holiday. All the men and women and children came down to the market place to look at the bell of justice. It was a beautiful bell, and it had been polished until it looked almost as bright and yellow as the sun.

"How we should like to hear it ring!" said the people.

Just then the King came down the street.

"Perhaps he will ring it," the people whispered among themselves. And everybody stood still, waiting to see what he would do.

But the King did not ring the bell. He did not even take the rope in his hands. When he came to the foot of the tower, he stopped and raised his hand.

"My people," he said, "this beautiful bell is *your* bell. I have bought it for you. But it must never be rung except in case of need. If any one of you is wronged at any time, that one may come and ring the bell; and then the judges shall come together at once, and hear your case, and give you justice. The bell is for you all, rich and poor, old and young, alike. But no one must ever touch the rope unless he knows that he has been wronged."

Years went by. Many times did the bell in the market place ring out to call the judges together. Many wrongs were righted, many ill-doers were punished. At last the hempen rope was almost worn out. The lower part of it was untwisted; some of the strands were broken; it became so short that only a tall man could reach it.

"This will never do," said the judges one day. "What if a child should be wronged? He could not ring the bell to let us know it."

The judges ordered that a new rope should be put upon the bell at once, a rope that should hang down to the ground so that the smallest child could reach it. But there was no such rope to be found in all Atri. They would have to send across the mountains for one, and it would be many days before it could be brought. What if some great wrong should be done before it came? How could the judges know about it, if the injured one could not reach the old rope?

"Let me try to fix it," said a man who stood by.

He ran into his garden, which was not far away, and soon came back with a long grape-vine in his hands.

"This will do for a rope," he said; and he climbed up into the tower, and fastened the vine to the bell. The slender vine, with its leaves and tendrils still upon it, trailed to the ground.

"Yes," said the judges, "it is a very good rope. Let it be as it is."

Now, on the hillside above the village, there lived a man who had once been a brave knight. In his youth he had ridden through many lands, and he had fought in many a battle. His best friend through all that time had been his horse—a strong, noble steed that had borne him safely through many dangers.

But the knight, when he grew older, cared no more to ride into battle; he cared no more to do brave deeds. He thought of nothing but gold; he became a miser. At last he sold everything he had, except his horse, and went to live in a little hut on the hillside. Day after day he sat among his money bags, and planned how he might get more gold. And day after day his horse stood in his bare stall, half starved and shivering with cold.

"What is the use of keeping that lazy steed?" said the miser to himself one morning. "Every week it costs me more to keep him than he is worth. I might sell him; but there is no one who wants him. I cannot even give him away. I will turn him out to shift for himself; he can pick grass by the roadside. If he starves to death, so much the better."

So the brave old horse was turned out to find what he could among the rocks on the barren hillside. Lame and sick, he strolled along the dusty roads, glad when he found a blade of grass or a thistle. Boys threw stones at him; the dogs barked at him, and in all the world there was no one to pity him.

One hot afternoon, when no one was on the street, the horse chanced to wander into the market place. Not a man nor child was there, for the heat of the sun had driven them all indoors. The gates were wide open; the poor beast could roam where he pleased. Soon his old eyes spied the grape-vine rope that hung from the bell of justice. The leaves and tendrils upon it were still fresh and green, for it had not been there long. What a fine dinner they would be for a starving horse!

He stretched his thin neck, and took one of the tempting morsels in his mouth. It was hard to break it from the vine. He pulled at it, and the great bell above him began to ring. All the people in Atri heard it. The sounds seemed to say—

Someone   has done me   wrong!
Someone   has done me   wrong!
Oh! come   and judge   my case!
Oh! come   and judge   my case!
Someone   has done me   wrong!

The judges heard. They put on their robes, and hurried through the hot streets to the market place. They wondered who it could be who would ring the bell at such a time. When they passed through the gate, they saw the old horse nibbling at the vine.

"Ha!" cried one, "it is the miser's steed. He has come to call for justice; for

his master, as everybody knows, has treated him most shamefully."

"He pleads his cause as well as any dumb brute can," said another.

"And he shall have justice!" said the third.

Meanwhile a crowd of men and women and children had come into the market place, eager to learn what cause the judges were about to try. When they saw the horse, all stood still in wonder. Then everyone was ready to tell how they had seen him wandering on the hills, unfed, uncared for, while his master sat at home counting his bags of gold.

"Go bring the miser before us," said the judges.

And when they brought him, the judges bade him stand and hear their decision.

"This horse has served you well for many a year," they said. "He has saved you from many perils. He has helped you gain your wealth. Therefore we order that one half of all your gold shall be set aside to buy him shelter and food, a green pasture where he may graze, and a warm stall to comfort him in his old age."

The miser hung his head. It pained him to lose his gold; he had no pity at all for his poor old horse. But the people shouted with joy. Justice had been done. The horse was led away to his clean new stall. He was given a fine, hearty dinner—a dinner such as he was now to have every day for the rest of his life, thanks to the ringing of the bell which had brought him justice.

The Cat Who Became Head Forester

By Arthur Ransome

IF YOU drop Vladimir by mistake, you know he always falls on his feet. And if Vladimir tumbles off the roof of the hut, he always falls on his feet. Cats always fall on their feet, on their four paws, and never hurt themselves. And as in tumbling, so it is in life. No cat is ever unfortunate for very long. The worse things look for a cat, the better they are going to be.

Well, once upon a time, not so very long ago, an old peasant had a cat and did not like him. He was a tom-cat, always fighting; and he had lost one ear, and was not very pretty to look at. The peasant thought he would get rid of his old cat, and buy a new one from a neighbour. He did not care what became of the old tom-cat with one ear, so long as he never saw him again. It was no use thinking of killing him, for it is a life's work to kill a cat, and it's likely enough that the cat would come alive at the end.

So the old peasant he took a sack, and he bundled the tom-cat into the sack, and he sewed up the sack and slung it over his back, and walked off into the forest. Off he went, trudging along in the summer sunshine, deep into the forest. And when he had gone very many versts into the forest, he took the sack with the cat in it and threw it away among the trees.

"You stay there," says he, "and if you do get out in this desolate place, much good may it do you, old quarrelsome bundle of bones and fur!"

And with that he turned round and trudged home again, and bought a nice-looking, quiet cat from a neighbour in exchange for a little tobacco, and settled down comfortably at home with the new cat in front of the stove; and there he may be to this day, so far as I know. My story does not bother with him, but only with the old tom-cat tied up in the sack away out there in the forest.

The bag flew through the air, and plumped down through a bush to the ground. And the old tom-cat landed on his feet inside it, very much frightened but not hurt. Thinks he, this bag, this flight through the air, this bump, mean that my life is going to change. Very well; there is nothing like something new now and again.

And presently he began tearing at the bag with his sharp claws. Soon there was a hole he could put a paw through. He went on, tearing and scratching, and there was a hole he could put two paws through. He went on with his work, and soon he could put his head through, all the easier because he had only one ear. A minute or two after that he had wriggled out of the bag, and stood up on his four paws and stretched himself in the forest.

"The world seems to be larger than the village," he said. "I will walk on and see what there is in it."

He washed himself all over, curled his tail proudly up in the air, cocked the only ear he had left, and set off walking under the forest trees.

"I was the head-cat in the village," says he to himself. "If all goes well, I shall be head here too." And he walked along as if he were the Tzar himself.

Well, he walked on and on, and he came to an old hut that had belonged to a forester. There was nobody there, nor had been for many years, and the old tom-cat made himself quite at home. He climbed up into the loft under the roof,

and found a little rotten hay.

"A very good bed," says he, and curls up and falls asleep.

When he woke he felt hungry, so he climbed down and went off into the forest to catch little birds and mice. There were plenty of them in the forest, and when he had eaten enough he came back to the hut, climbed into the loft, and spent the night there very comfortably.

You would have thought he would be content. Not he. He was a cat. He said, "This is a good enough lodging. But I have to catch all my own food. In the

village they fed me every day, and I only caught mice for fun. I ought to be able to live like that here. A person of my dignity ought not to have to do all the work for himself."

Next day he went walking in the forest. And as he was walking he met a fox, a vixen, a very pretty young thing, gay and giddy like all girls. And the fox saw the cat, and was very much astonished.

"All these years," she said—for though she was young she thought she had lived a long time—"all these years," she said, "I've lived in the forest, but I've never seen a wild beast like that before. What a strange-looking animal! And with only one ear. How handsome!"

And she came up and made her bows to the cat, and said,

"Tell me, great lord, who you are. What fortunate chance has brought you to this forest? And by what name am I to call your Excellency?"

Oh! The fox was very polite. It is not every day that you meet a handsome stranger walking in the forest.

The cat arched his back, and set all his fur on end, and said, very slowly and quietly,

"I have been sent from the far forests of Siberia to be Head-forester over you. And my name is Cat Ivanovitch."

"O Cat Ivanovitch!" says the pretty young fox, and she makes more bows. "I did not know. I beg your Excellency's pardon. Will your Excellency honour my humble house by visiting it as a guest?"

"I will," says the cat. "And what do they call you?"

"My name, your Excellency, is Lisabeta Ivanovna."

"I will come with you, Lisabeta," says the cat.

And they went together to the fox's earth. Very snug, very neat it was inside; and the cat curled himself up in the best place, while Lisbeta Ivanovna, the pretty young fox, made ready a tasty dish of game. And while she was making the meal ready, and dusting the furniture with her tail, she looked at the cat. At last she said, shyly,

"Tell me, Cat Ivanovitch, are you married or single?"

"Single," says the cat.

"And I too am unmarried," says the pretty young fox, and goes busily on with her dusting and cooking.

Presently she looks at the cat again.

"What if we were to marry, Cat Ivanovitch? I will try to be a good wife to you."

"Very well, Lisabeta," says the cat; "I will marry you."

The fox went to her store and took out all the dainties that she had, and made a wedding feast to celebrate her marriage to the great Cat Ivanovitch, who had only one ear, and had come from the far Siberian forests to be Head-forester.

They ate up everything there was in the place.

Next morning the pretty young fox went off busily into the forest to get food for her grand husband. But the old tom-cat stayed at home, and cleaned his whiskers and slept. He was a lazy one, was

192

that cat, and proud.

The fox was running through the forest, looking for game, when she met an old friend, the handsome young wolf, and he began making polite speeches to her.

"What had become of you, gossip?" says he. "I've been to all the best earths and not found you at all."

"Let be, fool," says the fox very shortly. "Don't talk to me like that. What are you jesting about? Formerly I was a young, unmarried fox; now I am a wedded wife."

"Whom have you married, Lisabeta Ivanovna?"

"What!" says the fox, "you have not heard that the great Cat Ivanovitch, who has only one ear, has been sent from the far Siberian forests to be Head-forester over all of us? Well, I am now the Head-forester's wife."

"No, I had not heard, Lisabeta Ivanovna. And when can I pay my respects to his Excellency?"

"Not now, not now," says the fox. "Cat Ivanovitch will be raging angry with me if I let anyone come near him. Presently he will be taking his food. Look you. Get a sheep, and make it ready, and bring it as a greeting to him, to show him that he is welcome and that you know how to treat him with respect. Leave the sheep near by, and hide yourself so that he shall not see you; for, if he did, things might be awkward."

"Thank you, thank you, Lisabeta Ivanovna," says the wolf and off he goes to look for a sheep.

The pretty young fox went idly on, taking the air, for she knew that the wolf would save her the trouble of looking for food.

Presently she met the bear.

"Good-day to you, Lisabeta Ivanovna," said the bear; "as pretty as ever, I see you are."

"Bandy-legged one," says the fox; "fool, don't come worrying me. Formerly I was a young, unmarried fox; now I am a wedded wife."

"I beg your pardon," says the bear, "whom have you married, Lisabeta Ivanovna?"

"The great Cat Ivanovitch has been sent from the far Siberian forests to be Head-forester over us all. And Cat Ivanovitch is now my husband," says the fox.

"Is it forbidden to have a look at his Excellency?"

"It is forbidden," says the fox. "Cat Ivanovitch will be raging angry with me if I let any one come near him. Presently he will be taking his food. Get along with you quickly; make ready an ox, and bring it by way of welcome to him. The wolf is bringing a sheep. And look you. Leave the ox near by, and hide yourself so that the great Cat Ivanovitch shall not see you; or else, brother, things may be awkward."

The bear shambled off as fast as he could go to get an ox.

The pretty young fox, enjoying the fresh air of the forest, went slowly home to her earth, and crept in very quietly, so as not to awake the great Head-forester, Cat Ivanovitch, who had only one ear and was sleeping in the best place.

Presently the wolf came through the forest, dragging a sheep he had killed. He did not dare to go too near the fox's earth, because of Cat Ivanovitch, the new Head-forester. So he stopped, well out of sight, and stripped off the skin of the sheep, and arranged the sheep so as to seem a nice tasty morsel. Then he stood still, thinking what to do next. He heard a noise, and looked up. There was the bear, struggling along with a dead ox.

"Good-day, brother Michael Ivano-vitch," says the wolf.

"Good-day, brother Levon Ivano-vitch," says the bear. "Have you seen the fox, Lisabeta Ivanovna, with her husband, the Head-forester?"

"No, brother," says the wolf. "For a long time I have been waiting to see them."

"Go on and call out to them," says the bear.

"No, Michael Ivanovitch," says the wolf. "I will not go. Do you go; you are bigger and bolder than I."

"No, no, Levon Ivanovitch, I will not go. There is no use in risking one's life without need."

Suddenly, as they were talking, a little hare came running by. The bear saw him first, and roared out,

"Hi, Squinteye! trot along here."

The hare came up, slowly, two steps at a time, trembling with fright.

"Now then, you squinting rascal," says the bear, "do you know where the fox lives, over there?"

"I know, Michael Ivanovitch."

"Get along there quickly, and tell her that Michael Ivanovitch the bear and his brother Levon Ivanovitch the wolf have been ready for a long time, and have brought presents of a sheep and an ox, as greetings to his Excellency . . ."

"His Excellency, mind," says the wolf; "don't forget."

The hare ran off as hard as he could go, glad to have escaped so easily. Meanwhile the wolf and the bear looked about for good places in which to hide.

"It will be best to climb trees," says the bear. "I shall go up to the top of this fir."

"But what am I to do?" says the wolf. "I can't climb a tree for the life of me. Brother Michael, Brother Michael, hide me somewhere or other before you climb up. I beg you, hide me, or I shall certainly be killed."

"Crouch down under these bushes," says the bear, "and I will cover you with the dead leaves."

"May you be rewarded," says the wolf; and he crouched down under the bushes, and the bear covered him up with dead leaves, so that only the tip of his nose could be seen.

Then the bear climbed slowly up into the fir tree, into the very top, and looked out to see if the fox and Cat Ivanovitch were coming.

The hare ran up and knocked on the door, and said to the fox,

"Michael Ivanovitch the bear and his brother Levon Ivanovitch the wolf have been ready for a long time, and have brought presents of a sheep and an ox as greetings to his Excellency."

194

"Get along, Squinteye," says the fox; "we are just coming."

And so the fox and the cat set out together.

They were coming; oh yes, they were coming!

The bear, up in the top of the tree, saw them, and called down to the wolf,

"They are coming, Brother Levon; they are coming, the fox and her husband. But what a little one he is, to be sure!"

"Quiet, quiet," whispers the wolf. "He'll hear you and then we are done for."

The cat came up, and arched his back and set all his furs on end, and threw himself on the ox, and began tearing the meat with his teeth and claws. And as he tore he purred. And the bear listened, and heard the purring of the cat, and it seemed to him that the cat was angrily muttering, "Small, small, small . . ."

And the bear whispers: "He's no giant, but what a glutton! Why, we couldn't get through a quarter of that, and he finds it not enough. Heaven help us if he comes after us!"

The wolf tried to see, but could not, because his head, all but his nose, was

covered with the dry leaves. Little by little he moved his head, so as to clear the leaves away from in front of his eyes. Try as he would to be quiet, the leaves rustled, so little, ever so little, but enough to be heard by the one ear of the cat.

The cat stopped tearing the meat and listened.

"I haven't caught a mouse today," he thought.

Once more the leaves rustled.

The cat leaped through the air and dropped with all four paws, and his claws out, on the nose of the wolf. How the wolf yelped! The leaves flew like dust, and the wolf leapt up and ran off as fast as his legs would carry him.

Well, the wolf was frightened, I can tell you, but he was not so frightened as the cat.

When the great wolf leapt up out of the leaves, the cat screamed and ran up the nearest tree, and that was the tree where Michael Ivanovitch the bear was hiding in the topmost branches.

"Oh, he has seen me. Cat Ivanovitch has seen me," thought the bear. He had no time to climb down, and the cat was coming up in long leaps.

The bear trusted to Providence, and jumped from the top of the tree. Many were the branches he broke as he fell; many were the bones he broke when he crashed to the ground. He picked himself up and stumbled off, groaning.

The pretty young fox sat still, and cried out, "Run, run, Brother Levon! . . . Quicker on your pins, Brother Michael! His Excellency is behind you; his Excellency is close behind!"

Ever since then all the wild beasts have been afraid of the cat, and the cat and the fox live merrily together, and eat fresh meat all the year round, which the other animals kill for them and leave a little way off.

And that is what happened to the old tom-cat with one ear, who was sewn up in a bag and thrown away in the forest.

"Just think what would happen to our handsome Vladimir if we were to throw him away!" said Vanya.

Juan Cigarron

(WHICH MEANS, IN ENGLISH, *JOHNNY CIGAR*)

By Ruth Sawyer

ONCE there was a poor couple who had many children.

The eldest was a clever rascal, always plaguing the younger ones, always turning a trick to benefit himself. At last when the thirteenth child was born, the father said to the eldest, "Juan Cigarron, you are a clever rascal. You can do your own whistling. Go and seek your fortune.

their game. He bore himself like one who consorted with magic. He fooled the world to perfection. Everybody believed in him because everybody wanted to believe in him; and so he became famous.

Now, it happened one day in the King's palace that all the silver plate disappeared. One day it was there and the King was eating from it, just as he had

There is no longer enough in the house to eat."

So into God's world went Juan Cigarron. As he followed this road and that, he said to himself, "I am such a good rascal, I will make a better wizard." So he served as an apprentice to all the wizards in Spain until he could beat them all at

eaten from it every day. The next day, the silver was gone—plates, goblets, trenchers, and tankards—as if the earth had swallowed them.

"Send for Juan Cigarron," said the King. "I have heard that he is the greatest wizard in Spain. I believe that he may be the greatest rascal. We will try him."

197

So a messenger was sent and Juan Cigarron was brought to the palace, straight to the hall where the King sat eating from a common clay dish.

"The royal silver is gone—stolen. You are to discover it, and who stole it," said the King. "But you will make your discovery locked in the deepest dungeon in the palace. Being a great wizard you can manage there as well as anywhere else to find it. If you should turn out to be a cheating rascal instead of a wizard, we will have you there safe, hide and hair, to hand as a fine example. Three days you shall have to find the royal silver."

The guards led Juan Cigarron to the dungeon. They fastened an iron ball and chain to his feet. They locked him in with a key as large as his thigh bone. They left him alone all day that he might better practice his magic, and all day his heart grew heavier.

"I am well caught," thought Juan Cigarron to himself. "There never was a wizard who died comfortably in his bed. Already, I feel a hempen collar about my throat. Ah, me!"

At the end of the day there came one of the King's pages to bring him food. In despair Juan Cigarron watched the jailor unlock the door for him to enter. He watched the page place the food on the bench before him, and watched him turn away. All the time he was thinking, "I

have paid dearly for my whistle. Three days of life granted me—no more, no less—and already one is completed." And he groaned aloud as the jailor unlocked the door for the page to go his way.

"Ay, by San Bruno, this is no fun;
Of the three—there goes one!"

Whereupon, hearing those words, the page took to his heels and ran as if the devil himself were after him. Finding the King's two other pages waiting for him in a corner of the palace wall, he told them breathlessly what Juan Cigarron had said. "Not a doubt of it. He is the greatest wizard on earth. He knows we three have stolen the silver and buried it in the graveyard. We are wholly undone. Let us go to him and confess."

"Never," said one of the others. "You are a weakling. Your ears did not hear right. Tomorrow I will carry his supper to him and then we shall see."

At the end of the second day the heart of Juan Cigarron had become as heavy as the irons on his feet. With what agony did he watch the second page enter his dungeon, leave his food, and depart. Counting off another day of life he groaned aloud:

"Now by San José, honest and true,
Of the three—I've counted two."

If one devil had been at the heels of the first page, a score were hounding the second. "He knows—he knows!" he screamed to the two waiting for him. "We are lost."

"Not yet," said the third and oldest page. "We wait. I myself will carry his supper tomorrow night. I shall not run from the cell. I shall stand beside him and mark his words with care."

At the end of the third day, so tightly could he feel the rope drawn about his neck, Juan Cigarron could not eat his supper for choking. Looking up from his bench and seeing the third page still at his elbow he thought—"Here is a lad who feels pity for me." And aloud he said:

"Good San Andras, counsel me.
They've come and gone—all three!"

The page threw himself at the jailed feet of Juan Cigarron. He groveled there. "Master wizard, pity us! Have compassion. Do not tell the King that it is his three pages who have stolen the silver. We will have our necks wrung tomorrow like so many cockerels if you do. Spare us and we will tell you where it lies buried and never, never again, will we commit such an indiscretion."

With great dignity Juan Cigarron rose to his feet. "Do you know that young rascals have a way of turning into old rascals. How do I know that by saving your necks now I shall not be sending you to purgatory later with more sins to atone for! Enough groveling. I will pardon you this time. But you must swear by all the saints never to steal again—not so much as an *ochavito*. Tomorrow when I appear before the King, bring the silver in secret to the dungeon here, every last piece of it."

So on the morrow Juan Cigarron was not hung. He told the King where the silver plate would be found, and there it was, sure enough. The King was more pleased than nothing. He embraced Juan Cigarron and kissed him on both cheeks.

"I did you a great wrong, but I will make restitution. From now on you shall be, not a wizard to all the world, but my own particular, royal wizard. You shall live with me always, in the palace, where you will be handy to turn a trick of magic when the occasion arises. You are great . . . stupendous . . . magnificent . . . more magnificent than all the wizards," and he embraced him again.

So Juan Cigarron lived in the palace, eating with the King, sleeping in his ante-chamber, going where the King went; and growing thinner and paler and more dejected every day. "What will I do when the next calamity falls. Ah me!" groaned Juan Cigarron, as each new hour in the day struck.

At last there came an evening when the King happened to be walking alone in his garden. He was smoking and think-ing that it was time Juan Cigarron should have his wits and his magic put to the test again. Thinking to practice a clever trick on him, the King took from his mouth the cigar and from his pocket his wallet. Into the wallet he stuffed his cigar; and back into his pocket went both of them. Then he sent a page for the wizard.

When Juan Cigarron stood before him, the King put him this question: "What did I have in my mind that I took out of my mouth and put for safe keeping in my wallet?" Meaning that he had been thinking of Cigarron, smoking cigarron and had put cigarron in his pocket.

But Juan Cigarron was in terror of his life. Here was the moment of his doom descending upon him. Hardly knowing that he spoke he muttered, more to him-self than to the King:

"What a fool is man to pretend—
Poor Juan Cigarron has met a bad end!"

How the King did laugh at that. He clapped his hand to his pocket, drew out the wallet and showed the cigar snuffed out, quite dead. Casting it from him, he embraced Juan Cigarron for a third time and said, "That was as clever an answer as ever I heard. I will grant for that any wish that is yours to make."

"Any wish?" asked Juan Cigarron.

"Any wish," confirmed the King.

"Then I wish to end my days as a wizard tonight—and begin them tomor-row as a simple man."

The Porcelain Stove

By "Ouida"

AUGUSTUS lived in a little town. He was a small boy nine years old, with rosy cheeks, big hazel eyes, and curls the brown of ripe nuts.

His mother was dead, his father was poor, and there were ten children to feed at home, beginning with Dorothy, a sweet dark-haired girl who kept house for them all, down to the three-year-old baby.

The children were always clean and happy, and the table was seldom without its big pot of soup once a day. Still, very poor they were, and their father's debts were many for flour, and meat, and clothing.

When indoors the children spent most of their time in a large room with a red brick floor that was bare and uneven. It had a wooden cupboard, a big deal table, and only a few stools for furniture.

But at the far end of the room sending out warmth and color, was a tower made of porcelain china shining with all the hues of a king's peacock and a queen's jewels.

The tower was ornamented with armed figures, and shields, and flowers, and a great golden crown stood on its top. There were also letters, H. R. H., which showed it had been made by a great potter many, many years before, and no doubt it had once stood in the palace of some Prince.

But of its past history nothing was known, except that Augustus' grandfather, who had been a mason, had dug it up out of some ruins where he was building, and, finding it quite whole, had taken it home. That was sixty years ago, and the stove had stood ever since in the big empty room, warming the children who clustered around it.

How the children loved the porcelain stove! In summer they laid a mat of fresh roses all around it, and dressed it up with green boughs and wild flowers.

And in winter they would sit close beside it, and cry, "Tell us a story, Augustus." And the boy, looking up at the noble tower, with all its pictures and flowers and crowns, would imagine the many adventures of the people who were pictured on its shining sides.

Augustus had never seen a story-book in his life, but he loved inventing stories, and the children never tired of listening to their brother's tales.

One cold winter's night, just a week before Christmas, in the midst of the

201

children's clatter and laughter, the door opened and let in a blast of frozen air as their father entered. Very weary he was, and Dorothy soon took the little ones to bed, while Augustus curled up in front of the warm stove, and lay silent so as not to disturb his tired father.

The cuckoo clock in the corner struck eight as Dorothy came downstairs, and the room was strangely quiet. Suddenly the father struck his hand on the table, and said in a husky voice, "I have sold the stove to a dealer for a hundred dollars. He saw it this morning when you were all out, and tomorrow he comes to pack it and take it away."

Dorothy gave a low shrill cry, and Augustus sprang to his feet, crying, "Oh, Father, it is not true! You are jesting, Father!"

But the father only gave a dreary laugh. "I owe money everywhere. We must have bread to eat. The stove is much too grand for a poor room like this. It is a stove for a museum, the dealer said, and to a museum it will go."

Augustus threw himself at his father's feet, and clasped his knees. "Oh, Father, you cannot mean what you say! To us it is not just a stove; it is a living thing— it is our fire-king. It loves us though we are only poor little children, and we love it with all our hearts. Give the money back to the man. Oh, Father, do you hear me, for pity's sake!"

"You are a foolish boy," said the

father. "Get up and go to bed. The stove is sold. There is no more to be said. The old black stove in the kitchen will warm you all quite as well as this painted thing. Go to bed, I say." Then he took the oil-lamp that stood at his elbow, and went upstairs to his room.

Augustus lay beside the stove he loved so dearly, covering it with kisses, and sobbing. What could he do? Nothing, nothing, nothing.

"Oh, Augustus," whispered Dorothy, "do not cry like that; you frighten me. Do come to bed."

"No, I shall stay here all night," he answered. "They might come to take it away." And alone he stayed through the long dark hours. The lamp went out, the fire in the stove slowly died, and the room grew cold as ice, but Augustus never moved.

There the children found him when they came downstairs in the morning. His father thrust him out into the back court when men came with straw and ropes to pack up and carry away the beloved stove.

Into the court an old neighbor hobbled to fetch water, and seeing the boy lying with his face hidden on the ground, he said, "Child, is it true your father is selling the big, painted stove?"

Augustus nodded his head, then burst into tears.

"Well, for sure he is a foolish man," said the neighbor. "It was worth a mint of money, for I do remember, in your

grandfather's time, that a stranger saw it and said it would bring its weight in gold."

"I do not care what its value was," sobbed Augustus, "I loved it!"

"Well, if I were you," said the old man kindly, "I would do better than cry. I would go after it. The world is a small place, after all, and your stove will be safe enough whoever gets it. When you are big you can follow it, and see your stove again." And the old man hobbled away.

The boy's heart gave a leap of hope. Yes, he would go after it. At once he hid himself in a doorway, and watched till he saw the straw-covered bundle carefully carried out by four men, and laid on a wagon. Then, unseen by Dorothy or his father, he followed it.

At the railway station Augustus heard the dealer arrange for the stove to be sent on a train that was due in half an hour, and he made up his mind that where his fire-king went he would go too. How he managed it he never clearly knew, but when the train left the station Augustus was hidden behind the stove in the great covered truck.

It was very dark and very crowded, and the truck smelled strongly of hams and hides that were packed in it. But Augustus was not frightened. He was close to his fire-king, and presently he would be closer still, for he meant to do nothing less than get inside it.

He had bought some bread and sausage at the station, and this he ate in the darkness, in spite of the lumbering, pounding, thundering noise of the train, which made him giddy, for he had never before been in any kind of train.

After he had eaten he set to work like a little mouse, to make a hole in the bands of straw that were wrapped round the stove. He gnawed and nibbled, and pulled, and pushed just as a mouse would have done, making his hole where he guessed the door of the stove would be. And get through them at last he did.

He slipped through the door into the inside of the stove, as he had often done at home for fun, and curled himself up to see if he could really hide there for many hours. He found he could, as plenty of air came in through the brass fretwork of the door.

He leaned out and drew the hay and straw together, so that no one could have dreamed that even a little mouse had been at them. Then he curled up again, and being safe inside his dear fire-king he fell fast asleep as if he were in his own bed at home.

For many a weary hour the train rolled on. It took all the long day, and all the long night, and half of the next day before their station was reached.

Then Augustus felt the stove lifted out of the truck, and very carefully it was laid on a wagon, which drove to a shop. The stove was then gently lifted down, and set upright on its four gilded feet in a small room.

"I shall not unpack it tonight," he heard a voice say. Then a key was turned in the lock, and there was silence.

After some time Augustus ventured to peep through the straw and hay which wrapped the stove, and he saw a room filled with many curious things. There were pictures, and carvings, old blue jugs, armor, daggers, china, and many other wonderful bits of furniture, all very old. But oh! there was not a drop of water, and Augustus was so thirsty.

There was a small window, and on the broad ledge outside he saw snow. Quickly he darted out of his hiding-place, raised the window, and crammed his mouth full of snow, broke off some icicles, then flew back to the stove, drew the hay and straw over the hole, and shut the door again.

It was not very cold in this lumber-room, and soon he slept again, and forgot how hungry and how tired he was. Midnight was chiming from all the clocks of the city when he awoke.

All the things in the room were alive and moving about! A big jug was dancing a polka with a fat blue jar. The tall clock was bowing to an old chair with spindle legs. A broken violin was playing to itself, and a queer little tune came from a piano.

Meanwhile, the bright light which filled the room shone from three silver candlesticks that had no candles in them. Strange to say, Augustus somehow did not feel at all surprised; all he longed for was to dance too!

Just then a lovely little china lady dressed in pink and gold and white tripped up to him and invited him to dance with her.

"I am a Princess," she said when the dance was over. And he took courage to say to her, "Princess, could you tell me why some of the things dance and speak, and some stand still and silent like lumber? Is it rude to ask?"

"My dear child," said the Princess, "is it possible you do not know silent dull things are imitation!"

"Imitation!" repeated Augustus.

"Of course," said the Princess. "They only pretend to be what we are. They are copies, so they never wake up."

"Oh!" said Augustus humbly, not sure that he understood yet, and he looked at his dear fire-king. Surely it had a royal soul within it!

"What will you be when you are a

man?" asked the Princess suddenly.

"I wish—I hope," said Augustus, stammering, "to be a painter, such as the master who painted yonder stove."

"Bravo!" cried all the real things in the room, for they all knew the name of the great artist who had made the fire-king. But the stove remained silent, and then a sickening fear shot through Augustus' heart.

Could it be that his beloved fire-king was only an imitation? "No, no, no," he said to himself stoutly, "that I will never believe." And he said it so loudly and sharply that the china Princess looked at him in surprise.

"Ah! if we could only all go back to our masters," sighed the china Princess. And somehow they all grew sad as they thought of the men who had made them and loved them so well.

Then from where the great stove stood there came a solemn voice. All eyes turned toward it, and Augustus' heart gave a great leap of joy.

"My friends," said the voice, "I have listened to all you have said. For over two hundred years I have not spoken, and I speak now only because I see a little human child who loves me, and I want him ever to remember this night and these words. I want him to remember that we are what we are because of these beloved masters who created us many, many years ago. They are all dead, these masters, but we live on— we, the things they made and loved. Through us they speak and live."

Then the voice sank away in silence. The light in the candlesticks faded and went out. The clocks of the city struck six, and Augustus awoke with a start to find himself lying on the bare brick floor of the room, while everything in it was still and silent.

Tramp, tramp, came heavy steps up the stairs. Augustus crept into the stove as the door opened. The dealer entered and began to wrap up the stove again in its straw and hay, and presently it was carried by six porters back to the railway station. There the precious bundle was hoisted into a great van, but this time the dealer and the porters stayed beside it.

The train rolled on with all its fuss and roar of steam, and in about an hour it stopped, and once more the stove was tenderly lifted out. It was now nearly ten o'clock, the sun had come out, and Augustus could see through the fretwork of the brass door that a large lake lay before them.

Soon the stove was gently placed in a boat, and the rowers pulled steadily for the other side of the lake. Presently they reached the pier. "Now, men, for a stout mile and a half," said the dealer to the porters, and the precious bundle was gently carried along a road heavy with snow.

It seemed a very long time to Augustus till they entered a house, and he knew by their movements that they were going upstairs. Warm air was about him, and there was a delicious fragrance of flowers. The stove was set down, all its wrappings were removed, and then the dealer and the porters left.

Presently Augustus heard a step beside him, and a low voice said, "Oh! how beautiful! No, it is not an imitation, it is indeed the work of the great master."

Then the hand of the speaker turned the handle of the brass door, and someone looked in. "What is this in it? A live child!" he heard the voice exclaim.

Augustus sprang out of the stove and fell at the feet of the speaker. "Oh! let me stay, let me stay!" he sobbed.

Some gentleman seized him, not gently, and a voice whispered, "Be quiet, it is the King."

They were about to drag him away, but the King said, "Poor little child, he is very young. Leave him alone. Let him speak to me."

The men let Augustus go, and looking up he saw a young man with eyes full of dreams. And this young man said to him, "My child, how came you here, hidden in the stove?"

"Oh, dear King," said Augustus, in a trembling little voice, "the fire-king was ours, and we have loved it all our lives, and Father sold it. I have come all the way inside it, and last night it spoke and said beautiful things. And I do pray you to let me live beside it, and I will go out every morning and cut wood for it, if only you will let me stay with it, for I love it so."

"Who bought the stove from your father, and what did they pay him?" asked the King. "A hundred dollars," said Augustus with a sob. "It was so much money, and we were so poor, and there were so many of us."

The dealer who had bought the stove was waiting downstairs, and the King sent for him. "How much did the gentleman who bought this stove for me give you for it?" he asked. "Ten thousand dollars, your Majesty," said the man.

The King then said, "You will give at once to this boy's father the ten thousand dollars you received, less the hundred dollars you paid him. You are a rogue. Begone, and be thankful you are not punished."

Augustus listened, but he understood little of what the King said. "Oh! do, please do, let me stay," he murmured when the King stood silent. And clasping his little brown hands together he knelt before the young King.

"Rise up, child," the King said in a kind voice. "Yes, you shall stay, and you shall live here and be taught at my own school. And if when you are twenty-one years old you have done well and bravely, I will give you your own stove back again."

He smiled and stretched out his hand, but Augustus threw his two arms about the King's knees and kissed his feet. Then he lost all sense of where he was, and fell down faint with hunger, and tiredness, and also with great joy.

—*Adapted*

Sir Cleges and His Gift

AN OLD ENGLISH CHRISTMAS LEGEND

By Arthur Guiterman

NOT IN the time of King Arthur, but in that still earlier day when King Arthur's father, the great Uther Pendragon, ruled Britain with a strong hand, there dwelt near the city of Cardiff, a strong, tall, fair, courteous, gentle knight, named Sir Cleges, with his good wife, Dame Clarys.

In his youth Sir Cleges had been a great champion. Right well had he served his king in the wars against the heathen invaders, the Northmen, and worthily had he won much wealth in lands and treasure.

But he cared little for wealth, loving to give rather than to hold in store. Both he and his wife loved to bestow bountiful alms on the poor and rich gifts to wandering minstrels. Each Christmas they held a great feast at which they gave presents of food and clothing to all who might come. But one Christmas morning Sir Cleges awoke to find that he had no more the means of giving, for all his treasure was spent, all his lands were gone, and little enough remained for himself and his wife.

So he went forth heavily from his door, and his sorrow was deepened as he heard on all sides the sounds of rejoicing and music celebrating the dawn of Christmas Day. Then out came the good Dame Clarys and comforted him, saying, "We have each other; and will not the Lord provide the little that we may need in our old age?" So they went in together and ate joyfully such food as they had.

And then Sir Cleges again went forth into his garden and, kneeling beneath a great cherry-tree, thanked God for all His mercies and prayed for the welfare of those he loved. As he arose he grasped the bough above him to help him to his feet; and as he looked upon that bough, behold! it was laden down with green leaves and rich red cherries—although it was December.

Then greatly he marveled and rejoiced, and told of this miracle to Dame Clarys.

Then said she, "Take this gift of Heaven to the king in his castle of Cardiff; I am sure it will greatly help us."

"Aye, good wife," replied Sir Cleges, "to Cardiff will I go and to the court where I have not been these many years. Much would it please me again to see my king at whose right hand I fought in my youth, though small chance is there that he will recognize his strong knight of the old wars in this poor garb and this long gray beard."

Sir Cleges gathered the cherries into a

huge basket, covering them with the leaves, and set out for Cardiff, poorly clad as he was and staff in hand for he had neither war-horse nor palfrey.

Now, when he came to the king's gate he found a proud porter. And the porter, seeing that he was ill clad, called to him gruffly: "Thou churl, withdraw thee smartly, without delay, or else shall I break thy head! If thou seekest again to come in, it shall rue thee, for then shall I beat thee!"

Sir Cleges answered mildly, though his heart was wroth, "Good sir, I pray thee, let me go in; for I have brought a present for the king. Behold it!" And he uncovered the basket.

Now the porter, seeing the cherries, knew full well that he that brought so marvelous a present would surely receive rich gifts in return. So he said: "Churl, thou comest not into this place unless thou grantest me a third part of that which the king shall give thee, whatever it may be."

As he needs must, Sir Cleges gave his word thereto and passed through the gate and on.

At the hall door he met the king's usher, holding his staff of office raised as if to smite, and saying, "Go back, thou churl, without tarrying, or I shall beat thee, head and body!"

Again answered Sir Cleges humbly: "Good sir, I have brought the king a Christmas gift that even this morning grew in my garden."

The usher lifted the leaves from the basket, beheld the untimely fruit, and marveled. "I tell thee truly, churl," said he with cunning, "even yet thou goest not in unless thou grantest me a third part of thy winning when thou com'st back."

Sir Cleges saw no other way, and so agreed. And with heavy heart he went on into the hall where there was feasting, harping, and singing. And the king sat on a raised seat at the great table, amid his knights and lords. Then came the steward bustling from among the richly clad nobles and went boldly to Sir Cleges. "Churl," said he, "who made thee so hardy as to come into this place? Thou art too bold. Withdraw thee with thine old clothes!"

Simply and sadly answered him Sir Cleges: "I bear a gift for the king," and showed it.

Then marveled the steward, "This saw I never at this time of year! But thou shalt come no nearer the king unless thou grantest me a third part of the gift that he shall give thee."

"Alas!" thought poor Sir Cleges, "among these thieves I shall have naught for my labor unless it be a dinner!" But, sighing sore, he answered: "So let it be. Whatever the king award, thou shalt have the third part, be it less or more."

Then the steward made way for him among the throng and hastened out beyond the curtains to await his returning. And Sir Cleges went up to the dais, where, kneeling before the king, he uncovered his basket, saying, "My lord, Heaven hath willed that earth should bear this fruit this very day, and sendeth it to thee with honor."

And the king said, "Heaven be thanked; and likewise do I thank the bringer. In truth, this is a fair sight and a great wonder."

Then he commanded that place be made for Sir Cleges at his board, and bade him feast and be merry. And he caused the cherries to be served bountifully through the hall; and never before had any tasted of such luscious fruit. And when the feast was done the king said to his squire, "Bring now before me the poor man that brought the cherries!"

So Sir Cleges came again before the king and fell on his knees, saying, "My lord, what is your will?"

Said the king, "I thank thee heartily for thy gift. Thou hast honored all my feast. So shall I grant thee whatever thou wilt have."

Now said Sir Cleges joyfully, yet somewhat grimly, "Gramercy, my liege king, right comforting is this to me. I tell thee truly, to have land or other riches is too much for such as I. So, if I may choose for myself, I pray thee grant me twelve strokes of my staff to be dealt where they are due; for fitting it is that men should pay their debts."

At that was King Uther troubled, for he loved not unseemly brawling. "Now do I repent my granting," said he. "Thou hadst better have gold or fee; more need of them thou hast than of sturdy blows, given or taken."

"My liege," answered Sir Cleges, "it was thine own grant; therefore am I full glad thereof. Yet do I promise, and pledge my head thereto, that these twelve strokes, thy gift, shall be bestowed only where they are rightly due. I pray thee to send after me two trusty knights who, unseen, shall note all that is said and done, and bear witness whether or not I keep my word."

Ill content was Uther, yet might he not gainsay that which he had granted; therefore he gave Sir Cleges leave to go, and bade two knights follow him secretly as he had desired.

While he was gone the king still sat with his lords in the hall, and the minstrels sang to them ballads of brave deeds; and the chief of them all sang of a gallant adventure of Sir Cleges. Whereat said the king: "Harper, tell me of this knight, Sir Cleges, since thou hast traveled widely; knowest thou him?"

"Yea, in sooth," answered the harper. "He was a true knight of yours, and fair of stature. We minstrels miss him greatly, for free was his bounty."

Then said the king, "I thought Sir Cleges was dead. I loved him much, for gentle he was, and stark in fight."

But now arose a great noise outside the hall; and presently in rushed the steward, the usher, and the porter, all crying for the king's justice upon a churl; and amongst them was not one head unbeaten. Behind them followed the two knights, holding their sides for laughter; and behind all strode Sir Cleges, grim and tall, tightly gripping his stout oak staff.

The king commanded silence and bade one of the two knights tell freely what he had seen and heard.

Then said the knight, when he could speak for merriment, "My liege, we two followed this good man whom these three varlets misname 'churl.' Hardly had he left the hall when up to him came the steward, seeing us not, for we were well hidden behind a curtain. 'Churl,' said he, 'now give me, according to thy promise, a third part of what the king hath given thee.' 'Aye,' answered the stout man, 'have here some strokes!' And four masterly strokes he laid on with good will, and left the steward blubbering. Then, as he went on his way, thy usher and thy porter in turn likewise demanded of him a third part of thy gift, and likewise did he deal with them. So do we two bear true witness, on the honor of our knighthood, that he hath paid these

211

strokes which were due according to his word. And truly do we see that no churl is he but a stout man-at-arms, for from his bearing may it be seen that his hand knoweth sword-hilt better than plow-handle."

Now loudly laughed the lords, both old and young, and louder laughed King Uther; and steward, usher, and porter crept away to nurse their broken heads in shame.

Then said the king: "What is thy name?"

And the man answered: "My name is Sir Cleges. I was thy knight till poverty came upon me."

Now the king came down from the dais and clasped both Sir Cleges' hands in his own. "Old friend," said he, "oft hast thou done me good service with sword and lance on the battlefield years ago when we both were younger and stronger than we are today, when each would have gladly given his life to save the other. But of all the timely and valuable services thou didst render me in the past, I have never received better service than thou hast done me this day when thy stout staff hath dealt justice on the grasping knaves who would stand betwixt true people and their king."

So he clothed Sir Cleges in fine robes befitting his rank, and bestowed upon him riches, together with the castle of Cardiff, and there the good knight and his wife dwelt long in peace, bounty, and honor, beloved by all the people.

The Wise King and the Little Bee

Retold by Rose Dobbs

MANY, many years ago there lived in the holy city of Jerusalem a mighty king whose name was Solomon. And his fame was in all the nations round about. For God had given Solomon a wise and understanding heart. He was wiser than any man who lived before him and any man who came after. And all the earth sought the presence of Solomon to hear his wisdom, and he always judged wisely and well.

Now, suppose I were to tell you that a little bee, a little, tiny, insignificant bee, once proved itself to be wiser than this wisest of men? You would probably not believe it. Yet it is true. There is an old, old story to prove it, and because Solomon was humble as he was wise, the story has a happy ending. And here it is:

It happened that among the countries which rang with the fame of Solomon's wisdom and riches was the country over which ruled the proud and beautiful Queen of Sheba. She longed to prove to everyone that Solomon was not the wisest man in the world. She would have liked to set him some difficult task which he could not perform, or better still, ask him a simple question which he would not be able to answer. She thought and she thought and at last an idea came to her.

She called together all the most skilled craftsmen in the land, and she com-manded them to fashion for her a bouquet of flowers. It was to be of roses of Sharon and lilies of the valley. And the flowers were to be made so beautifully, so perfectly, that no one standing within a few inches of them would be able to tell if they were real or false. The craftsmen went to work and shortly afterwards brought the bouquet to the queen. The little bells of the lilies of the valley and the purple blossoms of the roses of Sharon were so perfect that the queen could not believe they were not real. And her skilled workmen had labored long and hard to distil a perfume that matched perfectly the fragrance of the real flowers.

The queen was more than pleased. "Now we shall see," said she, "how wise Solomon truly is."

So she announced that she would pay him a visit; to do him honor, she said. And she came to Jerusalem with a very great train, with camels that bore spices and much gold, and with boxes full of precious stones.

Solomon received her graciously. The best rooms in the palace were offered to her and her companions. The finest musicians and dancers entertained her. And a lavish banquet was planned for her. On the evening of the banquet, the queen sent her most trusted servant to procure a bouquet of real roses of Sharon and lilies

214

of the valley. When the merry-making and feasting were in full swing, the queen left the gay company and soon returned with the two bouquets. Everyone gasped. Never had they seen such beautiful bouquets, such perfect flowers, and one the exact copy of the other.

"O, great and mighty king," said the Queen of Sheba, standing at a little distance from Solomon and holding out the two bouquets, "the whole world rings with stories of your wisdom. Tell me, you who can always see the truth, which of these bouquets is made up of real flowers and which of false?"

There was a deep silence in the vast hall. Not one person there could see any difference between the two bouquets. The little white bells of the lilies of the valley swayed gently in each and the lovely purple blossoms of the roses of Sharon sent out a faint perfume from each.

The deep silence was broken by a whispering and murmuring which started in one corner, traveled to another and soon filled the vast hall. Solomon leaned forward and wrinkled his brow. He heard the excited and anxious mutterings of his people, but both bouquets looked exactly alike. Perhaps they were both real? Or, perhaps they were both false? Suddenly, above the hum in the hall, Solomon's sharp ear caught another sound. It was made by a little bee buzzing against a window. Solomon smiled. He was wise enough to know that all wisdom comes from God and that God has given to each of His creatures a special wisdom of its own. So he motioned to one of his servants to open the window. No sooner was this done than the bee flew into the room. The king's eyes followed it. Straight and sure it flew to one of the bouquets and was soon lost to sight deep within the blossoms. So engrossed in watching the queen or in whispering to each other were the people that no one noticed what had happened.

The king sat up very straight and met the queen's mocking eyes.

"My gracious and honored guest," he said, "the true flowers are those," and he pointed to the bouquet chosen by the little bee.

The queen was astonished.

"It was a true report that I heard in my own land of your acts and of your wisdom," she said. "But I did not believe the words, until I came and have myself seen it. You have wisdom beyond the fame of which I have heard. Happy are your men, happy are your servants, happy are all those who stand before you always and hear your wisdom."

Then a great shout and roar of praise rang out from all the people. But the king himself was silent. In his heart he was giving thanks for the little bee that had come to help him.

To a Butterfly

By William Wordsworth

I'VE WATCHED you now a full half hour,
  Self-poised upon that yellow flower;
And, little butterfly, indeed
I know not if you sleep or feed.
How motionless! — not frozen seas
More motionless; and then
What joy awaits you, when the breeze
Hath found you out among the trees,
And calls you forth again!

This plot of orchard ground is ours;
My trees they are, my sister's flowers;
Here rest your wings when they are weary;
Here lodge as in a sanctuary.
Come often to us, fear no wrong;
Sit near us on the bough —
We'll talk of sunshine and of song,
And summer days when we were young;
Sweet childish days, that were as long
As twenty days are now.

On the Grasshopper and the Cricket

By John Keats

THE POETRY of earth is never dead:
  When all the birds are faint with the hot sun,
And hide in cooling trees, a voice will run
From hedge to hedge about the new-mown mead;
That is the grasshopper's — he takes the lead
In summer luxury, — he has never done
With his delights; for when tired out with fun
He rests at ease beneath some pleasant weed.
The poetry of earth is ceasing never:
On a lone winter evening, when the frost
Has wrought a silence, from the stove there shrills
The cricket's song, in warmth increasing ever,
And seems to one in drowsiness half lost,
The grasshopper's among some grassy hills.

216

Latin-American Legends

The Baker's Neighbor

A Story from Peru
Translated by Frank Henius

ONCE upon a time, more than a hundred years ago, there lived a baker in the city of Lima, in Peru. He was a very industrious man. At night he mixed the flour and kneaded the dough and baked his bread and pastries. Every morning when the sun rose, he stood in his shop and sold his appetizing wares to the townsfolk. He loved money better than anything else in the world. His next-door neighbor was quite a different kind of man. He did not like to work much and rather enjoyed sitting in the sun or listening to the birds, and he did not care much for money, unlike the stingy penny-pinching bread and pastry cook. The neighbor, who tried to enjoy life and take advantage of all the small and everyday joys it offered, took great pleasure in the splendid, aromatic smell of the freshly-baked rolls and cakes which the early breeze never failed to bring to his door.

After a night of hard work, the baker would go into the open air and sit down at a little table at the back of his house. He would pull out his purse, and, just as the sun rose over the horizon, he would count the money he had taken in during the preceding day. He would inspect each coin, and for more than an hour he would figure and fret and add and subtract. His jolly neighbor would get up the moment he heard the baker bang his door and go into his backyard to start his daily counting of coins. This was the signal for the neighbor to go downstairs also, lean easily against his door-frame and inhale the fragrant odors of the freshly-baked bread and rolls and cakes.

The baker knew full well that his neighbor was a bad customer in the shop, but that on the other hand he profited every morning by the breeze from the sea, which brought him the bakery's odors. The stingy breadkneader saw his neighbor's idle posture whenever he looked up from the money piled on the table in front of him. The baker was always angry when he thought how his blending of all the costly flour, sugar, raisins and other ingredients were enjoyed free and without charge by his neighbor, while he, the baker, had to work most of the night to provide such pleasure.

However, one fine day the baker decided he had stood it long enough. He would no longer silently allow himself to be deprived of the fruits of his labor and cost of his supplies, without any compensation. Going to the neighbor's house, he demanded a large sum of money for the splendid odors he had daily provided for him year after year, without ever sending a bill or collecting any payment. The jolly fellow at first did not seem to understand the bread and pastry cook, but when he at last realized what it all meant, he laughed right into the enraged baker's face. He laughed so loud and so long that all the other neighbors AND their wives came to ask what made him laugh so much? He told them his story, interrupted by his own and the others' loud guffaws. Especially the women seemed to enjoy the situation.

Naturally, this enraged the baker still more. He was not only disappointed that he had not at least obtained some kind of payment from his neighbor, but was angry because he had to stand all the chaff and the teasing of his neighbors, AND their wives, and even their children. When he came out of his shop to go on an errand, the little boys and girls would run after him. They would pretend to sniff at his clothes and his hands, then they would run in front of him and yell to ask him how much he wanted for the lovely smell they had just enjoyed. When he could not stand it any longer, he made another attempt to get some kind of payment from his neigh-

bor, so as to close the matter gracefully and put a stop to the ever-increasing, humiliating embarrassment the towns-folk were causing him. When he was quite unsuccessful, and on the contrary, was laughed at and teased more than ever, he decided to fight for the money he felt he was entitled to. So he took his case to court.

The Judge, like most of Lima's citizens, had heard of the baker and his complaint before it was ever brought to court. Nevertheless, as the laws of Peru demanded, he invited the baker to come to court and tell his story. The Judge, who had a great sense of humor, listened gravely and told the complainant that he would soon decide the case. The following week, keeping his promise, he ordered both the baker and his neighbor to appear in court. He ordered the latter to bring a bag containing one hundred gold coins. The news of the impending action and of the Judge's order soon spread through the whole town of Lima. The neighbor began to lose some of his gay, care-free spirits and behavior, trembling lest he was going to be made to pay for the pastry and bread smells he had been enjoying in the past. On the other hand, the baker rubbed his hands when no one was looking, counted the gold coins in his mind, and he went around happy and grinning. Inwardly, he gloated over their possession as if they were already jingling in his pocket.

At last, a week later, both were in court. All the neighbors and many other

citizens of Lima were there too, and they all felt sorry for the jolly fellow who looked so crest-fallen and sad at the smiling and beaming baker. The court-room hummed from all the noise and talk and whispering. However, when the clerk of the court announced the entry of the Judge, they all became silent and rose. After the Judge had ordered them to be seated, he had the plaintiff and defendant swear that they would tell the truth and nothing but the truth. Then the baker was told to repeat his complaint.

The baker, feeling that he must convince the Judge that the aromatic odors from his oven were worth at least the hundred gold coins he expected to receive, spoke for quite a while. He told all about his work in detail and explained how the odors the neighbor inhaled were the result of all his work and expenditure. The Judge listened gravely.

When the baker had finished his story, the Judge gave the defendant a hard look and asked him whether the morning breeze wafted these costly odors daily to his house? After this was admitted by the defendant, who was by now quite down-hearted, the Judge wanted to know if the freshly baked bread and rolls and pastry had a good, enjoyable or a bad, annoying smell? The neighbor of course could not but admit that the smells were very enjoyable indeed. As soon as he had thus confirmed the pleasantness of the aromatic odors, he regretted it, for the Judge now asked him to hand the bag with the hundred gold coins to the complainant. The latter, on hearing this order, almost fell over the witness-stand railing, so eager was he to grab the bag and get hold of the money. When he had at last clutched and pressed it tightly to his chest, and turned to leave and go home with the precious gold, the judge ordered him to step to a big table in front of the bench. There he was told to empty the bag, and to count the hundred coins, one by one.

The baker thought it very kind of the judge to give him this opportunity of making sure he had not been cheated.

So he emptied the bag on the large polished table and began to count. The gold coins glistened in the sunshine, and jumped and gave a fine, pleasant metallic sound as they hit the wood. Everyone could see the brightness of the coins and the sound of them was a feast for the eyes and music for the ears of the greedy pastry-cook. The Judge and the neighbor, and all the other neighbors and citizens of Lima, AND their wives, could plainly see with what gloating satisfaction the baker fingered each gold coin, how he could hardly get himself to drop it to pick up the next one. He was definitely and very evidently enjoying the touch of gold, its glint and glamor and its sound, as he counted and dropped the coins one by one onto the table, each ringing good and true.

Then he lovingly put the coins back in the bag and told the Judge that there were indeed one hundred coins and that not one was false. To make this declaration he had returned to the witness stand. Before leaving the court, he also wanted to thank the Judge for his fair and wise decision. But just then to his utter surprise and consternation, the Judge asked him to hand the bag back to the equally surprised defendant. The Judge now rose from his chair and putting on his black cap with the red ribbon, asked all those in court to stand up. They all rose, and stood silently and expectantly awaiting the decision. The Judge, lifting his voice, then in the name of the people of Peru solemnly pronounced his judgment and said:

"The court has heard the baker's complaint against the neighbor and the latter's admission that he did enjoy the aromatic and appetizing odors brought to his door, at sunrise, by the morning breeze. I therefore hereby declare that the case is now settled, Baker. Your neighbor has *smelled* your pastry and bread, and you have *seen* and *touched* his gold."

At first, no one fully realized the meaning of this wise judgment. But when they did, the hush in the court was suddenly broken and everyone was laughing, crying, shouting and congratulating the neighbor. The latter was still standing at the rail, quite dumbfounded at first, holding the bag with one hand and feeling it with the other to make quite sure that his savings had been returned to him. Then he began to laugh— to laugh loud and long, and soon the whole court was laughing except the baker. He had silently slipped out of the court, for he realized quicker than anyone else that he had lost his case. Then the clerk of the court brought down his gavel, and asked the people to be silent and to leave the court. But in front of the courthouse, they all stood and laughed and shouted until the neighbor came out. They hoisted him on their shoulders and with much noise and rejoicing carried him, gold and all, back to his house.

The baker, when he saw the procession entering his street, hid behind his curtains. He was crest-fallen. Henceforth, since he could no longer stand the sight of his life-loving, easy-going neighbor at sunrise, enjoying his bakery smells more than ever, he never went out into the morning-light himself. He brought the table and chair from the yard into his house, and counted his money inside.

But from that time many of the neighbors, their friends AND their wives, came to the jolly fellow's house every morning, their laughter and gaiety went straight through the door and window to the baker's ears, as he sat in a dark corner and counted his money by candlelight. The jolly neighbor himself enjoyed the morning breeze and its aroma more than ever.

Our Holy Lady of Good Grace

A STORY FROM THE DOMINICAN REPUBLIC

Translated by Frank Henius

ONE of the many ancient and picturesque small towns of the Dominican Republic is Villa de Salvaleón de Higuey. This town, with its many heraldic signs was founded at the beginning of the sixteenth century by the Spanish explorer, Juan de Esquivel. The most outstanding place of interest in the town is the ancient colonial church where the people go to worship the original image of Our Most Holy Lady of Good Grace, patron saint of the Dominican Republic. The annual festive day of this Holy Virgin is celebrated on the twenty-first day of January. On this day thousands of people from all parts of the country make a pilgrimage to the Sanctuary, either by automobile or on horseback. Many even walk, thereby doing penance, all in order to pay homage to the Virgin as she is represented by this miraculous image, and in this holy shrine.

The legend about the apparition of this Virgin tells us that some time during the sixteenth century, there lived in Duey, a region near Higuey, a rich Spanish gentleman who was very much esteemed and respected by the entire colony. In those days it was customary for the planters to make occasional trips to the capital of the colony, the city of Santo Domingo, to sell their cattle and farm products, and buy the things they needed in their households and on their plantations and cattle ranches.

On one of these occasions this fine Spanish gentleman, a planter and cattle-breeder, went on a journey to the capital, for just that purpose. Before his departure, he asked his daughters what he should bring them from the shops in the town.

The older of his two daughters asked him to bring her clothes and ribbons, and other things to adorn herself with, including a bracelet and some earrings. But the younger daughter, who was called Niña by her family and friends, was of a very religious and pious mind. She did not ask for clothes or finery, but begged her father to bring her an image of the Holy Virgin of the Good Grace. This seemed quite strange to her father, for he had never heard of a Virgin by that name, but of course, as he loved his little daughter dearly, he promised to find and bring her the desired image.

When he was returning home with his arms full of presents for his older

223

daughter, he thought sadly about his inability to fulfill his younger daughter's wish for an image of Our Holy Lady of Good Grace, for he had not found anyone who knew anything about her. Not even the Canons nor even the Archbishop himself had ever heard of any image of the Holy Virgin known by that name.

He stopped at a town called Los Dos Rios, where he was to spend a night at the house of a friend. During the evening the two men discussed the strange request of little Niña. Her father told his friend how sad he felt at being unable to comply with the girl's wish.

It so happened that an old man with a flowing white beard, a pilgrim, was also spending the night at the house in Los Dos Rios. And when he heard his host and his friend speak of the image of the Holy Virgin that was impossible to find, he brought out of his saddle bag a beautiful image of the Virgin wearing a cloak of heavenly blue and adoring a new-born child. A star shone upon her over her left shoulder. Behind her, on the right and in the shadows, St. Joseph, holding a candle, was keeping guard over both the Virgin and the Infant. On each side of the Virgin there was a beautiful white lily.

The old man handed the image to the planter. He told him that it was what he and his friend were looking for —the image of Our Holy Lady of Good Grace.

Next day, the gentleman, before leaving his friend's house, looked for the pilgrim to thank him for his precious present. But to his surprise and the surprise of the entire household the old man was gone, without bidding goodbye to anyone.

Little Niña had been waiting for the return of her father with great eagerness. Daily, while she waited, she would sit under a beautiful orange tree which was in full bloom. Together with her friends she prayed that her father would return safe and sound, and bring with him the image of the Virgin.

It was the twenty-first day of January when Niña's father returned. He found her among her friends under the blossoming orange tree, praying and waiting for him. It gave him the greatest delight to present the beautiful image to his daughter and see how happy it made her.

The image of the Holy Lady of Good Grace was afterwards known as Niña's Virgin, and soon after she received it a sanctuary was built for it under Niña's own orange blossom tree which still stands.

The image, in a gold frame, was moved some years ago to Santa Domingo, the capital city, where it may be seen by great numbers of people every day.

Altagracia, which means Good Grace, is a popular name for Dominican Republic girls. And the national flag of that country bears the three colors of the Holy Lady of Good Grace, blue, white and red, in the shape of a cross.

Sumé

A STORY FROM BRAZIL
Translated by Frank Henius

ONCE upon a time when the Tamoyo tribe was gathered in great numbers on the beach to celebrate a victory, they looked up and beheld on the ocean, coming from the direction of the sun, a towering figure, more like a god than a human being. The figure was that of a venerable old man, bright as the light of day, with a long snow-white beard spread over his breast down to his feet and touching the waters of the sea.

Great was the astonishment of the Tamoyos at seeing a man like themselves walk thus upon the waters as fearlessly as upon the land. It was Sumé, messenger of Tupan, Lord of Heaven and Earth. Sumé it was who worked the most unheard-of wonders. At his approach the thickest forests would open of their own accord to make a path for him. When the sea was at its wildest, seething and lashing with wrath, Sumé could bring it into instant submission by a simple motion of his hand. His presence could quiet storms, quench rains and stop droughts. Even the savage beasts of the forests would crawl submissively to his feet and lick his hands. And the Tamoyos, captivated by his good-

ness, enthralled by the wonder of his miracles, took Sumé for their counselor.

Sumé loved those simple-minded people, free from vice and sin. He praised their victory in war and their moderation in peace. He wanted to make them happy by teaching them how to live in abundance.

Sumé said, "The earth is the great mother, the great and generous mother. It is enough to cherish her, to love her, to caress her, for her to pour out lavishly upon us all manner of riches and happiness."

An old medicine man, wise in the lore which common mortals do not know, said, "How so, holy one, when up to now she has given us only thorns and reptiles?" And Sumé answered, "That is because up to now you have never loved her with fervor and effort. Dig the earth and water it with your sweat. At once it will open, not to swallow you but to give you new life. Come with me and see."

They followed him. And on all sides they saw that the land was wild and hostile. Dense, tangled jungles rose up out of its bosom; in them serpents hissed

226

and jaguars howled, and all primitive nature was the enemy of man. Armed against him, it sharpened the teeth of its savage beasts and the thorns of its thickets. Sumé ordered the Indians to attack the forest and lay it low with the same bravery and the same vigor that they would use in attacking the hordes of a cruel enemy. Then he ordered them to harrow and smooth the land and gave them various seeds to cast lavishly on the breast of the great mother.

Thus Sumé traveled the whole length of the coast, followed by all the able-bodied men of the tribe. Days went by. Months went by. Years went by. The vast multitude of men toiled from sun to sun, possessed by a common zeal, impelled, captivated, enthralled by the goodness and kindness of one man. When Sumé arrived at the great bay that marked the southern boundary of the dominions of the Tamoyos, he stopped. Calling the laborers together, he said:

"It is time to retrace our steps. Now you are going to see how the land repays you in abundance and happiness for the sweat of your brow."

They turned back. And soon the tribe was carried away by wonder. For behold, the earth was transformed. The nearer they came to the place of depar-

227

ture, the more they marveled at the strange vegetation and the fruits, the like of which they had never seen before. And when they arrived at the camp it was to find their women and children dancing and singing and their granaries full to overflowing. The sky seemed more beautiful, and the sea, too, and all nature more beautiful because the whole tribe looked upon nature through the spirit of joy that is the child of happiness. From the seeds furnished by Sumé grew great clusters of banana trees, laden with fruit, manioc roots, golden ears of corn, cotton, beans, peas.

Sumé, not satisfied with what he had already done, taught them the art of making meal and grinding manioc, and revealed to them the secrets of navigation. He improved the rude dugout boats, providing them with sails that, like the wings of birds, made them fly like the wind. He showed them how to make rudders that, like the tail of a fish, helped the boat to cut through the waves. The whole tribe blessed Sumé, and every day at sunset when the sun dyed blood-red the waters of the sea, the tribe danced to the sound of their drums around the old man, the blessed son of Tupan, Father of all growing things.

But time passed. And as the years passed, so passed the gratitude of the tribe.

The medicine men, jealous of the power of Sumé, poisoned the people's minds against him.

"What!" they cried. "Shall this tribe that is so strong that its war-cry is enough to terrify all other nations remain forever under the domination of one man, and he a stranger?"

And around about Sumé there spread a cloud of slander, and the net of intrigue was drawn closer and closer.

He heard and smiled. His great soul, full of love and compassion, understood and pardoned the ingratitude of the people.

One morning when Sumé came out of his hut he saw all the Tamoyos lined up against him, crying out and threatening. Their faces showed nothing but hatred.

Sumé tried to speak, but before he could open his lips an arrow pierced his breast. The Saint smiled. He drew out the arrow and threw it on the ground. He turned away toward the sea.

When he reached the beach he entered the sea. His figure looked large as he walked upon the waters, and still traveling backward, receded smiling instead of cursing the ungrateful people to whom he had brought abundance.

The people, paralyzed with wonder and awe, stood transfixed. They saw him softly swaying on the waters that the rising sun dyed blood-red. They saw him grow smaller and smaller and at length vanish on the horizon—the gentle being with skin as white as the light of day and a long snow-white beard spread over his breast down to his feet and touching the waters of the sea.

The Princess Bird

By J. A. Rickard

MANY boys and girls have wished to be princes or princesses, so that they might have wonderful times and wear crowns, but not many of them ever wished that they could be birds. Yet there was once a princess who became a bird—a beautiful bird, like those red-necked and white-necked ones we often see hopping about in the fig tree. At any rate, that is the way the story goes.

It all happened many hundreds of years ago, when the Maya and the Aztec Indians lived in the land of Mexico, and when there really were kings and queens and other great people like them.

But in the land of Uxmal there was great sorrow, for their kind King Copano had become blind. His wife, Queen Teo, tried many many remedies and used many medicines, but none of them did him any good. She called many doctors, but not one of them could restore his sight.

At last in despair the Queen sent word throughout the land that help was wanted. She promised that whoever could cure him would be given anything that he might ask, if it was possible to give it. In order to make everyone believe in the Queen's promise and want to do something, the King put his great seal on the proclamation, and swift runners went everywhere telling the news.

Many people came from far and near, and they tried many remedies, but still King Copano remained blind. Nothing that any of the strangers suggested seemed to help him.

One day while she was walking in the palace grounds with the little Princess Tula and wondering what to do next, she met a large dog. She was about to walk on without looking at him, when to her great surprise he spoke to her.

"I have heard of King Copano's blindness," he said, "and I know a remedy that will cure him."

"Oh, please tell me what your remedy is," begged Queen Teo. "I will give you anything if he is cured."

"Will you give me the hand of the Princess Tula in marriage?" asked the dog.

This shocked the Queen, but so anxious was she to have the King see again that she replied, "I will, as soon as she is old enough to marry."

"Then listen closely and do exactly as I say," cautioned the dog. "Turn around and go back to the palace. Every time you take a step with your right foot, pull up any flower or plant that you step on. Place all these in a pot and boil them in water two hours. Rub the water on the king's eyes once each day for fifteen days. On the fifteenth day he

will see again."

The Queen thanked the dog and did exactly as he had told her to do. She watched the King's eyes every day, and on the fifteenth day, sure enough, his sight was restored completely. The King and Queen were very happy, and the people of Uxmal were happy too.

The years passed, and the Princess Tula grew into a beautiful lady. One night she and her friends were making merry. The palace was brightly lighted, and there was music and dancing in the patio. A large brown dog came up and stood watching the scene. One of the servants tried to make him leave, but he refused to go and asked to see the Queen.

When at last Queen Teo stood before the dog, she knew he was the one that had given her the cure for the King's eyes fifteen years before.

"I have come for my reward," said he.

The Queen told him that it was not possible to do as he asked and ordered him to leave. He refused to go, though, even when the servants beat him with sticks.

Finally the King heard the noise and came to see what was wrong. The Queen now told him for the first time the story of how he had been cured and the promise she had made.

When he heard the story he said, "We have given our solemn promise, and the word of the King and Queen must not be broken. Call Princess Tula."

When the beautiful Princess Tula came, she too was told the story, and she remembered it and agreed that the marriage should take place at once.

The poor Queen was grief-stricken at the thought of such a terrible thing, but there was nothing else to do except carry out the King's command. The Princess did not know of anything else to do but obey. She began to prepare for the ceremony.

It was indeed a strange wedding. The Princess, dressed in a long trailing gown, leaned on the arm of the King as they marched down the aisle to the altar. The solemn padre read the ceremony, and the dog-groom took a ring in his paw and placed it on the finger of the Princess.

As the last words of the ceremony were said, a wonderful thing happened. The dog stood up on his hind legs and shook himself. Off fell his skin as though it had been a robe, and lo! a handsome Prince stood there. We may be sure that as soon as the Princess saw him she made no objection when he turned and kissed her. Then he seized the old skin that had fallen to the floor, and before the crowd could understand what had happened, he and the Princess had run out

of the church and were off on their honeymoon.

The Princess was very happy when two weeks later she proudly brought back the handsome Prince Tezco to live at the palace. The king and queen were happy, too, for they had no son of their own. Now, with such a handsome Prince to rule the kingdom later, all would be well.

But alas! Their happiness did not last long. One day when the Queen was gathering up the clothes for the wash-woman, she saw the robe that Prince Tezco had thrown off at the time of the wedding. Wishing to get rid of it and buy him a newer and better one, she burned it.

When Prince Tezco learned of this, he moaned, "Oh, what have you done? That robe protected me from a witch who once had me enchanted. As long as I had it she could not harm me, but now she can. In fifteen days she will come after me."

Sure enough, in fifteen days, a haggard old witch rode her broomstick through the sky to the palace. Straight through its walls she came, as if nothing had been there, and she did not stop until she stood in front of the royal family.

"I have come for the Prince," she croaked.

The Queen begged, and the Princess pleaded. The King offered the witch a house full of gold, and finally he offered her his palace. But to all these offers the old witch only gave a hollow laugh and said, "I have a palace and gold of my own. The Prince must come with me."

So strongly did the Princess plead, though, that finally the old witch promised to let her see him once each week. In order to do this, she had to turn him into a bird, so that he could fly from the home of the witch to the palace and back.

Thereafter each week the Princess went to the woods to seek her beloved Prince in the form of a bird. She always looked for one that had a red neck and a white bill, for she knew he was her Prince.

One day she decided to follow him and learn where he lived. Without letting him know what she had in mind, she asked him to fly high and slowly, so that she could see him longer. He did so, and she followed him.

After many hours of travel, she saw him fly into the huge home of the witch, deep in the forest. Then she boldly went up to him. In vain did he beg her to leave. He told her that she too would fall into the power of the old witch if she were found there, but she only shook her head.

"I will never leave you again," she said.

When the old witch came out of the house, Princess Tula begged her to give her back her Prince, but this she would not do.

"Then," said the Princess, "make me into a bird just like him, so that we may be together. Make his neck red and mine white."

Her wish was granted, and they have been together ever since. Maybe they are happier than they would be if they were still humans. Who knows?

The Old Aztec Story Teller

Stories of North America

Grinding the Ax

By Benjamin Franklin

ONE COLD MORNING in winter, when I was a little boy, a smiling man with an ax on his shoulder stopped me, saying, "My pretty boy, has your father a grindstone?"

"Yes, sir," said I.

"You are a fine little fellow!" said the

man. "Will you let me grind my ax?"

Pleased with the flattery, I answered, "Oh, yes, sir. The grindstone is down in the shop."

Patting me on my head, he said, "Will you get me some hot water?" I ran and brought the hot water.

"How old are you, and what is your name?" he inquired, without waiting for a reply. "I'm sure you are one of the finest lads I have ever seen. Will you turn the grindstone a few minutes for me?"

Tickled with the flattery, I went to work with a will. It was a new ax, and I toiled and tugged till I was almost tired to death. The school bell rang, but I could not get away. My hands were blistered; still the ax was not half ground.

At last, however, it was sharpened. Then the man turned to me and said, "Now, you little rascal, you've played truant! Scud to school, or you'll be sorry!"

"Alas!" thought I. "It was hard enough to turn a grindstone this cold day, but now to be called a rascal is too much."

The memory of turning the grindstone that winter's morning sank deep into my mind. I have thought of it since. Now, whenever I hear words of flattery, I say to myself, "That man has an ax to grind."

The Goat that Went to School

By Ellis Credle

WHEN the clouds hung heavy about the mountains, Hubert could step outside the cabin and wash his face in their damp white mist. That was how high up he lived. His Pappy's little log house was built on the steep side of old Thunderhead Mountain so far up that the valley down below looked misty blue like an opal. The houses down there in the settlement seemed tinier than matchboxes. It was easy to pick out the schoolhouse from the others for its new tin roof glittered in the sun and sent up shafts of light like a diamond.

Hubert sat on a rock ledge in front of his home and stared downward at the bright roof longingly. He was ten years old and he had never been to school.

Around by the road it was a far piece to the school in the valley. It took a whole day to get there. But Hubert knew a short cut. Even though it was a steep and toilsome way zigzagging down the face of the mountain, Hubert could make it in an hour.

But when he pleaded with his mother to let him go down and get some learning she always said,

"I'm afeared—I'm afeared for you to walk it alone in the winter-time. If the snow began to fly, pretty soon the trail would be covered as smooth and as white as a fresh-made feather bed and you'd not know which-a-way to turn. You'd go wandering on these vast and rugged mountains until you were lost and frozen in the cold. No, no, you'll have to make out for a while longer with what your Pappy and I can teach you."

But Hubert could not forget his desire to go down to the school in the valley. All the boys down in the valley went there. They learned how to read stories out of books, tales of cowboys, and hunts and other things that boys like to read of. And they played games down there in the valley, fox-in-the-war, and baseball; and at the end of the year they had a "speaking" and each pupil would go up and say a little piece, all dressed in his best. It was something to wish for!

"Can't I just *start* this year, Mammy," begged Hubert, "and go until the days begin to get cold and it looks like snow?"

"Well, I suppose there'd be no harm in that," said his Mammy. "You can go during the month of September. There's never any snow in September." Hubert was joyful. Even one month in school was something to look forward to.

Now, Hubert began to worry about his clothes. All he had to wear was a pair of blue overalls and a homespun shirt. The other boys in the school would have on short store-bought pants and nice striped shirts. And then there were books.

235

Where would he get money for books?

There was always plenty to eat in the little cabin on Thunderhead Mountain, for Pappy raised everything they needed. There were warm clothes, too, for Mammy spun the wool from their own sheep and wove it into cloth. But there was never any money to spare, and Hubert did want some clothes like the other boys' and some books so that he could study his lessons.

If there were only a way he could earn a little money! Hubert cudgeled his brains. One day he said to his Mammy,

"I think I'll go ask Mr. Honeycutt if he would like a little help picking his apples and loading 'em into the wagon to take to town. Maybe I could make me a little money to buy some store clothes and some books."

"Go right ahead," his Mammy nodded. "Asking wouldn't hurt."

Hubert set off plodding around the mountain to his neighbor's home in the next cove.

"Why, yes, I can use a little help loading my apples," said Mr. Honeycutt, twisting his handle-bar mustaches.

Hubert set to work picking up the sound apples from the ground, plucking the ripe ones from the tree, sacking them and helping Mr. Honeycutt to hoist them into his covered wagon. When it was loaded high, Mr. Honeycutt hitched his old brown mule between the shafts, then he climbed into the driver's seat.

"I'll not forget you when I sell my apples in the town," he promised as he cracked his whip and went creaking down the rough mountain road. "I'll be back in two or three days and I'll stop by your house with your pay."

During the time that Mr. Honeycutt was away, Hubert wondered if he would get a good price for his apples. He hoped so, for if he did, he might pay enough for picking them to buy all his things.

"If he pays me only enough to get part of them," he thought, "I'll buy me the store-bought pants first." A homespun shirt wouldn't look so outlandish if he had a pair of proper pants to go with it. After that he would buy a reader.

On the third day when he heard the rumble of Mr. Honeycutt's wagon wheels coming around the mountain, he ran to the cabin door.

"Whoa!" cried Mr. Honeycutt, pulling up in front of the door. "Well, Hubert, I've got your pay!" He was smiling so that his handle-bar mustaches spread out over his face.

"He must have got a good price and he's going to pay me a lot," thought Hubert, taking note of his good humor. He ran out to the covered wagon and looked up expectantly.

Mr. Honeycutt leaned into the back of the wagon behind the white canvas top and began to pull something forward. "Well, here's your pay."

Around the edge of the wagon top peeped a neat fur-covered head with two dainty horns. A goat! A trim little brown beard wiggled merrily as his jaws worked. The goat was chewing busily upon the end of something white. It was Mr. Honeycutt's shirt tail.

236

"Here! Here! How did you get a-holt of that!" Mr. Honeycutt cried, pulling it away from his passenger and stuffing the ragged edge back into his trousers.

"Well, how do you like him?" he asked, turning back to Hubert. "He cost a little more than I ought to pay for having my apples picked, but then I remembered how a boy loves a goat."

Hubert was surprised but it would not do to let Mr. Honeycutt see that he was disappointed to get a goat instead of money. Besides, it was a pretty, neat-looking little goat and he had always wanted one.

"Gee, Mr. Honeycutt, he sure is a fine goat. I thank you, I sure do!" He took the goat's rope and the trim little animal bounded gracefully out of the wagon.

"Landsakes! What have you got there!" asked Mammy when she saw the goat stepping along into the house beside Hubert.

"Well, I've got me a goat, though it's not what I expected. It's my pay for picking Mr. Honeycutt's apples."

"But I thought you wanted some money to get yourself some clothes to wear to school, and maybe some books."

"It's what he brought me," said Hubert, "and I'd as soon have him."

The goat made himself right at home. Hubert fixed him a nice bed of leaves in a corner of the woodshed and he fed him some corn or oats every day and let him crop grass in front of the cabin.

The goat was never too busy eating to stop for a tussle with Hubert, for he was frisky and full of fun. He would rear up on his hind legs and butt at Hubert playfully and sometimes, when Hubert bent over to pick up something, he ran at him from behind and sent him tumbling.

One time he did it when Hubert was pouring a bucket full of buttermilk for the pigs. Over Hubert went, sprawling into the trough full of buttermilk. He went squishing and squashing to the house with streams of buttermilk running from his clothes, his hair and his ears.

When she saw the mischief the goat had done, his Mammy said, "That goat's going to be a nuisance. You had as well take him down to town and sell him. Then you'd have money to buy things."

Hubert shook his head. Naughty as the goat was, he had learned to love him. He did not like to think of selling him, even for some new clothes and his books. There must be another way of making money.

One day he had a bright idea. "I think I'll go along to Mr. Posey's place and see if he needs some help with his molasses."

"It won't hurt to ask," said Mammy. And so off Hubert went. He was hardly out of his own yard when he heard a scampering of small feet and the goat ran alongside. Hubert was pleased to have his company and soon they arrived at the Posey cabin.

"Well now, I might need someone to help me," said Mr. Posey, rubbing his bald head. "It's a lot of work making molasses, cutting the sugar cane in the fields, driving the mule around and around to squeeze the juice in the home-made molasses mill, then standing over the juice and boiling and boiling it until it gets thick and sweet and heavy. I've already made one big barrelful. It was a sight of trouble but if I do say so, it's good molasses. Would you like a taste?"

"Yes, sir," Hubert nodded and the old man leaned over and dipped into the barrel with a large spoon.

It was a nice invitation to the goat. He stood off a little way, then came at Mr. Posey with a rush. He sent him sprawling headfirst into the barrel of molasses.

Mr. Posey floundered out looking like a tar-baby, covered from head to foot with thick black molasses.

"Get along!" he sputtered, wiping the molasses out of his face. "Get along home with that mischievous goat!"

Sorrowfully Hubert walked along home, the goat mincing beside him.

"Just see what you've done," he said. "But for you, I'd have had a chance to make me a little money."

"Baa, baa, baa!" said the goat, as cheerfully as though he had not just butted his master out of a good job.

"Just as I told you, you had better take him down to the town and sell him," urged Mammy when she heard of the mischief the goat had done. "He'll never be anything but a nuisance. Then you could buy your things."

238

But Hubert did not care to part with his goat. "He'll not be naughty again," he said. "I'll try him a while longer."

The next day he went about his tasks with a thoughtful face. He was trying hard to think of another way to earn some money. After a while he had a bright idea. "I think I'll go a-berrying," he said to his Mammy. "Maybe I can pick enough to sell in the town and then I could buy my things."

"It's worth trying," said Mammy.

Before he left to go a-berrying, Hubert took a stout piece of rope and tied the goat to a tree.

"You're a troublemaker," he said, "and you'd best stay here out of mischief."

Off he started with a big basket over his arm. He was only halfway to the peak where the biggest blackberries grew when he heard a clattering behind him. He turned and looked and there was the goat tripping up the steep stony trail dragging his rope all frayed and chewed.

"How did you get loose, you naughty goat?" cried Hubert, but just the same he was half glad to see his friend. All day long he picked berries on the high mountainside and the goat was as good as could be. When his basket was full, Hubert set off for home.

"Mammy, Mammy, come and see!" he cried when he got there. "Come and see how many berries I've got! And they're nice ones. I'll get a good price for them." He set his basket on the edge of the porch and ran to find his Mammy.

When he got back, he found the basket tipped over. His berries were spilled on the ground and all scuffed and crushed. The goat's mouth was stained with blackberry juice.

"I told you," cried Mammy, when she saw the mischief. "That goat is nothing but a nuisance. Why don't you take him down to the town and sell him?"

Hubert looked at his naughty goat regretfully. Perhaps he should take Mammy's advice. He'd likely get enough money for the goat to buy everything he needed, even a green striped shirt and books. But the more he thought about it, the more he hated to part with his pet.

"I think I'll give him another chance," he decided.

For a while the goat would go along as good as yellow gold. But as surely as Hubert would think up a way to make a little money, he would break out with a piece of naughtiness and spoil all Hubert's chances.

That was the reason that on the first day of September Hubert set off sadly for the school, wearing the same old homespun shirt and his old blue overalls. He left the goat at home shut up tight in the woodshed. But not quite tight enough, for when he was only about halfway down the mountain he heard a quick trip-tripping behind him. He looked around and there was the goat prancing merrily after him.

Hubert frowned at him. "If it hadn't been for you I would have been going to school with some new store-bought pants and a nice striped shirt," he said, "and books to study from."

"Baa, baa, baa!" bleated the goat, as gaily as though his master were dressed in some brand-new clothes. Down, down, they wound until they came to school.

"Oh, look!" cried the children. "A new boy! And he has a goat!" They crowded around Hubert. No one noticed his faded shirt and his old blue overalls for they were much too busy asking questions about the goat.

The goat pranced with delight at seeing so many children. He stood upon his hind legs and butted the boys. He chased the girls. Then he let each one ride upon his back. Everyone wanted to be friends with Hubert and his goat.

When the school bell rang, the goat lay down on the porch and waited while the children marched in for their lessons. Hubert went uneasily. "What shall I do for books?" he thought. But as soon as he was seated the teacher handed him a pile of them. There was an arithmetic, a speller, and a reader.

"They are yours for the year," she smiled at him. "The State furnishes all our books. You're only supposed to keep them nice and clean so that next year another boy can use them."

Every day during the month of September when the leaves were turning red and gold and brown on the shaggy mountainsides, Hubert wound happily down the trail to the schoolhouse with the goat beside him. He did not mind the long hard trip, and neither did the goat. Hubert studied his lessons hard for he knew that pretty soon cold weather

would come and the danger of snow. He wanted to learn as much as he could.

If only he could keep on going! Perhaps if he put his mind to it, he could think up a way. But think as he would, not an idea came into his mind.

Then came the end of September. It was his last day in school. Hubert told his friends good-by and started for home.

As he climbed slowly up the mountain he noticed that the sky was dark and leaden. He was hardly halfway home when soft feathery flakes began to float downward among the tree trunks. Snow in September! It could not be! As the white flakes flew thicker and thicker, Hubert hurried his footsteps. He remembered what his mother had said about getting lost.

"Baa, baa, baa!" bleated the goat, as happily as though the whirling flakes were not fast covering up the ground, hiding the trail, making everything look strange. Hubert stopped and looked all around. His eyes were wide and frightened.

Everything looked white and cold and unfamiliar. He could not tell which way to go. Any way he turned might start him rambling and he would be lost—lost in a snowstorm on shaggy Thunderhead Mountain.

But the goat seemed not to have a worry in his head. He frolicked ahead, bleating at Hubert, "Baa, baa, baa!" Now and then he returned to nip at his trouser-legs. It was as though he were saying, "Come on, what are you waiting for?" It gave Hubert a glint of hope.

"Perhaps he knows the way," Hubert thought. He put his hand on the smooth back and stumbled along where the goat led. They climbed and climbed. With his eyes half-closed to keep the snow from blinding him, Hubert did not know where he was going. But the goat stepped confidently as though he were sure of the ground and at last Hubert felt himself on a level place.

Could it be that they had reached the clearing where the cabin was? Hubert's heart gave a leap. He shielded his eyes with his arms and peered about. Dimly through the falling snow he could make out a building straight ahead. It was—yes, it was the cabin! He broke into a run.

When he pushed open the door, his mother started up. She cried joyfully, "Hubert!" She hugged him tight. "Your Pappy was just setting off to look for you!

241

I was afeared you were lost in the snow!"

"Not with a goat like this," cried Hubert, flinging the door wide so that his pet could come in and warm himself beside the hearth fire. "I couldn't tell which-a-way or where to turn, but he stepped right out and led me straight along home!"

"If that goat could lead you through a storm like this," spoke up Pappy, "he could lead you through anything! And you never need fear getting lost between here and the schoolhouse."

"I reckon you're right," agreed Mammy.

After that there was nothing to keep Hubert from going to school during the rest of the year.

Every day through the fall, the winter, and the spring, he and his goat zigzagged down the mountain trail together. Hubert learned to write and to figure sums and to read. But for all the time the goat spent in school, the only thing he ever learned was how to chew tobacco.

But the goat was never left out of anything, not even from the speakings on

the last day of school. The children went into the woods that day and gathered armfuls of bright red mountain laurel, and pale pink rhododendron. They plucked great bunches of shiny heart leaves and then made garlands to hang about the little stage at the end of the schoolroom. When they were finished it looked beautiful.

The lamps were lighted that night. The mothers and fathers and all their kin were there to hear the children speak their pieces and hardly anybody made a mistake. When his turn came Hubert walked proudly out upon the stage. But before he reached the center he heard a trip-trip-tripping. He turned and looked and there was the goat stepping along behind him.

"Go back where you belong," whispered Hubert, but the goat did not care to go back. He stood quietly while Hubert recited his piece. Hubert finished without a mistake and all the people clapped.

"Hurray! Hurray for Hubert!" they shouted.

Hubert bowed politely as the teacher had taught him to, and marched from the stage, but the goat, spying the beautiful green garlands hanging upon the wall, went over and took a nip. Finding them tasty, he braced himself, pulled them down from the wall and stood in the bright light in the middle of the stage, chewing with gusto.

"Hurray! Hurray for the goat!" shouted all the people, laughing and clapping as the curtain went down.

Balto's Race Against Death

By Irma H. Taylor

THE pale face of Dr. Curtis Welch grew very serious as he looked about the hospital room. He knew that he faced a hard fight—and all alone! He was the only doctor in the little town of Nome, Alaska, that bitter, cold winter in 1925.

Already three people were dead.

On the hospital beds lay twenty-five sick people. They had diphtheria, a terrible throat disease. If it should get out of control, it would sweep like wildfire over hundreds of square miles. Eleven thousand Eskimos and white people were in danger!

"We've got to have help," Dr. Welch said in a worried voice. "I mean help from the outside!"

"Yes, it's getting away from us," agreed a nurse. "Maybe some town can send us more doctors. If we were only on the railroad, or if the sea weren't frozen! This load is too much for you alone."

"It is not doctors or nurses we need," said Dr. Welch. "It is medicine. I have hardly five shots of antitoxin left, and that is six years old. Maybe it is no good." He clasped his thin fingers. If he could shoot fresh antitoxin into the arms of the people who were well, they probably would not get sick.

The nurse spoke eagerly. "Can't you radio to the United States for antitoxin?"

"Yes, but it will take six weeks to get here. By that time we may have one of the worst disasters in history."

"But, Doctor, couldn't they reach us sooner with airplanes?" broke in the nurse.

"Not through this weather. No pilot could make it, and it is fifty degrees below zero." The doctor looked very grave. "Our only hope is to get antitoxin from some place closer. Take care of that Eskimo woman's throat while I call the radio station."

A few minutes later the cry for help was flashing across the snows. As people heard the bad news, they were much alarmed. Nome was up in the Arctic Circle, four hundred miles from the nearest railroad and frozen in by the sea. Yet help must be sent at once.

A doctor in southern Alaska heard the message. He happened to have a good supply of antitoxin, and immediately wired Dr. Welch: "I am sending antitoxin to Nenana on today's train." Nenana was the town closest to Nome on the railroad.

So the precious twenty-pound package was started on its journey. After the three hundred miles by train, it must be carried six hundred and fifty miles over the cruel

243

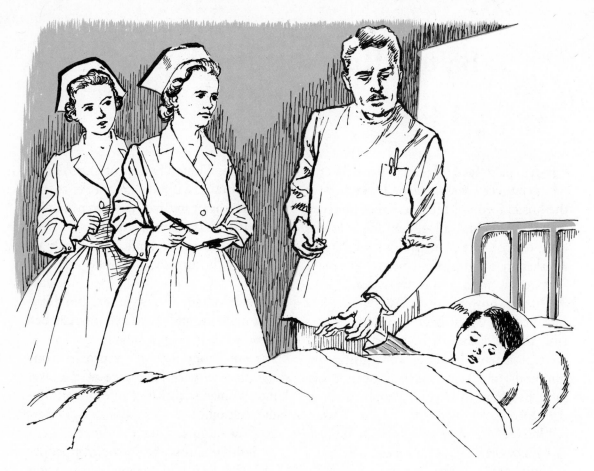

snowbound trail stretching between Nenana and Nome.

Only dogs could make it!

Again the radio sent out a call—this
time for drivers of dog teams. These
drivers are known as mushers and their
dogs as huskies, the right name for what
are sometimes called Eskimo dogs. At
once brave mushers picked out their
strongest dogs, hitched them to their
sleds, and hurried to the trail. The six-
hundred-and-fifty mile trail had never
been covered in less than nine days. But
this was a race against death, with eleven
thousand lives at stake!

At eleven o'clock on Tuesday evening,
January 27, the package on which so
many lives depended was taken off the
train. The first musher, waiting with his
dog team, took it eagerly and set out on
the trail.

The great relay race had begun. Each
musher would struggle on until he reached
the next man, twenty-five to one hundred
miles away.

We do not know much about the first
heroes who carried the medicine. We
know their names and the route they
took. But the greatest honor has been
paid to the two mushers who bore the
most dangerous part of the journey. Of
course, their skill and daring would not

244

have been enough. The others had to do their part also, but to these two fell the greatest tests of heroism. Their courage and that of the huskies who led their teams would have been hard to equal.

Shannon was the first musher. Every inch of the trail was familiar to him as he hurried down a frozen stream bed toward the Yukon River. Even in the dark he recognized which Indian dwelling he was passing. He knew he was making good time—more than five miles an hour.

Wednesday noon Shannon, tired but happy, turned the package over to the second musher. It was time for Shannon to stop, because his dogs were worn out. Losing no time, the second stout team plunged down the trail. By seven o'clock in the evening they had reached the Yukon River.

One hundred and fifty miles in twenty hours!

If the next teams could only keep up the pace! Just twenty-four hours later the antitoxin was three hundred and fifty miles on its way.

Friday afternoon it was placed in the hands of Leonard Seppala, known far and wide as "the king of dog-team drivers." This daring musher had come out from Nome to meet the medicine. He had covered two hundred miles of difficult trail in four days. Now, with no chance to rest, his picked team of Siberian dogs turned back on the trail.

Seppala hoped to carry the antitoxin all the way back to Nome so that it would get there Saturday afternoon. This would mean covering those two hundred miles in one day! Even in the fresh fallen snow! And with the temperature down below zero.

His team soon came to the edge of the ice-covered Norton Bay. Anxiously he looked out over the frozen surface, for the direct route to Nome lay across this bay. It would be safer to take the land route around it, but that would add almost another hundred miles. If he followed the land, maybe the antitoxin would arrive too late. Seppala decided quickly. It would be the short, dangerous way.

"Gee, Togo!" he cried, and the beautiful forty-eight-pound husky dog headed over the ice.

The musher watched the sixteen-year-old dog with a thrill of pride. Togo was a natural leader. He was a wonder at picking up the trail, and the other dogs knew they must obey him.

It was now dark. The condition of ice worried Seppala. Any minute it might break up and drift out to sea. Sometimes before they realized that the ice was free, travelers have been carried for miles on a loose ice cake. Some have been blown out into Bering Sea and drowned.

Horrible thoughts crowded into Seppala's mind. "Suppose the bay ice should suddenly crack up. We would be carried to open water and drift helplessly all night. Nobody could rescue us. My dogs would freeze to death—and so would I— if we did not drown first. And the antitoxin would be lost, somewhere on the bottom of the sea. They trusted it to me, and I must get through."

Speed—there lay his safety. Togo

picked his way carefully as the team raced along. Each husky seemed to know that Seppala was depending upon him. They loved this master who never struck with a whip.

Midnight came. Seppala wondered whether they were halfway across. How cold it was! Didn't he hear a cracking noise? His heart stood still! Togo raced on as if he knew the danger.

At last the sky turned gray. The musher looked eagerly for signs of land. Ahead lay only an icy stretch.

No, wasn't that a shadowy coast line a bit to the right? A few minutes later he was sure. Another mile slipped by. They would make it safely—the ice would hold!

"My good dogs!" he cried proudly. "Gee, Togo!"

Togo led the team up on the snowy bank, and the treacherous bay ice was left behind. Seppala hummed a little song. Now if this team he loved could only go the rest of the way.

Suddenly, as he rounded a turn, he saw a dog team and musher waiting on the trail. Much as he would have liked to press on himself, he knew it would be wiser to let this fresh team of dogs take over.

"Hello, Olson," he called, stopping his sled beside the new team. "Here is the antitoxin." He smiled cheerfully as he handed over the package to the musher.

"Things are worse in Nome . . . another death!" said Olson. His fingers were busy tying the package to his sled. "You made wonderful time, Seppala."

Olson and his seven dogs were off. Before their twenty-five-mile run was over, these dogs were almost frozen.

With great relief Olson handed the antitoxin to the last musher. Gunnar Kasson, who lived in Nome, had been waiting in an empty cabin for two days and nights. He had not even lain down, because he was afraid he might fall asleep and then miss Olson. Thirteen stouthearted dogs made up his team.

He said to Olson, "I am going to take the antitoxin into the cabin for a few minutes. The terrible wind may have frozen it."

Although the men waited inside the cabin for two hours, the weather kept getting colder. It was thirty degrees below. Snow began to fall. Every time they looked outside, the flakes were pelting down all the faster. A snowstorm meant dangerous going, Kasson knew. But he said, "There is no use waiting any longer."

Stepping outside, he called his lead dog, "Hey, Balto!"

Thirteen balls of fur scrambled out of their warm nests in the snow.

"Here, Balto. Here, boy!"

A handsome husky with a glossy coat ran to his place at the head of the traces. As Kasson fastened the dog into the harness, he said, "Tonight we'll have a hard pull. We have to make it through, boy!"

The dog pricked up his ears and raised intelligent eyes as if he understood.

Thirty-four miles away lay the next town, a little place called Safety. They must reach it before snowbanks could pile up and block the trail.

"Mush!" cried Kasson.

The dogs headed out bravely on the trail following the coast. It was terribly hard pulling. Although animals and sled sank into the heavy snow, the team struggled on.

"Whew, I never felt a colder wind!" thought Kasson, trying to pull his long reindeer coat closer around him. Sealskin boots reached to his hips, and over these he wore sealskin trousers. His head was protected by a reindeer hood. But the fierce eighty-mile gale whipped right through the skins.

Their way led straight into the wind. How could he or the dogs face it? He feared they would all freeze to death. Even though they kept going, how long could they stay on the trail?

Something else made Kasson very uneasy. The ice under his feet was in constant motion from ocean ground swells. He turned the dogs in closer to the shore line. Now he was crossing the mouth of a frozen river.

Suddenly he realized that Balto was in trouble.

The lead dog had stepped into a pool of water, an overflow that had run up on the ice. Unless Balto's feet could be dried off immediately, the skin would stick to the ice and be torn off. Then he would have to drop out—and he was the only lead dog in the team. It was a bad moment. Just then Kasson saw the one thing which could save Balto's feet—a snowdrift a few yards away

"Gee, Balto!" he shouted, and the dog turned sharply to the right.

When Balto felt the soft snow, he knew just what to do. He worked his paws in the snow until they were dry. Now the skin was safe. Kasson breathed a sigh of relief.

Starting off again, he headed the team up a six-hundred-foot hill. Here there was nothing to stop the fury of the wind howling in off the sea. Kasson's lips set tightly. This hill was the spot he feared more than any other. Near the top he discovered that his right cheek had no feeling. It was frozen. He grabbed some snow and rubbed the cheek until it felt alive again.

He was glad to leave the hill behind. Next came a flat stretch six miles long. He wondered whether they would ever get across it, for the wind was picking up masses of snow and hurling them. Kasson was choked and blinded. He strained to catch sight of the dogs. The dog nearest the sled was not even a blur. He held up his hand—no use, he could not see it!

His heart sank. Lost—he was hopelessly lost. The antitoxin would never reach Nome.

Yet the sled was moving steadily on. There was one hope left—that the dogs could keep the trail themselves. Kasson thought, "Balto will not fail me!"

The heroic lead dog never hesitated. Hurrying straight ahead, he scented the trail on the glaring, wind-swept ice. For two hours the musher held to the sled and trusted everything blindly to Balto.

They entered the tiny village of Solomon. Kasson did not even see the cabins. In this village a message was waiting for

him: "Stop in Solomon until the storm clears. Then go on to Safety. Ed Rohn is there with a fresh team. Let him finish the race."

Kasson sped on through the storm, not knowing that he had passed Solomon—not dreaming he had missed an important message.

If anything, the wind grew more bitter in the next twelve miles. Kasson was filled with joy when finally he caught sight of an old log store. He was in the village of Safety. His wonderful Balto had followed the trail!

Kasson saw that all the houses were

dark. Not knowing that another musher was waiting here, he thought, "Shall I stop for help? It would mean a long delay. There may not be any dogs in town strong enough to mush through the storm. Balto knows the trail; there is no other dog like him."

Speeding past the dark hotel, the team soon left Safety behind. Just twenty-one miles to go. The trail followed the shore of Bering Sea.

An angry wind whipped in from the sea. "I will tear you off the sled!" it seemed to cry. Kasson clung the tighter.

He was growing very tired. The dogs too, were slowing up, almost worn out by the long, cruel grind. Deep drifts made the pulling terribly hard. Yet they struggled bravely on. They would reach the goal—or die in the traces!

Kasson was thinking of many things;

the rosy flames of a warm fire, how wonderful it would feel when he got to Nome. Would all his dogs make it through? Too bad to lose even one—it must not be Balto! What wouldn't he give for a drink of steaming hot coffee? How far away was Nome? Fifteen miles? Twelve miles? How many more sick people had died? He must hurry—hurry—

Just then Kasson felt the sled pitch roughly. The next instant he was flung into the snow. As the sled overturned in a great drift, Balto slowed down and stopped the team. The dogs began to bark and fight, tangling up their harness.

Kasson jumped up and put the sled back on both runners. Then, lashing his whip, he quieted the dogs. It took him some time to straighten their harness in the dark. When they were ready to start again, he reached down to see whether the antitoxin was securely fastened.

What a horrible moment—the antitoxin was gone!

Crawling on his hands and knees, he hunted frantically in the snow. The sled had turned over on the right. Surely he would find the metal can there—if he had not lost it miles back on the trail. Could that have happened?

No, thank heaven, here it was!

His heart began to beat again. This time he tied the package very securely.

As they set out, the snowfall seemed lighter. At times he could see a bit of trail ahead. Then in the half-light he saw that two dogs were suffering—the two that had been frozen a few weeks before. The poor creatures were limping stiffly. Stopping the team, he fastened rabbitskin covers over these two dogs; but it didn't help much, for the cold went right

through. If they should die, he would leave them and press on. If all the dogs should die, he would still go on, carrying the antitoxin in his arms. Nome—he must get to Nome!

He wished for morning as the hours dragged by. Now he was running behind the sled, for the team was staggering. "Keep going, Balto!" he cried. "We're almost there!" It seemed that the team could not last another mile.

He was straining his eyes looking for the lumber mill at the edge of Nome.

At last it appeared out of the falling snow. Thank God, they had made it— they had made it to Nome! It was 5:36 in the morning of Monday, February 2—

just five and a half days after the start at Nenana.

The dogs seemed to know that the end of the great race was here. They hurried past the mill, past a row of wooden houses. Kasson heard people shouting, knew they were running after him. He turned to the left—there was the hospital. The next thing he knew, Dr. Welch was wringing his hand. "You got here in time!" said the doctor joyfully. The crowd shouted.

Half frozen and almost blinded Kasson dropped down into the snow. With tears in his eyes he started to pull ice splinters out of Balto's paws.

"Balto!" he cried. "Wonderful dog! You brought us through!"

Billy, the Dog That Made Good

By Ernest Thompson Seton

He was the biggest fool pup I ever saw—chock-full of life and spirits; always going at racing speed; generally into mischief; nearly breaking his neck over some small matter; breaking his heart if his master did not notice him; chewing up clothing, hats, and boots; digging up garden stuff that he could not eat; going direct from the pigsty to frolic in the baby's cradle; getting kicked in the ribs by horses and tossed by cows; but still the same, hilarious, rollicking, good-natured pup, and given by common consent the name of Silly Billy.

It was maddening to find on the first cold morning that he had chewed up one's leather glove; but it was worse to have that good-natured little idiot come wagging his tail, offering the remaining glove as much as to say that one glove was enough for anyone. You had to forgive him, and it did not matter much whether you did or not, for the children adored him. Their baby arms were around his neck as much of the time as he could spare from his duties, and, in a sense, those protecting arms were around him all the time. The father realized this fact when one day the puppy pulled down a piece of sacking that hung on the smoke-house pipe, upsetting the stove and burning up the smoke-house and all the dry meat in it. Bob Yancy was furious, for his whole winter's meat stock was gone. He took his shotgun and went forth determined to put that fool dog forever out of mischief. But he met the unexpected. He found his victim with two baby arms about his fuzzy neck; little Ann Yancy was hugging her "doggy," and what could *he* do? "It's my Billy! You shan't touch him! Go away, you naughty daddy!" And the matter ended in a disastrous defeat for daddy.

Every member of the family loved Silly Billy, but they wished that he might soon develop at least a glimmer of common dog sense, for he was already past the time when most bull terriers' puppyhood is ended. Although he was in time to take a place among his master's hunting dogs, he was not yet ready for this honor.

Bob Yancy was a hunter, a professional. His special line was killing bears, mountain lions, lynxes, wolves, and other "varmints" for whose destruction the state pays a bounty. He was ever ready to increase the returns by taking with him amateur hunters who paid him well for the privilege of being present.

Much of this hunting was done on what is commonly called the chase. The morning rally, the far search for a trail, the warming hunt, the hot pursuit, and the finish with a more or less thrilling

251

fight—that was ideal. But it was seldom fully realized. The mountains were too rough. The game either ran off altogether, or, by crossing some impassable barrier, got rid of the hunters, and then turned on the dogs to scatter them in flight.

That was the reason for the huge bear traps that were hanging in Yancy's barn. Those dreadful things would not actually hold the bear prisoner, but when, with a convenient log, they were gripped on his paw, they held him back so that the hunters, even on foot, could overtake the victim.

The dogs, however, were the interesting part of the pursuit. Three kinds were needed: perfect trailers, whose noses could follow with sureness the oldest, coldest trail; swift runners for swift game; and intelligent fighters. The fighters had, of course, to be brave, but intelligence was more important, for the dogs were expected to nip at the victim from behind and spring back from his counter blow rather than to close at final grips.

Thus there were bloodhounds and greyhounds as well as a bulldog in the Yancy pack, together with a few half-breeds. Most of the pack had marked personality. There was Croaker, a small lady hound with a sensitive nose and a miserable little croak for a bay. You could not hear her fifty feet away; but fortunately Big Ben followed her everywhere, and he had a voice like the bell for which he was named. He always stuck close to

Croaker and translated her feeble whispers into tones that all the world within a mile or two could understand.

Then there was Old Thunder, a very old, very brave dog, with a fine nose. He was a combination of all good gifts and had been through many fights, but had escaped destruction, thanks to his shrewdness. Though slow and feeble now, he was the acknowledged leader of the pack, respected by dogs and men.

The bulldog is known for his courage rather than for his good judgment; hence the post of "bulldog to the pack" was often open. The last bulldog had been buried with the bones of the last grizzly. But Yancy had secured a new one, a wonder. He was the perfect product of a long line of fighting bulldogs, kept by a famous breeder in another state. When the new leader arrived, it was a large event to all the hunters. He was no disappointment; broad of head and chest, massive in the upper arm, and hard in the flank—a perfect beast of the largest size. The hunters at Yancy's knew at once that they had a fighting treasure in the Terrible Turk, who was even more surly and savage than most bulldogs.

It was with some distrust that he was turned loose on the ranch, because he was so unpleasant in his manner. There was a lack of dogginess about him in the gentle sense, and never did one of his race display a greater haughtiness. He did not try to hide his sense of superiority, and the pack seemed to accept him at his own value. Clearly they were afraid of him. He was given the right of way—avoided, indeed—by his future comrades. Only Silly Billy went bounding in hilarious friendliness to meet the great one, and a moment later flew howling with pain to hide in the arms of his little mistress.

In the next two weeks that passed about the ranch the Terrible Turk had quarreled with nearly every hound in the pack. There was only one that he had not actually injured, and that was Old Thunder. Even they met once or twice when Thunder was gnawing a bone, but each time he stood his ground and showed his teeth. There was a certain dignity about Thunder that even a dog will feel, and in this case the Terrible Turk retired.

In October word came that Old Reelfoot, a famous cattle-killing grizzly, had reappeared in the Arrow-Bell Cattle Range, and was up to his old tricks of destroying livestock. A big reward was offered for his destruction, several times as much as for an ordinary bear.

Bob Yancy was ablaze with hunter's fire when he heard the news. His only dread was that some rival might get ahead of him. It was a spirited procession that left the Yancy claim that morning, headed for the Arrow-Bell Ranch, the pack straggling along or forging ahead till ordered back in line by the huntsman. There was the venerable Thunder trotting by the heels of his old friend Midnight, Yancy's coal-black mare; and just before was the Terrible Turk with his red-rimmed eyes upturned at times to measure his nearness to the powerful, black mare's hoofs. Big Ben was near Croaker, of course. Next was a pack horse loaded with a huge steel

253

bear trap on each side, followed by pack horses with the camping outfit, and other hunters, the cook, and the writer of this story.

Everything was in fine shape for the hunt, and we were well started when trouble tumbled in among us. With many a yap of glee, there, bounding, came the foolish bull terrier, Silly Billy. Like a June bug among honeybees, like a crazy schoolboy in a council room, he rollicked and yapped, eager to be first, to be last, to take liberties with Thunder, to chase rabbits, ready for anything but what was wanted of him—to stay at home and mind his own business.

Bob might yell "Go home!" till he was hoarse. Silly Billy would only go off a little way and look hurt, then make up his mind that the boss was "only fooling" and didn't mean a word of it, and start in louder than ever.

No one wished him to come, but there was no way of stopping him; so Silly Billy came to have a place in the first bear hunt of the season.

That afternoon they arrived at the Arrow-Bell Ranch, and the expert bearman was shown the latest kill, a fine heifer barely touched. The grizzly would surely come back for his next meal. Yes, an ordinary grizzly would, but Reelfoot was an extraordinary animal. Just because it was the bear fashion to come again soon,

254

he might not return for a week. Yancy set a huge trap by this kill; but he also found the kill of a week gone by, five miles away, and by that set another trap. Then all retired to the ranch house.

Who that knows the grizzly will be surprised to hear that the night brought the hunters nothing, and that the next was blank? But the third morning showed that the huge brute had come to his older kill.

I shall not forget the thrills of that time. We passed the recent carcass near the ranch. It lay untouched and little changed. We rode on the five miles to the next. And before we were near, we felt there was something unusual in the air, for the dogs seemed excited. I could see nothing; but, while yet a hundred yards away, Bob was exclaiming, "A catch this time, sure enough."

Dogs and horses were all inspired. The Terrible Turk breasted his way to the front, and the rumbling in his chest was grand as an organ. Ahead, behind, and all around him was Silly Billy, yapping and tumbling.

There was the carcass still untouched. The place of the trap was vacant; log and all were gone; and all around were signs of an upset, many large tracks, so many that scarcely any were clear; but farther on we got the sign most sought, the thirteen-inch track of a monster grizzly, and the bunch on the right paw stamped it as Reelfoot's trail.

I had seen the joy blaze in Yancy's eyes before, but never as now. He glowed with the hunter's heat, and let the dogs run free, and urged them on with whoops and yells of "Sic him, boys! Ho, boys! sic him!" Not much urging was needed; the dogs were possessed of the spirit of the day. This way and that they circled, each for himself. The bear had walked around awhile before going off. It was Croaker that first had the real trail. Big Ben was there to let the whole world know; then Thunder indorsed the statement. Had it been Plunger that spoke, the rest would have paid no heed; but all the pack knew Thunder's voice, and his judgment was not open to question. They left their different tracks and flocked, behind the leader, baying deep and strong at every bound, while Turk came hurrying after, and Silly Billy tried to make up in noise for all he lacked in judgment.

Away we went, with the bawling pack as guides. The country was a wilderness of rocky gullies, dense thickets, and down timber, where fire and storm had piled the mountain slope with dead forest. But we kept on, and before an hour the dinning of the pack announced the bear at bay.

Creeping from trunk to trunk we went forward. The thought flashed up, "Which of us will come back alive!" What a din those dogs were making! Every one of them was in the chorus. They were yapping and baying, high and low, swaying this way and that; this meant that the bear was charging back and forth and still had some freedom.

"Look out now! Don't get too close!" said Yancy. "Log and all, he can cover fifty feet while you make ten, and I tell

255

you he won't bother about the dogs if he gets a chance at the men. He knows his game."

There were more thrills in the woods than the mere sounds accounted for. My hand trembled as I scrambled over the down timber. It was a moment of fierce excitement as I lifted the branches and could look so big), and charged his tormentors. They scattered like flies when one strikes at a swarm of them. But the log on the trap caught on a stump and held him, the dogs surged around, and now my view was clear.

This is the moment of all in the hunt. This is the time when you size up your

got my first view. But it was a disappointment. There was the pack, bounding, seething, yelling, and back of the brush was some brown fur; that was all. Suddenly the brushwood swayed and a shaggy mountain of flesh rushed forth, a tremendous grizzly (I never knew one hounds. This is the fiery furnace in which the metals all are tried. There was Old Thunder baying, tempting the bear to charge, but ever with an eye to the safe retreat; there was Croaker doing her duty; there were the greyhounds, yapping and nipping at his rear; there in the background, wisely waiting, saving his power for the right time, was the Terrible Turk; and here and there, bounding and yapping, was Silly Billy, dashing into the very jaws of death again and again, but saved by his restless activity, and proud of the bunch of bear's wool in his teeth.

Round and round they went, as Reelfoot made his short, furious charges, and Turk still kept in the background, baying hoarsely, biding his time for the favorable moment. And whichever side Old Thunder took, there Turk went too. Yancy rejoiced at this, for it meant that the fighting dog had good judgment.

The fighting and the baying swung behind a little bush. I wanted to see it all and tried to get near, but Yancy shouted out "Keep back!" He knew the habits of the bear and the danger of coming into range. But his shouting attracted the notice of the bear, and he charged straight for Bob.

Many a time before had Yancy faced a bear. This time he had his gun, but, perched on a small and shaky rotten log, he had no chance to shoot. As he swung for a clearer view he raised his rifle with a jerk, but the rotten log crashed under him, and Bob fell sprawling among the tumbled logs. The grizzly now had him in his power, and we were struck with horror. We had no power to stop that certain death; we dared not fire—the dogs and the man himself were right in line. The pack closed in. Their din was deafening; they sprang on the huge, haired flanks; they nipped the soggy heels; they hauled and held, and did their best; but they were as flies on a badger or as rats on a landslide. They held him not an instant. The small logs cracked as he rushed forward, and Bob would in a moment more be smashed with that huge paw, for now no human help was possible. Good Old Thunder saw the only way. It meant sure death for him, but it was the only way. He ceased all halfway dashing at the flank or heel and leaped at the bear's throat. One swift sweep of that great paw sent him reeling back, bruised and shaken. Still he rallied, rushed as though he knew it all must turn on him; when Turk, the mighty warrior, the hope and valor of the pack, who long had held back, sprang forward now and gripped with all his strength—on the bear? NO! shame of shames!—how shall I say the truth?—on *poor Old Thunder*, wounded, battered, winded, downed, seeking to save his master! On him the bulldog fastened with a grip of hate. This was what he had waited for; this was the time of times that he took to vent his pent-up jealous rage. He sprang from behind, dragged Thunder down, and held him, gasping, in the brushwood. The bear had freedom now to take revenge, for his only foe was gone; what could prevent him? But from the reeling, yapping pack there sprang a small white dog, not for the monster's heel, not for his flank, nor even for his massive shoulder, but for his face—the only place where a dog could count in such a sudden attack. He seized with an iron grip above the monster's eye, and the huge head jerking back made that small dog go flapping like a rag; however,

the dog hung on. The bear reared up to claw, and we realized for the first time that the small white dog was Silly Billy, none else, hanging on with all his might and weight.

Bob scrambled to his feet, escaped! The huge brute seized the small white body in his great paws, which looked like stumps of trees, just as a cat might seize a mouse. He wrenched him, quivering, and hurled him like a bundle far to one side, and wheeling for a moment paused to seek the greater foe, the man. The pack drew back. Four rifles rang, a long, deep snort, and Reelfoot's huge bulk sank limp on the storm-tossed logs. Then Turk, the traitor Turk, with chesty gurgle as a war cry, closed bravely on the dead brute's haunch and tore out the hair, while the pack sat lolling back, the battle done.

Bob Yancy's face was set. He had seen nearly all the fight, and we supplied the rest. Billy was wagging his tail, shaking and shivering with excitement. There were some red-stained slashes on his ribs. Bob greeted him affectionately, "You dandy. It's the finish that shows up the stuff a bear-dog is made of, and I tell you there isn't anything too good on Yancy's ranch for you. Good Old Thunder has saved my life before, but this is a new one. I never thought you'd show up this way."

"And you," he said to Turk, "I've just two words for you. Come here!" He took off his belt, put it through the collar of the Terrible Turk, and led him to one side. I turned my head away A rifle cracked, and the big, strong bulldog was no more. He had been tried in the fire and found wanting—a bully, a coward, a thing not fit to live.

In the triumphal procession heading homeward, on the front of Yancy's saddle was Billy, the hero of the day, his white coat stained with red. His body was stiff and sore, but his spirits were not lessened. He probably did not fully understand the feelings he had aroused in others; but he did know that he was having a glorious time, and that at last the world was returning the love he had so bounteously given to it. Old Thunder was riding on a pack horse. It was weeks before he got over the mauling he had had from the bear and the bulldog, and he was soon afterward put into honorable retirement on account of his age.

Billy was all right again in a month. A half year later he had shed his puppy ways, and his good dog sense came forth in strength. He had proved himself brave as a lion, full of energy, affectionate, true as steel. Within two years he was leader of the pack. They do not call him "Silly" now, but "Billy, the dog that made good."

Coronado's Ghost

By Robert M. Hyatt

STANDING in the doorway of the trailer, John Nelson shaded his eyes against the blazing glare of sun on alkali flats and confessed to a moment of fear. Death Valley? So vast, so deadly silent, so ominous! Maybe he had been rash in starting out on this foolhardy treasure hunt . . . certainly without water they would be in a bad spot.

He turned to the tanned, khaki-clad youth seated at the table littered with maps. "Ronnie," he said, "how far are we from Fool's Well?"

Ronnie made a rapid calculation. "About a hundred miles, Dad. We should make it tomorrow some time."

"I only hope we have enough water left to fill the radiator," the elder man said. "What luck breaking that hose."

Chuck Williams, Ronnie's California cousin, had just finished repairing the broken water hose. He grinned at the two Easterners.

"All set!" he sang out. "Let's fill 'er up and shove off. I'm nearly roasted!"

"We've got just about enough left in the tank," Ronnie told him. "We'll probably get a little thirsty tomorrow——"

"Not much!" Chuck exclaimed. "We'll reach Fool's Well by noon."

Late the next day the three parked their trailer near the base of the towering Funeral Mountains. The big moment had almost arrived. According to the yellowed parchment in John Nelson's possession, an ancient Spanish silver mine lay hidden somewhere in this great waste. Riches awaited them if they could find the secret cañon that held "a small circular valley twenty leagues northwest of Fool's Well."

Earlier in the forenoon they had come upon what they firmly believed to be "Fool's Well." Chuck, piloting the car, had sighted it from the rutty trail, a small oasis some five hundred yards below them, in the middle of which they could see a tiny pool of clear blue water. Taking buckets, Chuck and Ronnie had set off. But when they were within fifty yards of the oasis, which was nothing more than a scraggy clump of ocotillo, they discovered the reason for the name. As they reached a lower level, the "well" vanished into thin air. It was a "fool's" well indeed —a most convincing mirage!

However, now they were sure they were on the right trail. Twenty leagues due northwest, they had halted the car and trailer. And now came the breathless search for that long-lost silver mine.

"Let me see that map again," said John Nelson. "It says here that a dry stream bed leads to the mouth of a narrow cañon 'on the walls of which appear Indian pictographs. . . .' Now to find the dry stream bed."

A half hour's hard going brought them to a depression that proved to be the bed of an ancient river. Such rivers were quite common in the Southwest. Water had once filled them, but with the coming dryness the water seeped below, and they became known as "lost rivers."

They followed the river bed for a half dozen miles and came at last to an abrupt turn in its course. Ahead, fifty yards, rose the walls of a flinty cañon and between them the "river" lost itself. Near sundown they reached a portion of the cañon where the walls rose to dizzy heights above them. Their very tops were dyed a vivid flame by the sunset glow, but lower there was the growing twilight that is so sudden in this country. Soon darkness would be upon them.

"Let's hurry," urged John Nelson. "We haven't much water for tea; maybe there's a spring farther on." They had noticed a slightly cooler atmosphere as they entered the cañon, and on both sides green growths, mostly bizarre thorny bushes, raked them.

A faint wind had risen and, as they walked on, it grew in volume until it resembled the wailing of some awful demon.

"Br-rrr!" exclaimed Chuck. "Good thing I don't believe in ghosts! Did you ever hear anything like that?"

It was almost night when they stepped out into a vast circular valley that seemed, with the speck of lavender sky far above, like some abysmal well. It was then that the phenomenon of the howling wind was made clear. Directly in the middle of the valley they could barely see a funnel-like whirlwind. It was a sort of maelstrom, caused by some freak of the wind. In the gathering gloom it was a weird sight, its top lost far above the well-like valley.

"Gosh!" breathed Ronnie. "Do you suppose that goes on all the time? It looks like one of those Florida cyclones."

John Nelson set his pack down with a sigh of weariness. "I don't know how you boys feel, but I'm fagged out. Let's find a place to camp and explore tomorrow."

The suggestion was hailed with delight, for both boys were tottering with fatigue. Not far from the entrance of the round valley, they found a shallow cavern and, too tired to look for water, they drank sparingly from their canteens and munched a few crackers. Tomorrow would be a big day!

Dawn roused them from deep slumbers. The valley had become a place of beauty, with patches of lush green grass and small, strange-looking trees. It might have been another world. The mighty whirlwind, that could well have been revolving since Time began, was now a thing of living gold in the vivid sunshine.

After a hearty breakfast, and a drink of clear, cold water from a tiny spring they had found bubbling a hundred yards away, they set out to find the lost mine of the Spaniards. The walls of the cañon leading into the valley were covered with strange hieroglyphics—symbols of a vanished race of aborigines. Ronnie took several photographs of them. His enthusiasm was boundless, but it was John Nelson who made a startling discovery. They had been walking slowly, intending to make a circuit of the valley to find signs of the ancient mine workings, when he suddenly halted.

"Look here," he said, pointing to a large rock. "This is Spanish, isn't it, Chuck?"

Young Williams peered closely at the faint tracings on the rock and then shouted, "Jupiter! Listen to this: 'I, Francisco Vasquez de Coronado, in the year of grace 1542, found within this valley the Tower of Winds'!"

Ronnie gasped. "Imagine—the great Coronado was here! Was right here beside this rock and wrote those words!"

"I suppose this was during his search for the Seven Cities of Cibola," said John Nelson, "but I never knew he had entered California."

"Say," exclaimed Chuck, "maybe it was Coronado who found the silver mine we're looking for. Maybe——"

"No, Chuck," said John Nelson. "I hardly think so. It must have been discovered much later than the sixteenth century. Still, why was this strange whirlwind never reported?"

Ronnie, who had made several pictures of the ancient legend, had gone on ahead. Suddenly they heard him shout.

"I've found it!" he cried. He was dancing a jig as they came up. "Look— the mine! Coronado's old mine!"

There were, indeed, indications of an ancient mine. There was the huge slag pile, and beyond that a framework of rotted wooden beams.

"But where are the bars of silver stored?" Chuck wanted to know. "Or did they make bars then?"

"A fine mining engineer you are!" snorted Ronnie. "Think you ought to find them lying all around? Come, let's explore the dark tunnel there."

John Nelson had lighted a small storm lantern. "Be careful," he advised. "Most anything may be using that cave as its home—an old rattler at least."

The entrance of the cave was quite small. Fifty feet beyond, it became a large chamber where their voices echoed and bounded back and forth in a weird manner. Far above them, they could see, in the bright rays of the lantern, monstrous stalactites that sparkled in a thousand colors. The floor was damp and the air of the place chilly. Two offshoots of the main cavern they explored to their ends.

John Nelson joined the boys in the big main room. "Well," he said, "it's possible the silver isn't stored here at all, you know. But wait!" He drew the map out of his pocket and holding the lantern close, began reading it.

'Aha!" he exclaimed after a moment. "The silver is here—somewhere. Listen to this: '. . . ore in goodly quantity where the sun falls. . . .' The words are faded out here. Now, just what does that mean, 'where the sun falls'?"

Chuck shook his head. "It's got me."

"I know!" Ronnie started for the opening of the mine. "Look," he said. "The sun only shines down in here for a short time each day. It would depend upon the time of year—during the winter it wouldn't shine in here at all."

Chuck laughed. "All very clear, Dr. Watson, but what time of year did the writer of this thing mean?"

"There's just one way to settle it," observed John Nelson. "We'll watch. It's about noon now, and if the sun passes overhead at all, it will be an easy matter to see where any stray beams fall."

But the sun didn't appear overhead. So each one of the three started for a point where it seemed likely the sun's rays might touch. About three in the afternoon they returned to the starting place. They had found nothing.

"The only thing I found, besides hot sand and rocks," said Chuck, "was a big pile of reeds that must've been chopped down where some spring once bubbled."

"Well," said John Nelson with a note of disappointment, "I guess our mine venture has been a will-o'-the-wisp. But we've had a lot of fun anyway."

Deciding to remain the night and start

back in the morning, the three made their camp comfortable, ate dinner, and settled down for a quiet chat. But Ronnie was restless. Picking up a flashlight, he sauntered off, bent on making another search.

It was near twilight that John Nelson and Chuck heard strange sounds from the cañon. At first it seemed as if the ever-wailing wind had suddenly grown louder, but soon they heard something else—something that made their hearts pound. Yells, fierce blood-thirsty yells. They grew in volume.

"In heaven's name, what's that?" queried John Nelson.

Chuck sat as if turned to stone.

Then into the valley, hoofs thudding against the rocks, poured a strange procession. Men on horseback appeared, bronzed men, with blankets flying and long streamers of feathers. Indians! They rode like the wind, blasting the air with frenzied yells.

Chuck leaped up. John Nelson followed him. The words of the latter were almost drowned in the din: "Chuck, am I dreaming? Or am I crazy?"

Chuck, stiff with fright, could make no answer. He stood as if rooted to the spot. And then into the valley came another sight that made their brains whirl: A full hundred mounted men in armor. Armor! Bright, gleaming steel armor! They followed the Indians, whose column had swerved to the other side of the valley.

Another procession entered the valley —a string of heavily laden pack horses and more mounted men. They were talking and singing gaily. As they disappeared, Ronnie came running up, breathless, his face blanched.

"Did you see 'em?" he panted. "Those men in armor. It was Coronado and his army! Coronado!"

It was all beyond conception. The three withdrew to the darkest corner of their camp and listened to the sounds of another camp in the making across the valley.

"What do you suppose it all means?" asked Chuck.

"I think we've gone crazy—or else time has turned backwards." Ronnie's voice was filled with awe.

"Well," said John Nelson, "we might as well get some sleep. We'll probably know in the morning."

But they got little sleep that night. Strange, unearthly sounds rent the stillness and by dawn they were in a state bordering panic.

When, about seven o'clock, they saw two men riding toward them, John Nelson took charge. "I don't know what this means," he said, "but let me handle it."

"Hello!" sang out one of the strangers. "Didn't know anybody was in here." This was no man from some dim page of history—he was, rather, quite modern in appearance.

"Suppose you thought you were having a nightmare last night, eh?" he laughed.

"That we did," answered John Nelson. "We're still not sure that we didn't."

"Well, it's all quite tame," replied the newcomer. "We're shooting a picture up here—called 'Coronado's Ghost.' "

"Then all this—Indians and every-thing," Nelson began, "are merely——"

"Props," said the picture man. "A few of the redskins are real, from the reservation; but most of 'em are fresh from wild Hollywood!" he grinned. "Well, I guess we'll get started shooting. This is a swell spot for our last sequence. See you later!" The two strangers rode off.

"Pooh," said Chuck. "A movie outfit—'Coronado's Ghost,' huh? Well, it's an appropriate place."

Ronnie had wandered off again. Suddenly they heard his shout. He was turning cartwheels when they reached him.

It was at the pile of old reeds. They were scattered all about and some of them were broken. Ronnie held one out.

"Look!" he cried. "Here's our silver!"

John Nelson whistled. "My word, it's true. Look at that, will you! Why, there's hundreds of pounds of silver in those reeds. Come on, lads, let's get busy."

"How did you discover it, Ronnie?" Chuck asked, as he began breaking the dried shell from a long strip of silver.

"I didn't," answered Ronnie. "Coronado did. His horses ran through this pile and scattered the reeds about. Good old Coronado!"

Sah-mee and the Rabbit Hunt

By Muriel H. Fellows

THE BIG, round sun came peeping over the edge of the purple mountain, making the sky all pink and orange and gold. It shone brightly on the dry, sandy desert at the foot of the mesa. The sun tried to shine into the mud and stone houses of the Indian pueblo on top of the mesa. But the sun's rays had a hard time getting inside the houses because the windows were so very small.

However, when at last one ray of sunshine did find its way into his room, Sah-mee awoke. He yawned and stretched, and then crept out of the warm blankets and woolly sheepskins of his bed. He pulled on his white trousers, red shirt, and soft deerskin moccasins.

Sah-mee's black eyes shone with excitement as he fastened his silver belt around his waist. He remembered that something very pleasant was going to happen that day. Sah-mee's father had promised to take him on a rabbit hunt, and had made him a little curved rabbit stick, with which to kill rabbits. Sah-mee hoped that some day he would be able to throw his rabbit stick as well as Father threw his. Sah-mee tied a red band around his head and ran to find Moho.

Moho was Sah-mee's little sister. She was helping Mother cook breakfast. Mother was making puvulu. She put corn meal, sugar, and water into a bowl, and then Moho stirred and stirred until she had made a thick dough. While Moho was making the dough, Mother put a pan of water over the fire. When the water was very hot, she put some mutton fat into it and then dropped little balls of the dough into the hot water and mutton fat.

"Breakfast is ready, Sah-mee," said Moho.

The puvulu smelled good to Sah-mee for he was very hungry, but he was so excited that he could hardly eat.

"Father will be ready to start on the hunt very soon," said Mother.

"I wish that I could go with you, Sah-mee," said Moho.

Sah-mee laughed. "Girls do not hunt," he said. "You must stay here and help Mother get the fire ready for rabbit stew. We shall have a big feast tonight. You must help Mother carry water from the spring, too."

"Sometimes I wish I were a boy," sighed Moho.

While Sah-mee was eating breakfast, Father came home. He had been down to the cornfield, looking after his corn plants and loosening up the hard, dry earth with a sharp-pointed digging stick.

When Sah-mee was ready, he and Father started down the steep trail which led into the desert. Many other men and boys from the pueblo were also going rabbit hunting. They walked swiftly over the desert trail, their soft moccasins making no noise on the hard, dry earth and rough stones. Little prairie dogs chattered and scolded when they came near, and then with a little flip of their stubby tails, they disappeared into their burrows.

Sah-mee was only seven summers old, but he felt very, very old indeed! How much he wanted to catch a rabbit! He wanted to hear Father say, "Sah-mee, you are a great hunter! Some day you will be the greatest hunter in the pueblo!"

When Sah-mee and Father had gone away, Moho and Mother found many things to do. Moho helped her mother brush the floor very clean with a queer little broom made of twigs. They shook and folded the blankets and washed the cooking bowls.

"We shall need some water from the spring, Moho," said her mother, pointing to an empty water jar.

"It is hard work to carry water," sighed Moho as she went to get her heavy olla. It was not hard work to go down the hill with the empty jar. For there Moho could look up at the blue sky and the fluffy white clouds. But when she had filled the olla at the spring, the jar was very heavy indeed.

Moho wrapped the olla in a blanket and lifted it to her back. Some women who were filling their ollas at the spring, helped her to hold the jar on her back by a strap which they fastened across her forehead.

The hot sun beat down upon her as she climbed the trail. Her feet slipped in the hot sand. But Moho knew that this was the only way in which her family could get water, except for the little rain water which they were able to store in big clay jars, or the water which they obtained from melted snow in the winter.

"I think my leggings should be cleaned, Mother," said Moho, when she came back with the water. "I splashed mud on them when I was getting water at the spring. While you are cleaning them, I am going to hunt for some little colored stones in the desert."

"No, Moho," said her mother. "Do not go until I have finished cleaning your leggings. Never go into the desert without them. Think how those thorny plants would scratch your legs!"

"And the snakes! I forgot about snake bites," said Moho with a shudder.

"Snakes can't bite through buckskin," said Mother as she smeared white clay over Moho's leggings.

When she had finished this cleaning, Mother sat down in the bright sunshine in front of the house and began to make a clay bowl. Moho wrapped the strips of white buckskin around her legs and went down to the desert to gather colored stones and pebbles. When she was tired, she came and watched Mother as she rolled the soft clay between the palms of her hands, and wound the coils round and round until the clay bowl grew higher and higher.

"When will Sah-mee come home?" asked Moho.

"When the sun begins to sink down into the desert and the purple shadows

fall over the mesa," answered her mother.

Sah-mee had never been on a rabbit hunt, but he had heard Father tell about it many times, so he knew just what to do. Father had said that the men and boys would beat the bushes and make a great noise. This would frighten the rabbits and they would try to get away. Then the men and boys would throw their rabbit sticks and kill the rabbits.

Sah-mee was excited. His black eyes sparkled. He beat the bushes and shouted. Just then a little animal ran out of the bushes. It was very much frightened. It ran toward Sah-mee instead of running away from him. Sah-mee saw that the little animal was a baby fox. Sah-mee forgot that he wanted to kill a rabbit. He forgot that he wanted to be a great hunter. He thought only of the poor, little, frightened baby fox.

Sah-mee saw that the little thing was too tired and frightened to run away. He took it up in his arms.

"Poor little fox," he said, gently. He stroked its ears, and the little animal tried to get away. "I will not harm you," he whispered. "I will take you home to Moho and she will keep you for a pet."

Sah-mee looked around for Father but could not find him. Father and the others had gone farther away into the desert in search of rabbits. Sah-mee was not frightened. He knew the way home. He could not hunt and take care of the baby fox, too. Besides, he was more tired than he had ever been before.

Sah-mee started up the steep trail to the village. He held the baby fox tightly in his arms. When he was about halfway up the trail, Sah-mee remembered that he had left his rabbit stick lying under a sage bush in the desert.

"I will go back and get it tomorrow," he thought to himself.

The trail seemed very steep and rough and rocky to Sah-mee. He could feel the heart of the frightened little fox thumping against his own.

"We will soon be home," he whispered into the little brown ear.

Moho was waiting for Sah-mee to come home. When she saw him coming, she ran out of the house to meet him. "How many rabbits did you bring home, Sah-mee?" she called.

Then suddenly, she caught sight of the little brown bundle of fur in Sah-mee's arms. Moho was very much excited. "What have you there?" she asked.

"It isn't a rabbit," answered Sah-mee. "It is a little fox. I couldn't kill him, Moho, for he is only a baby. I brought him to you for a pet."

Moho understood. She reached out and took the little animal in her arms. "I always wished for a little fox for a pet," she said.

By and by Father and the other men and boys came home, bringing many rabbits with them. They had missed Sah-mee and had hoped to find him at home, so they were glad to see him waiting for them.

The Indian women were all ready to make the rabbit stew.

Sah-mee was a little worried. He wondered what Father and the others would say. To go on a rabbit hunt and not bring home one rabbit! To go on a rabbit hunt and bring home a fox! He hoped that the boys would not laugh at him.

"I caught a little fox," said Sah-mee to Father. "I could not kill him because he is just a baby. I brought him to Moho for a pet."

Father smiled. He put his hand on Sah-mee's head. "You are a good boy, Sah-mee," he said. "We killed so many rabbits that there will be food enough for all for many days. I am glad that you remembered that a good Indian never kills a baby animal."

Onawandah

By Louisa M. Alcott

Long ago when hostile Indians haunted the great forests, and every settlement had its fort for the protection of the inhabitants, in one of the towns on the Connecticut River lived Parson Bain and his little son and daughter.

The wife and mother was dead; but an old servant, Becky, did her best to make Reuben and Eunice good children. Her direst threat, when they were naughty, was, "The Indians will come and fetch you if you don't behave." So they grew up in great fear of the red men. Even the friendly Indians, who sometimes came for food or powder, were regarded with suspicion by the people. No man went to work without his gun near by. On Sundays, when they trudged to the meeting-house, all carried the trusty rifle on the shoulder, and while the pastor preached, a sentinel mounted guard at the door, to give warning if canoes came down the river or a face peered from the wood.

One autumn night, when the first heavy rains were falling and a cold wind whistled through the valley, a knock came at the minister's door and, opening it, he found an Indian boy, ragged, hungry, and foot-sore, who begged for food and shelter. In his broken way, he told how he had fallen ill and been left to die by enemies who had taken him from

his own people, months before; how he had wandered for days till almost sinking; that he had come now to ask for help, led by the light in the parsonage window.

"Send him away, Master, or harm will come of it. He is a spy, and we shall be scalped by the murdering Injuns who are waiting in the wood," said old Becky, harshly; while little Eunice hid in the old servant's ample skirts, and twelve-year-old Reuben laid his hand on his cross-bow, ready to defend his sister if need be.

But the good man drew the poor lad in, saying, with his friendly smile: "Shall not a Christian be as hospitable as a godless

savage? Come in, child, and be fed; you sorely need rest and shelter."

Leaving his face to express the gratitude he had no words to tell, the boy, whose name was Onawandah, sat by the comfortable fire and ate like a famished wolf, while Becky muttered and the children eyed the dark youth from a distance. Something in his pinched face, wounded foot, and eyes full of dumb pain and patience, touched the little girl's tender heart, and, yielding to an impulse, she brought her own cup of new milk and, setting it beside the stranger, ran to hide behind her father, suddenly remembering that this was one of the dreaded Indians.

"That was well done, little daughter. Thou shalt love thine enemies, and share thy bread with the needy. See, he is smiling; that pleased him, and he wishes us to be his friends."

But Eunice ventured no more that night, and quaked in her little bed at the thought of the strange boy sleeping on a blanket before the fire below. Reuben hid his fears better, and resolved to watch while others slept; but was asleep as soon as his curly head touched the pillow, and dreamed of tomahawks and war-whoops till morning.

Next day, neighbors came to see the waif, and one and all advised sending him away as soon as possible, since he was doubtless a spy, as Becky said, and would bring trouble of some sort.

"When he is well, he may go wherever he will; but while he is too lame to walk, weak with hunger, and worn out with weariness, I will harbor him. He can not feign suffering and starvation like this. I shall do my duty, and leave the consequences to the Lord," answered the parson, with such pious firmness that the neighbors said no more.

But they kept a close watch upon Onawandah, when he went among them, silent and submissive, but with the proud air of a captive prince, and sometimes a fierce flash in his black eyes when the other lads taunted him with his red skin. He was very lame for weeks, and could only sit in the sun, weaving pretty baskets for Eunice, and shaping bows and arrows for Reuben. The children were soon his friends, for with them he was always gentle, trying in his soft language and expressive gestures to show his good will and gratitude. They defended him against their ruder playmates, and, following their father's example, trusted and cherished the homeless youth.

When he was able to walk, he taught Reuben to shoot and trap the wild creatures of the wood, to find fish where others failed, and to guide himself in the wilderness by star and sun, wind and water. To Eunice he brought little offerings of bark and feathers; taught her to make moccasins of skin, belts of shells, and pouches gay with porcupine quills and colored grass. He would not work for old Becky—who plainly showed her distrust—saying: "A brave does not grind corn and bring wood; that is squaw's work. Onawandah will hunt and fish and fight for you, but no more." And even the request of the parson could not win obedience in this, though the boy would

271

have died for the good man.

Winter came, and the settlers fared badly through the long months when the drifts rose to the eaves of their low cabins, and the store, carefully harvested, failed to supply even their simple wants.

But the minister's family never lacked wild meat, for Onawandah proved himself a better hunter than any man in the town, and the boy of sixteen led the way on his snow-shoes when they went to track a bear to its den, chase the deer for miles, or shoot the wolves that howled about their homes in the winter nights.

"Be of good cheer, little daughter; I shall be gone but three days, and our brave Onawandah will guard you well," said the parson, one April morning, as he mounted his horse to visit a distant settlement where the bitter winter had brought sickness and death to more than one household.

The boy showed his white teeth in a bright smile as he stood beside the children, while Becky croaked, with a shake of the head, "I hope you mayn't find you've warmed a viper in your bosom, Master."

Two days later, it seemed as if Becky was a true prophet, and that the confiding minister *had* been terribly deceived; for Onawandah went about to hunt, and, that night, the awful war-whoop woke the sleeping villagers to find their houses

burning, while the hidden Indians shot at them by the light of the fires kindled by dusky scouts. In terror and confusion the whites fled to the fort; and, while the men fought bravely, the women held blankets to catch arrows and bullets, or bound up the hurts of their defenders.

It was all over by daylight, and the red men sped away up the river, with several prisoners and such booty as they could plunder from the deserted houses. Not till all fear of a return of their enemies was over did the poor people venture to leave the fort and seek their ruined homes. Then it was discovered that Becky and the parson's children were gone, and great was the bewailing, for the good man was much beloved by all his flock.

Suddenly the smothered voice of Becky was heard by a party of visitors, calling dolefully, "I am here, betwixt the beds. Pull me out, neighbors, for I am half dead with fright and smothering."

The old woman was quickly extricated from her hiding-place, and with much energy declared that she had seen Onawandah, disguised with warpaint, among the Indians, and that he had torn away the children from her arms before she could fly from the house.

"He chose his time well, when they were defenseless, dear lambs! Spite of all my warnings, Master trusted him, and this is the thanks we get. Oh, how can I tell him this heavy news?"

There was no need to tell it; for, as Becky sat moaning and beating her breast on the fireless hearth, and the sympathizing neighbors stood about her, the sound of a horse's hoofs was heard, and the parson came down the hilly road like one riding for his life. He had seen the smoke afar off, guessed the sad truth, and hurried on, to find his home in ruins and to learn by his first glance at the faces around him that his children were gone.

When he had heard all there was to tell, he sat down upon his door-stone with his head in his hands, praying for strength to bear a grief too deep for words. The wounded and weary men tried to comfort him with hope, and the women wept with him as they hugged their own babies closer to the hearts that ached for the lost children. Suddenly a stir went through the mournful group, as Onawandah came from the wood with a young deer upon his shoulders, and amazement in his face as he saw the desolation before him. Dropping his burden, he stood an instant looking with eyes that kindled fiercely; then he came bounding toward them, undaunted by the hatred, suspicion, and surprise plainly written on the countenances before him. He missed his playmates, and asked but one question:

"The boy? the little squaw?—where gone?"

His answer was a rough one, for the men seized him and poured forth the tale, heaping reproaches upon him for such treachery and ingratitude. He bore it all in proud silence till they pointed to the poor father whose dumb sorrow was more eloquent than all their wrath. Onawandah looked at him, and the fire died out of his eyes as if quenched by the tears he would not shed. Shaking off the hands

Few words, but they were so solemnly spoken that the most unbelieving were impressed. The youth laid one hand on the gray head bowed before him, and lifted the other toward heaven, as if calling the Great Spirit to hear his vow.

A relenting murmur went through the crowd, but the boy paid no heed as he turned away, and with no arms but his hunting knife and bow, no food but such as he could find, no guide but the sun by day, the stars by night, plunged into the pathless forest and was gone.

Then the people drew a long breath, and muttered to one another:

"He will never do it, yet he is a brave lad for his years."

"Only a shift to get off with a whole skin, I warrant you. These varlets are as cunning as foxes," added Becky, sourly.

The parson alone believed and hoped, though weeks and months went by, and his children did not come.

Meantime, Reuben and Eunice were far away in an Indian camp, resting as best they could, after the long journey that followed that dreadful night. Their captors were not cruel to them, for Reuben was a stout fellow and, thanks to Onawandah, could hold his own with the boys who would have tormented him if he had been feeble or cowardly. Eunice also was a hardy creature for her years, and when her first fright and fatigue were over, made herself useful in many ways among the squaws, who did not let the pretty child suffer greatly.

Life in a wigwam was not a life of ease,

that held him, he went to his good friend, saying with passionate earnestness:

"Onawandah is *not* traitor! Onawandah remembers. Onawandah grateful! You believe?"

The poor parson looked up at him, and could not doubt his truth; for genuine love and sorrow ennobled the dark face, and he had never known the boy to lie.

"I believe and trust you still, but others will not. Go, you are no longer safe here, and I have no home to offer you," said the parson, sadly, feeling that he cared for none unless his children were returned.

"Onawandah has no fear. He goes; but he comes again to bring the boy, the little squaw."

and fortunately the children were accustomed to hardships that all endured in those early times. But they mourned for home till their young faces were pathetic with longing, and their pillows of dry leaves were often wet with tears in the night. Their clothes grew ragged, their hair unkempt, their faces tanned by sun and wind. Scanty food and exposure to all weathers tried the strength of their bodies, and uncertainty as to their fate saddened their spirits; yet they bore up bravely, and said their prayers faithfully, feeling sure that God would bring them home to father in His own good time.

One day, when Reuben was snaring birds in the wood, he heard the cry of a quail, and followed it deeper and deeper into the forest, till it ceased, and, with a sudden rustle, Onawandah rose up from the brakes, his finger on his lips to prevent any exclamation that might betray him to other ears and eyes.

"I come for you and little Laraka," the name he gave Eunice, meaning "Wild Rose." "I take you home. Not know me yet. Go and wait."

He spoke low and fast; but the joy in his face told how glad he was to find the boy after his long search, and Reuben clung to him, trying not to disgrace himself by crying in surprise and delight.

Lying hidden in the tall brakes they talked in whispers, while one told of the capture, and the other of a plan for escape; for, though a friendly tribe, these Indians were not Onawandah's people, and they must not suspect that he knew the children, or they might be separated.

"Little squaw, you watch her. Tell her not to cry out, and speak me any time. When I say come, we go—fast—in the night. Not ready yet."

These were the orders Reuben received, and, when he could compose himself, he went back to the wigwams, leaving his friend in the wood, while he told the good news to Eunice and prepared her for the part she must play.

Fear had taught her self-control, and the poor child stood the test well, working off her relief and rapture by pounding corn in the stone mortar till her little hands were blistered, and her arms ached for hours afterward.

Not till the next day did Onawandah make his appearance, and then he came limping into the village, weary, lame, and half starved after his long wandering in the wilderness. He was kindly welcomed, and his story believed, for he told only the first part, and said nothing of his life among the white men. He hardly glanced at the children when they were pointed out to him by their captors, and scowled at poor Eunice, who forgot her part in her joy, and smiled as she met the dark eyes that till now had always looked kindly at her. A touch from Reuben warned her, and she was glad to hide her confusion by shaking her long hair over her face, as if afraid of the stranger.

Onawandah took no further notice of them, but seemed to be very lame with the old wound in his foot, which prevented his being obliged to hunt with the men. He was resting and slowly gathering strength for the hard task he had set

himself, while he waited for a safe time to save the children.

At last, in the early autumn, all the men went off on the war-path, leaving only boys and women behind. Then Onawandah's eyes began to kindle, and Reuben's heart to beat fast, for both felt that their time for escape had come.

All was ready, and one moonless night the signal was given. A cricket chirped shrilly outside the tent where the children slept with one old squaw. A strong hand cut the skin beside their bed of fir boughs, and two trembling creatures crept out to follow the tall shadow that flitted noiselessly before them into the darkness of the wood. Not a broken twig, a careless step or a whispered word betrayed them, and they vanished as swiftly and silently as hunted deer flying for their lives.

Till dawn they hurried on, Onawandah carrying Eunice, whose strength soon failed, and Reuben manfully shouldering the hatchet and the pouch of food. At sunrise they hid in a thicket by a spring and rested, while waiting for the friendly night to come again. Then they pushed on, and fear gave wings to their feet, so that by another morning they were far enough away to venture to travel more slowly and sleep at night.

The children who had learned to love and trust the Indian boy in happier times, adored him now, and they came to regard him as an earthly Providence, so faithful, brave and tender was he; so forgetful of himself, so bent on saving them. He never seemed to sleep, ate the poorest morsels or went without any food when provision failed; let no danger daunt him, no hardship wring complaint from him; but went on through the wild forest, led by guides invisible to them, till they began to hope that home was near.

Twice he saved their lives. Once, when he went in search of food, leaving Reuben to guard his sister, the children, being very hungry, ignorantly ate some poisonous berries which looked like wild cherries and were deliciously sweet. The boy generously gave most of them to Eunice, and soon was terror-stricken to see her grow pale and cold and deathly ill. Not knowing what to do, he could only rub her hands and call wildly for Onawandah.

The name echoed through the silent wood, and, though far away, the keen ear of the Indian heard it, his fleet feet brought him back in time, and his knowledge of wild roots and herbs made it possible to save the child when no other help was at hand.

"Make fire. Keep warm. I soon come," he said, after hearing the story and examining Eunice, who could only lift her eyes to him, full of childish confidence.

Then he was off again, scouring the woods like a hound on the scent, searching everywhere for the precious little herb that would counteract the poison. Anyone watching him would have thought him crazy as he rushed hither and thither, tearing up the leaves, creeping on his hands and knees that it might not escape him, and when he found it, springing up with a cry that startled the birds, and carried hope to poor Reuben, who was trying to forget his own pain in his anxiety for Eunice.

"Eat, eat, while I make drink. All safe now," cried Onawandah, as he came leaping toward them with his hands full of green leaves, his dark face shining.

The boy was soon relieved, but for hours they hung over the girl, who suffered sadly and lay as if dead. Reuben's courage failed then, and he cried bitterly. Even Onawandah lost hope for a while, and sat like a bronze statue of despair, with his eyes fixed on his Wild Rose.

Suddenly he rose, stretched his arms to the west, where the sun was setting splendidly, and in his own musical language prayed to the Great Spirit. The Christian boy fell upon his knees, feeling that the only help was in the Father who saw and heard them even in the wilderness. Both were comforted, and when they turned to Eunice there was a faint tinge of color on the pale cheeks, the look of pain was gone, and she slept quietly without the moans that had made their hearts ache.

"He hears! he hears!" cried Onawandah, and for the first time Reuben saw tears in his keen eyes, as the Indian boy looked at the sky in gratitude.

In the morning she was safe, and great was the rejoicing; but for two days the little invalid was not allowed to continue the journey, much as they longed to hurry on. It was a pretty sight, the bed of hemlock boughs spread under a green tent of woven branches, and on the pillow of moss the pale child watching the flicker of sunshine through the leaves, listening to the babble of a brook close by, or sleeping tranquilly, lulled by the murmur of the pines. Patient, loving and grateful, it was a pleasure to serve her, and both the lads were faithful nurses. Onawandah cooked birds for her to eat, and made a

277

pleasant drink of the wild raspberry leaves to quench her thirst. Reuben snared rabbits, that she might have nourishing food, and longed to shoot a deer for provision, that she might not suffer hunger again on their journey. The boyish desire led him deeper into the wood than it was wise for him to go alone, for it was near night-fall, and wild creatures haunted the forest in those days.

The fire, which Onawandah kept constantly burning, guarded their little camp where Eunice lay; but Reuben, with no weapon but his bow and hunting knife, was beyond this protection when he at last gave up his vain hunt and turned homeward. Suddenly, the sound of stealthy steps startled him, but he could see nothing through the dusk at first, and hurried on, fearing that some treacherous Indian was following him. Then he remembered his sister, and resolved not to betray her resting-place if he could help it, for he had learned courage from Onawandah, and longed to be as brave and generous as his hero.

So he paused to watch and wait, and soon saw the gleam of two fiery eyes, not behind, but above him, in a tree. Then he knew that it was an "Indian devil," as they called a species of fierce wild-cat that lurked in the thickets and sprang on its prey like a small tiger.

"If I could only kill it alone, how proud Onawandah would be of me," thought Reuben, burning for the good opinion of his friend.

It would have been wiser to hurry on and give the beast no time to spring; but the boy was overbold, and, fitting an arrow to the string, aimed at the bright eye-ball and let fly. A sharp snarl showed that some harm was done, and, rather daunted by the savage sound, Reuben raced away, meaning to come back next day for the hoped-for prize.

But soon he heard the creature bounding after him, and he uttered one ringing shout for help, feeling too late that he had been foolhardy. Fortunately he was nearer camp than he thought. Onawandah heard him and was there in time to receive the wild-cat, as, mad with the pain of the wound, it sprung at Reuben. There was no time for words, and the boy could only watch in breathless anxiety the fight which went on between the brute and the Indian.

It was sharp but short, for Onawandah had his knife, and as soon as he could get the snarling, struggling beast down, he killed it with a skilful stroke. But not before it had torn and bitten him more dangerously than he knew, for the dusk hid the wounds, and excitement kept him from feeling them at first. Reuben thanked him heartily, and accepted his first words of warning with grateful docility; then both hurried back to Eunice, who till next day knew nothing of her brother's danger.

Onawandah made light of his scratches, as he called them, got their supper, and sent Reuben early to bed, for tomorrow they were to start again.

Excited by his adventure, the boy slept lightly, and waking in the night, saw by the flicker of the fire Onawandah binding

278

up a deep wound in his breast with wet moss and his own belt. A stifled groan betrayed how much he suffered; but when Reuben went to him, he would accept no help and sent him back to bed, preferring to endure the pain in stern silence, with true Indian courage.

Next morning they set out and pushed on as fast as Eunice's strength allowed. But it was evident that Onawandah suffered much, though he would not rest, forbade the children to speak of his wounds, and pressed on with feverish haste, as if he feared that his strength might not hold out. Reuben watched him anxiously, for there was a look in his face that troubled the boy and filled him with alarm, as well as with remorse and love.

In three days they reached the river, and, as if Heaven helped them in their greatest need, found a canoe, left by some hunter, near the shore. In they sprang, and let the swift current carry them along, Eunice kneeling in the bow like a little figure-head of Hope, Reuben steering with his paddle, and Onawandah sitting with arms tightly folded over his breast, as if to control the sharp anguish of his wound.

Hour after hour they floated down the great river, looking eagerly for signs of home, and when at last they entered the familiar valley, the little girl cried for joy and the boy paddled as he had never done before. Onawandah sat erect with his haggard eyes fixed on the dim distance, and sang his death-song in a clear, strong voice—though every breath was pain—bent on dying like a brave, without complaint or fear.

At last they saw the smoke from the cabins on the hillside and, hastily mooring the canoe, all sprang out, eager to be at home after their perilous wandering.

But as his foot touched the land, Onawandah felt that he could do no more, and stretching his arms toward the parsonage, the windows of which glimmered as hospitably as they had done when he first saw them, he said, with a pathetic sort of triumph in his broken voice: "Go. I can not. Tell the good father, Onawandah not lie, not forget. He keep his promise."

The Peddler's Clock

By Mabel Leigh Hunt

MILES, Ezra, and Timothy Bellamy needed no clock to tell them when it was time to bring the cows home. It would have done them no good to wish for one, either, for Father was stubborn about having a clock in the house. He was jealous for the big silver watch which his own father had bought in Boston town sixty years before.

Sometimes, when Father wound the watch at night, he would allow the children to hold it, vigilant all the while to see that no harm came to his precious heirloom. When he went off on any kind of journey, he always wore the watch, looking very grand with the thick silver chain looped across his vest. But such occasions were rare. Most of the time the watch ticked away in its bulky leather case, hidden in the top drawer of the tall desk that stood in the parlor of the Connecticut farmhouse where the Bellamys lived in 1822.

So, for the most part, the days were measured for the family by the position of the sun in the sky, by the shadows which were cast by this or that familiar object. When the sun stood, as it seemed to Timothy, about a foot from the dark line of forest that lay to the westward, he knew that it was time for him and his brothers to bring Daisy and Sukey and Muley home for the milking.

Miles, who was the eldest, claimed Daisy for his cow. Ezra pretended that Sukey belonged to him. Muley, a gentle creature without horns, was the pet and special charge of Timothy.

Each boy milked his own cow, morning and night, and carried in the brimming pails.

Mother had been provoked with Father on the day that he had bought Muley. "Another cow?" she exclaimed. "When Daisy and Sukey give us all the milk we need? I declare, Jonathan, you are foolish over cows. I would much rather you had brought us a clock."

But Father said, "We have one perfectly good timepiece in the house. That is enough. And a cow is valuable property, whereas a clock is just an ornament!"

"Tush, Jonathan," said Grandmother Bellamy, "thee exaggerates to suit thine own argument. A clock is certainly more than an ornament, and Elizabeth doesn't want just the works of a clock, that folks call a 'wag-on-the-wall.'"

"No," said Mother, "I want a clock in a nice case with pictures painted on the glass." Mother's eyes shone a little, as if she could plainly see the clock of her dreams.

"'Tis a frivolous wish, Elizabeth," reproved Father, "and not in keeping with your good judgment. Clocks are expensive luxuries, and I can ill afford to buy one."

"But, Father," said seventeen-year-old Prudence, timidly, "these new shelf-clocks with wooden works are much less dear."

"A clock would be company," murmured Mother. At that everyone had to laugh, for Mother certainly never lacked for company, with the house full of young ones.

"Lay not up for yourselves treasures upon earth," said Father, pompously. Surely a quotation from the Bible would put a stop to all arguments.

There were mischievous twinkles in Grandmother's eyes as she said slyly, "What about thy silver watch, Jonathan?"

Only Grandmother dared to talk back to Father. For though he was kind, he was also stern, the lord and master of his household, as fathers were in those days.

So Mother continued to do without a clock, and Muley, the cow, stayed on the farm.

One summer morning a few weeks later, Father, dressed in his best, with his silver watch in his pocket, set off early for Colchester on a matter of business. He wanted to attend a public meeting as well, and planned to stay the night with one of his kinsmen. It always seemed strange on the farm without Father, the days longer than ordinary days, and the nights more still and lonely.

Toward evening of this day, when the milking had been done and Mother had supper almost ready, there came the sound of hoofs in the lane, and there was someone hallooing outside. Everyone crowded to the door. A tall, lean fellow was alighting from his horse.

"A peddler, I think," said Mother.

"A good day to you, Mistress," said the

peddler, with a quick stiff bow. "And to all that dwell in the house," he added and he looked at the children with a little twinkling smile. He took his pack off the horse. He laid it down on the grass of the door yard. Carefully he drew out something and unwound the wrappings. There was—a clock!

Up to the door he marched, carrying the clock. Mother backed away a little, as if she knew that here was Temptation, with a capital T.

"I represent Ebenezer Plumb, clockmaker, silversmith, and bellcaster of Wethersfield," said the peddler. "I am almost at my journey's end. I have sold every buckle, every candlestick, every spoon, every clock that I had when setting forth from the shop a week ago. All, good Mistress, but this shelf-clock and three cowbells. What will you offer for this fine clock, the best of the lot?"

He laid the clock in Mother's arms, and, as she looked down on it, a little smile played about her lips. It was the clock of her dreams! In a cherry case it was, smoothly polished and beautifully carved, with a graceful scroll at the top. There were slender pillars at the sides, surmounted with balls. Little pink rosebuds were painted on the face, and a wreath of full-blown roses bloomed on the glass door. It seemed as if the hands that pointed the hours must have been hammered on a fairy forge by fairy fingers, so delicately carved they were.

"Just set it up in the house somewhere," said the peddler, "and I will start it going and let you hear how it sounds when it strikes the hour."

Mother could not resist this suggestion. She stood it up on the dresser in the kitchen. And presently the wooden pendulum, overlaid with brass, was swinging back and forth, gleaming within the circle of roses.

"Now," said the peddler, "when the minute-hand points exactly to figure twelve, and the hour-hand exactly to ten, the clock will strike the hour."

Timothy held his breath, waiting, while the minute-hand moved, second by second. And sure enough, when it pointed to figure twelve, there fell upon the listening ears ten cheerful notes. Everyone, including the peddler, looked at Mother. She stood with clasped hands, gazing at the clock. Her cheeks were pink, her eyes bright.

"Now," said the peddler, "let me set it for you."

"Alas," said Mother, sighing as if she were renouncing a box of jewels, "I have no money, and my husband is not at home." She turned her back to the clock and looked at the peddler with tragic eyes. "You had best go," she said.

It really made one feel dreadfully sorry to see Mother giving up the beautiful clock.

"Oh, Mother," cried Prudence, "maybe the man would trade something for the clock."

"I might consider it," said the peddler. "What have you to trade?"

Mother looked at Prudence. She looked at Grandmother. She held a corner of her apron to her mouth, thinking. Then she threw up her chin. She spoke breathlessly, "I have a cow!"

"Elizabeth!" gasped Grandmother.

"Mother!" gasped Prudence.

"Mother! Which cow?" Timothy's voice was a frightened squeak.

But Mother looked straight at the peddler. "Are you interested in such a trade?" she asked.

"If it is a good cow," answered the peddler.

"We have only good cows," said Mother. "Come. You may see for yourself." She led the way to the barn and Timothy trotted after her. Ezra started, too, and one of the girls, but Mother turned swiftly. "Go back into the house, children," she said. "This bargain is between me and the peddler."

Timothy stood at the window, his heart almost bursting with anxiety. He caught his breath as Mother and the peddler came out of the barn. The peddler was leading Muley!

"Oh-h-h, Grandmother," moaned Timothy, "he's taking my cow!"

Grandmother seized him just as he was dashing out of the door. "Timothy! Thee is not to say a word. Muley is not really thy cow. And thy mother is doing what she thinks best. At least, she is doing what she wants to."

And there was the peddler going off down the lane, the horse's reins in one hand, and the rope which led Muley in the other.

"Now we'll have supper," said Mother.

"How can she be so calm about it all?" thought Timothy. Off he dashed after the peddler, who heard the boy's shouts and drew rein. Timothy looked up, breathless. "You don't even know her name!" he cried. "It's Muley."

"I might have guessed," laughed the peddler, "since she hasn't any horns. That's one reason I wanted her."

Timothy dug his bare toes in the dust of the road. "You—you'll be good to her, won't you?"

"She'll be Ebenezer Plumb's cow, not mine, boy. But never fear, the master will be good to her."

"Let me pet her just once," cried Timothy. He leaned against the cow, stroking her. "Good-by, Muley," he whispered.

"I guess you feel sort of bad to see her go," said the peddler. "Here, I'll give you a present." He fished into his pack and pulled out the three cowbells.

"Much obliged," said Timothy, jingling the bells. And for a moment he felt a warm glow of happiness from the unexpected gift. But as the peddler disappeared at a bend of the road, the thought came to Timothy: three cowbells, but only two cows!

Still, the evening seemed festive. To have the new clock there on the dresser was like having a cheerful and honored guest in the house. The eyes of everyone were constantly turning to it. They watched the minute-hand as it traveled miraculously around, the slow creep of the hour-hand. The shine of the polished case, the golden gleam of the swinging pendulum, the dainty pink of the painted roses gave an air of luxury to the big, plain kitchen.

As the hours of six, and seven, and eight were told, all were silent, giving ear to the measured notes that filled the room with a music sweeter far than that of Ezra's jew's-harp.

But the next morning there was no Muley to milk, and Timothy felt lost. As the day wore on, and the hour of Father's return drew nearer, an atmosphere of strain became evident among the Bellamys. They stole looks at each other, and at Mother's straight mouth.

It was late afternoon when Father returned. He was happy to be at home again. He put his watch carefully away in its case, changed his clothes, and they all sat down to supper in the kitchen.

"There isn't anyone can cook like you, Elizabeth," he said, and he was just on the point of taking a great bite of food when the clock struck six. He lowered his fork.

"What's that?" he demanded.

"That's the new clock, Jonathan," said Grandmother in her most soothing tone. "Doesn't it sound nice?"

Miles gave a small embarrassed snicker.

Father looked at the clock, frowning. "Where did it come from?"

"I got it from a peddler," answered Mother, "representing Ebenezer Plumb of Wethersfield."

"And what, may I ask, did you give him for it?" asked Father, coldly.

"One of the cows," said Mother. "Muley."

Father pushed back his chair and stared at Mother. "You—you mean you traded Muley for that fancy contraption yonder?"

"Yes," said Mother.

Father's face was like a thundercloud. He stood up. "I won't say what I think. The children—" and he strode out of the house, walking to the barn with long rapid steps.

It was an unhappy evening. Everyone went to bed very early.

The next morning was rainy. At breakfast Father said, pointedly, "Since there is no cow for you to milk, Timothy, you may come and help me grease axles."

In the barn, Timothy said, "Father, I thought it was a terrible piece of bargaining, too. The cow's worth lots more than the clock."

Father coughed. "You must never criticize your mother, Timothy."

"No, Father," answered Timothy. "I do think the clock is nice. But, Father, I want to tell you. Last night, in bed, I planned how we can get Muley back. I could go and be an apprentice to Ebenezer Plumb and work out the price of Muley."

"That would take a long time, Son," said Father. "And you were never cut out for a craftsman. You're a born farmer, like your father." He gave Timothy a look that made the boy's heart beat high with happiness.

They worked in silence for a few moments. Then Father spoke again. "Son, run to the house and bring me a gourdful of soft soap and my coat and hat."

After Father had washed his hands at the trough and put on his coat and hat, he saddled his horse. "Now, Timothy, I'm going away. You can say that I shall be

284

back by evening." And Father was off, in the rain.

All day Timothy wondered where Father had gone. Mother looked pale and distressed, too, for there had been never a word of farewell.

The new bells that Daisy and Sukey wore made a pleasant jangle as they came across the pasture and into the barnyard that evening. The clouds had broken in the west. There was a rainbow in the sky. Timothy was standing in the barn doorway watching it, while his brothers did the milking, when suddenly, there was Father with Muley.

"Here, Timothy," he said, "here's your cow! Take her into her stall."

"Father!" cried Timothy, his face shining with joy. "How did you get her back?"

"I went to the clock-maker's shop and paid him what the clock was worth."

Father ate a hearty supper that evening.

He got up from the table and stretched.

"Ho-hum!" he yawned. Then he said, "That's a handsome clock, Elizabeth, mighty handsome! Come winter, and I will make you a nice shelf for it. How would you like that?"

"I'd like it very much, Jonathan."

Mother and Father smiled at each other, and suddenly it seemed as if the whole house were filled with sunshine. The children began to laugh and chatter, and Grandmother's face was lit with a quiet happiness.

Timothy was happiest of all. He took the pail and ran out to the barn. First he tied the extra bell around Muley's neck. "Three bells—three cows," he said. He sat down on the milking stool and pressed his head against Muley's smooth flank. The sound of the milk hissing against the sides of the pail was sweeter to Timothy's ears than the golden chimes of any clock could ever be.

The Royal Greens

By Russell Gordon Carter

O<small>N A COOL</small> misty autumn morning in the year 1777, as David Wethervale led the small black mare from the stable, his father said to him, "After today I reckon you'll have to go to school afoot."

David's hand tightened on the bridle, and he swallowed hard. He said, "Then —you have at last found a buyer for her?"

"Aye," Seth Wethervale replied. "A man from over Danbury way is coming tomorrow. I'm sorry, lad, for your sake."

David made no comment, knowing the futility of further pleas and arguments. His father had made up his mind to sell the mare almost a year earlier, soon after Uncle Charles had died from wounds at the hands of Johnson's Tories in York State, leaving the horse to his brother-in-law. At that time Seth Wethervale had said, "She's too light for farm work. I'll have to sell her."

As David rode slowly westward toward the schoolhouse at the Corners, some three miles distant, he was miserable. No one knew the full depths of his feelings for the little mare that had enabled his uncle to carry dispatches for Washington's army. "Hobgoblin," she was named, because of her swift ambling gait and her curious facial markings—a generous spattering of little white flecks that gave her a strange and frightening look.

Yet, in spite of name and appearance, she was one of the gentlest horses in western Connecticut. And now, after almost a year of wonderful comradeship, he was about to lose her! It made David feel completely miserable.

Halfway to school, as they were crossing the old wooden bridge over the swift waters of Dog Creek, one of the rotten planks gave way under Hobgoblin's weight, and she stumbled and pitched her rider sidewise into the stream. David scrambled out, breathless and shaken, his hose and breeches dripping. Hobgoblin gazed at him wonderingly, then began to nuzzle at his shoulder. Her manner seemed regretful and apologetic.

David threw an arm impulsively over her drooping neck. " 'Twasn't your fault," he said. " 'Twas that rotten plank. Lucky you didn't break a leg!"

He removed his shoes and proceeded as best he could to squeeze the water out of his clammy breeches. Half an hour passed before he mounted again.

School was in session when David tethered the mare in a pine grove across the road. As he entered the small square building, Mr. Verrill, the schoolmaster, frowned and tightened his thin lips.

"What made you late?" he demanded. "Did you dawdle?"

"No, sir, I pitched off my horse,"

David replied. "She went through a plank in the bridge, and I landed in the water."

Several of the smaller girls tittered.

Mr. Verrill glowered at them, and the sound subsided at once. "Take your seat," he said to the boy.

After David had sat down between Mary Jacobus and Joseph Trumbull, the schoolmaster reopened the brown-covered speller on his desk and proceeded to call upon the pupils at the front of the room. But David's mind was not on the lesson. He was thinking of Hobgoblin, wondering miserably what would become of her. Would the man from over Danbury way treat her kindly? Would he put her to heavy work?

"David! Stand up and spell 'independent.'"

Joseph Trumbull's elbow against his ribs roused David to the realization that the schoolmaster had called on him. He got slowly to his feet. What was the word Mr. Verrill had asked him to spell? He heard Mary Jacobus whisper something.

"Indignant," he began. "I-n-"

"The word was 'independent!'" Mr. Verrill broke in sharply.

David's thoughts cleared. "Oh, yes, sir. Independent. I-n-d-e-p-e-n-d-a-n-t."

"Wrong!" cried the master. "Who can spell it correctly?"

The schoolroom buzzed with eager voices.

"Now try it again, David."

The boy wrinkled his forehead. Even amid the buzz of eager voices his thoughts had again strayed to the mare. He began

uncertainly. "I-n-d-i-g-"

Mr. Verrill sprang from the chair, his face flushed. Seizing his birchwood ruler, he motioned with it to a corner. "Stand over yonder with your face to the wall!" he ordered. "Maybe 'twill help you gather your wits."

David was ashamed of himself. Yet even now, as the lesson resumed, he was unable to give his full attention to it. As he shifted uncomfortably from one foot to the other, his thoughts were once more for Hobgoblin: If only there were something he could do to make his father change his mind.

Half an hour dragged past. With head against the wall, David was listening to Mary Jacobus trying to spell "beatific," when she suddenly uttered a startled exclamation and then began to laugh. Glancing sidewise, he saw a surprising sight. Through the open window close to Mary protruded Hobgoblin's white-flecked head, her ears twitching, her jaws gently chewing a wisp of grass that hung from her lips. Others began to laugh, but a sharp crack of the ruler on the desk brought sudden silence in the schoolroom.

"David!"

"Yes, sir?"

"Why did you not tie up your horse?"

"I—I did, sir."

"It does not look so!"

"She must have freed herself, sir."

"Well, go and tie her up again! You and your horse are a vexation!"

David hurried outside. He thought he had tied the bridle rein securely enough to a young pine, but here it was hanging free. Gathering it up, he led the horse away from the schoolhouse—not back to the pine grove, however, but up the hill to where a solitary apple tree stood above grass that was still long and green.

"There now," he said as he secured the rein to a limb. "You can graze here all you please."

He lingered, caressing Hobgoblin's smooth neck and letting her nibble playfully at his shoulder. Must he leave her and return to the schoolroom? With a renewed sense of misery, he allowed his gaze to wander far off. To the east he could see the clustered houses of the village and, to the north of it, the round powderhouse built of field stones. Close by stood Amos Thatcher's big barn, which now held all the supplies for the militia. His own house lay out of sight in a valley beyond the town. His gaze lowered to the road winding among patches of woodland, dropping to Dog Creek, then gradually twisting upward toward the Corners.

Suddenly he stiffened and caught his breath. There on the road a quarter of a mile from the Corners a body of men were marching—men with muskets, upwards of two score of them and all clad in dusty green uniforms! He stared with mouth agape, almost unable to believe his eyes. Men in green uniforms marching toward the town!

His throat went abruptly dry as the explanation leaped to his mind. Tories! A detachment of the Royal Greens, Johnson's Tories, who had fatally wounded his uncle a year earlier! They must have come up the old logging road that joined the main road some two hundred yards below the Corners. Now they were doubtless on their way to destroy the militia supplies while the menfolks were at work in the fields!

David jerked the bridle free from round the limb. A moment later his leg was across the gray blanket that served as saddle, and he was on his way down the slope, circling toward the west in order not to be seen from the road.

Mr. Verrill, ruler in hand, was at the door when the boy reached the schoolhouse.

"What is the meaning of this?" he demanded. "I told you—"

"There's a party of Royal Greens down yonder on the road!" David interrupted him breathlessly. "They aim to raid the town—"

"Eh, what? I say—here, now! David, where ye goin'—" The schoolmaster's voice trailed off into a blur of sound as horse and rider went quartering down across the field.

Reaching the main road, David drew rein and held Hobgoblin to a slow walk. He knew exactly what he would do. Just beyond Dog Creek a second logging road joined the main road from the north. He would follow the raiding party at a safe distance until he was across the bridge, then he would strike northward up the logging road till he came to open

country and then push eastward as fast as possible. He was sure he could reach the town in time to give the alarm.

David was riding now through an old beech wood, the mare's hoofs making hardly a sound on the soft earth at the right of the road. Ahead of him he could hear Dog Creek tumbling over its stony bed as it raced southward to join a branch of the Housatonic. The sound grew louder as he approached the base of the valley. Overhead a pair of crows called raucously.

Just ahead of him the road turned to the right before it dropped steeply to the creek. David drew rein and listened, but heard nothing except the roaring of the creek and the calling of the crows. Probably the raiders were by now already across the bridge. He urged the horse round the turn and then jerked her to a sudden halt, his heart almost in his throat. Less than fifty yards in front, on the near side of the bridge, marched the raiders! Several in the rear glanced backward and, spying him, called to those ahead.

For an instant David sat rigid, viewing the collapse of his careful plan. He could never reach the north logging road now, and if he were to turn back, the surprise of the town would be complete. The thought was intolerable! Acting on swift impulse, he clapped both heels to the mare's flanks, and away she went straight down the incline.

The suddenness of his charge took the Tories unawares. He saw green-clad figures drawing hurriedly apart in front of him. The wind sang in his ears. The woods rang with the clatter of hoofs and the shouts of men as Hobgoblin thundered downward, her haunches straining, her mane flying, sparks leaping outward from beneath her pounding feet. Something slashed at him as he bent low over her neck. A musket butt glanced off his shoulder. Another swished through the air and struck the mare's haunch, causing her to leap sidewise. A branch raked his face as he swung her back in the middle of the road again.

Only one man was between him and the bridge! He saw the fellow raise his musket threateningly, but before he could fire, Hobgoblin struck him with her shoulder, sending him spinning. The bridge now was only a score of yards distant and seemed to David to be rushing at him at wild breakneck speed. In a terrified instant he pictured what would happen if one of Hobgoblin's feet should go through the hole. Then he steeled himself. He had taught her to jump. She must jump now—for her life! Almost at the edge of the bridge he tightened his legs under her and let his weight fall backward. "Now, girl, now!"

Hobgoblin responded beautifully, landing almost in the center of the bridge. Then she was thundering up the slope beyond. Two or three musket shots rang out as she reached the first turn, and he heard the bullets snap overhead. A moment later horse and rider were round the turn—safe!

But there was no time to waste. David dug his heels against the mare's flanks, urged her to her utmost. When they reached the first house on the outskirts of the town, she was wet and glistening.

A woman appeared in the doorway, wide-eyed.

"Tories!" David shouted, slowing down. "A big band of them on the road!"

Through the heart of the town he clattered, shouting the warning on all sides: "Tories! Two score of the Royal Greens!" Then he made off across the fields toward where he saw men working.

"Tories!" he shouted. "They're on their way up the west road!"

Somewhere in the town a bugle blared, the uncertain notes quivering across the countryside. On a rise of ground David brought the mare to a halt. He had done his best. From all directions, from the woods to the north and the fields to the east and south and west, men in shirt sleeves were running toward the town—sun-browned, resolute men with scythes or axes in their hands. He saw the first arrivals enter Amos Thatcher's barn, saw them emerge with muskets and powder horns. Others joined them, and as they formed ranks, he caught sight of his father.

It was only when David saw the hastily formed column moving off down the road to the west that he realized the full significance of what was happening. There would be a battle. Men would die, his father, perhaps. He felt suddenly faint. Slipping from Hobgoblin's back, he led her to a gully and sat down heavily on a rock.

How long he sat there he never was able to determine. From the west came the sound of firing, first a volley, then a second volley, then scattered shots at long intervals, then silence. The faint odor of burnt powder presently touched his nostrils. He stood up, then sat down again. He was cold, too cold to sit still.

He rose to his feet once more and, clutching Hobgoblin's bridle, made his way slowly to the town. Women and young children gathered bewilderingly about him, and he tried as best he could to answer their excited questions. Finally one of the women said, "Let him be now. He's overwrought. Sit ye down here on the step, David, whilst I go and warm some milk for ye."

It was not until well past noon that the militiamen began to return. David saw them come straggling up the hill, and in one group, to his profound relief, he spied his father.

Seth Wethervale came forward at a quick walk. His face was powder-stained.

David ran to meet him. "The Tories—" he began.

"They're in York State by now, them as is left," his father replied grimly. Then his rough hand reached forth and clutched his son's shoulder.

"Lad, I be proud o' ye!" he said. "What ye done an' all—"

David smiled and shook his head. " 'Twas Hobgoblin," he protested.

Seth Wethervale nodded. "I know all about it! Mr. Verrill told how you rode headlong down the road right through

292

the midst o' them—"

" 'Twas Hobgoblin," David repeated.

For a long moment father and son looked full at each other—a moment vibrant with understanding.

Finally Seth Wethervale said, "I reckon ye're right. The mare shares the credit." Then he added in a tone meant to be matter-of-fact, "And I reckon, after what's happened, 'twould be a mite unfair to part the two o' ye."

David felt the warm blood come flooding into his face. "You—you mean you'll not sell her after all?"

"Aye, lad, that is what I mean. You've earned the keep of her."

David stared with eyes bright and lips parted, too deeply moved to speak. With a boisterous shout, he suddenly whirled and ran to where Hobgoblin was patiently waiting. A moment later his arm was across her neck and her soft lips were against his shoulder as he told her the joyous news.

Storm Flight

By Rutherford G. Montgomery

THE NAPIER lurched and bounced as her low wings cracked the rough air that backwashed from Mount Kirby. Tommy wiped the usual smile from his lips and glanced at the flight bubble. Ahead lay trouble! It was written all over the spruce-choked side of the mountain. Gray-black clouds piled high in the notch toward which the Napier was heading. And there was no other crossing for a hundred miles along the divide, aside from the narrow pass. Heavily loaded, the Napier did not have ceiling enough to top the ridges towering above the storm.

Barrows, who sat beside Tommy, leaned over and shouted. His voice sounded like a whisper as it cut through the scream of the hurtling winds.

"Do you want to turn back?"

Tommy shook his head and gave the Napier all she had. Her big, radial motor shook the sills inside her fuselage as it responded. Had the ship been loaded within her weight limit, the Napier would have

taken clearance, and Tommy could have zoomed above the onrushing wall of storm that was rolling up out of the valley beyond the pass.

"People are starving across the hump! We must get this food through to them! We've got to!" shouted Barrows.

Tommy's eyes shifted to the gray mass that swirled down upon them. Barrows' face was expressionless. If Tommy cracked up the Napier, it would mean a loss of seven thousand dollars for Barrows, to say nothing of the danger to their lives. Barrows had picked Tommy to fly the load of rescue food into Happy Valley where a mountain community was stormlocked and starving.

Barrows was not a flier, himself. He had come along because he would not ask anyone to fly into a danger he would not face. He had picked Tommy from a recruit line because he was certain that the slender, steel-muscled boy with the curly hair and blue eyes would not turn back.

The Napier shoved her slicing propeller into a swirling mass of powder-dry snow. The particles hurtled against the glass panes of the cabin. The Napier shifted suddenly, and one wing lifted with a sickening lurch. Tommy fought to keep her level and to hold his altitude.

Barrows settled back in his bucket seat and stared out of the little window at his side. Like a flash the walls of the mountain were wiped out by the swirling mass of snow. No landmark showed the way to the pass. On both sides granite walls lurked in the white mists. Tommy would have to feel the Napier through the notch

or crack up. Barrows looked across at his pilot and caught Tommy's eyes. He grinned at the storm.

Tommy leveled off and the Napier bore the storm. Suddenly the white wall ahead scattered like the mass of a jig-saw puzzle that has been roughly shaken. A wall of granite, studded with scrub growth, came hurtling at them through the storm! Tommy laid the Napier over sharply and she lifted high into the air. The upward lift shot them into the storm again and blotted out all vision. Desperately Tommy put her nose down again. He must see where he was going! Again the clouds cleared and this time no walls of granite loomed ahead. Tommy sent the big ship roaring over the tops of the tall spruce toward the pass.

Flying close to the tops of tall spruce in a raging storm is a tough job, and Tommy felt a strange coldness in the region of his belt. Then he remembered the starving folks in Happy Valley and his lips set tight. Barrows was unmoved.

Tommy sucked in a breath of cold air. He could see the notch ahead, a low-lying valley that curved down from high ranges on either side. The Napier was bouncing and jerking as she hit the pass and roared through with less than five hundred feet of ceiling. Barrows reached over and slapped Tommy on the back. He bent close and roared into Tommy's ear.

"You get a regular job from now on!"

"Thanks!" Tommy shouted back. A regular job with Barrows meant flying into places that were considered as impossible, but Barrows paid top wages and had the best planes.

The Napier was almost clear of the mountain side when the updraft of the storm hit her. A howling demon of lashing air clutched at the ship, hurling it high into the air, turning it over on its side and crashing Barrows against the little window at his side.

The Napier came out of the clutches of the storm with sickening suddenness. Her tail swept up and she spiraled dizzily, then she plunged downward and buried her nose in the white wall of storm that was sweeping up through the pass. Tommy fought to level off, but the wind was too powerful and he could not right the ship. For two or three sickening seconds they hurtled downward, then a rending crash shook them and a jarring impact jerked them sharply. Black lights flickered before Tommy's eyes.

When Tommy opened his eyes, he was numb with cold and icy particles were pelting his face. He sat up dizzily. A sharp pain shot through his left side. He shouted loudly: "Barrows! Barrows!"

Only the howling of the wind answered him. He staggered to his feet and looked around. Little could be seen through the driving storm. The Napier lay twisted and battered, her nose buried in a deep drift and her tail elevated. Tommy realized that he had been thrown through the window and side plates. He thanked his padded suit for being alive as he plowed to the ship to look inside.

Barrows lay sprawled over the controls. Much of the packed food had piled upon him. Tommy fought back the numbing pain in his side and began pulling Barrows free of the plane. Barrows groaned and opened his eyes as Tommy laid him in the snow beside the wrecked Napier. A wavering smile came to his lips.

"Have to have a fire. Feet cold— cold——" Barrows slumped back and his eyes closed.

Tommy found plenty of logs in the snow. Hurriedly he swept clear a space and built a fire. He dug a heavy blanket from the wreck and fixed a shelter. Tommy guessed that Barrows was internally injured, but he had no way of knowing how seriously. Tommy watched and hoped that his boss would recover consciousness. But Barrows did not come to. His lips moved but he did not speak.

Tommy faced the danger coolly. He knew they could not be rescued for perhaps a week. The dwellers of Happy Valley did not know they were coming, so there was no hope of help from them, though the plane must be close to the settlement.

Tommy stood up. Night was beginning to darken the swirling storm. Grimly Tommy fixed the shelter over his boss. He knew what Barrows would order if he were conscious, and he meant to follow that course. Hesitating only a moment, he plunged into the storm heading down the mountain. Their objective was still ahead, and Barrows would expect him to carry on.

Through the first drift he wallowed, always going downhill. His side pained and weakened him, and he began to think

he had acted the fool in braving the storm and leaving Barrows unconscious, possibly dying beside the fire. The storm raged about him, shutting out the world and piling drifts in the open spaces.

But fate cares for those who dare greatly, and when their cause is mercy bound they are oftentimes lucky. Tommy fell into a drift. He raised himself wearily and wiped the snow from his face. Then he saw a light glimmering ahead. Eagerly he staggered forward and threw himself against a snowcovered cabin.

Rough mountain men met him at the door. They were gaunt from hunger but they dragged him inside and placed him on a bunk. He had found the outmost cabin of the settlement. Tommy refused to rest until they back tracked to the Napier. They were wildly joyous when they heard the ship was loaded with food.

In a very short time Tommy and the men of Happy Valley had rescued Barrows, unloaded the welcome supplies, and returned to the waiting community. All of Happy Valley was rounded up to share the food they so badly needed.

Late that night Barrows and Tommy sat beside a roaring fire and sipped tinned soup that was simmering hot. Barrows was bandaged and at rest. Tommy's side had ceased to pain.

"You have what it takes to fly for me," Barrows said.

"Thanks!" Tommy said, and went on sipping his soup.

The Yellow Shop

By Rachel Field

ALL her neighbors on Cranberry Common advised Miss Roxanna Robbins against adopting the twins.

"You're not so young as you were," Miss Peters, who lived next door, told her, "and two children will eat you out of house and home."

"Oh, I guess not," said Miss Roxanna. "Besides they're my brother's children and I don't want they should go to strangers."

"How old are they?" asked Mrs. Winterbottom, the Doctor's wife. When Miss Roxanna said they were going on nine, she shook her head very knowingly. "Just the age to get mumps and measles and chicken pox and whooping cough.

"But they've had all those already," said Miss Roxanna. "It's in this letter."

"I don't believe it for a minute," said Mrs. Winterbottom, "but even if it's true you ought to have your roof mended first."

"It won't leak any worse because two more are under it," Miss Roxanna told her, "and they're coming day after tomorrow."

So Will and Rebecca came.

They had been living with her nearly a year. The roof still leaked, but they all knew just where the rain was likely to come in. They took turns sleeping in the room with the biggest leak. There was an old umbrella always kept within easy reach that could be set up at the first drop on the pillow.

Although they were twins they did not look at all alike. Will had blue eyes and sandy hair and freckles and he could whistle more tunes than any other boy in the brick schoolhouse. Rebecca had dark eyes and brown hair and she could make boats and birds and windmills out of paper quick as a wink. Miss Roxanna liked the tunes and paper birds and boats very much indeed, but all the neighbors said something useful would be more to the point. It was overhearing Miss Peters saying this to Mrs. Winterbottom that made the children decide to open the little yellow shop.

It stood down by Miss Roxanna's gate and it had been boarded up for so many years that only a few people remembered that it had once done a thriving business.

"Why don't we keep store?" they said to each other as they walked home from their last day of school.

So the next morning they were up early and at work. Will pried the boards off the door and window and they went inside. It was just the way Miss Roxanna's brother Timothy had left it years before.

"It's just the right size for us," said Rebecca.

"Yes," agreed Will, "and that's as nice

298

a counter as I ever saw and those drawers behind will hold a lot."

All that morning they worked away on it, Rebecca with the broom and dustpan, and Will with pail and scrubbing brush. It was spick and span by noon when they called their Aunt out to see. Although it

was so small, it had drawers and shelves and a small rusty black iron stove with a chimney that stuck out of the roof. Best of all, on one shelf they found a box half full of clay pipes, and an old china teapot, and two blue glass jars. On still another there was a bolt of red-and-white gingham.

"Well," said Miss Roxanna when they showed her, "I'd forgotten all about that teapot and the jars. Timothy used to keep molasses drops and peppermint sticks in them, and that gingham looks like new."

That was how the store started, though if it had not been for Silas Bean there would have been very few customers. Silas Bean lived down the road all by himself, and everyone said he was the handiest man for miles around. That very evening after supper Will and Rebecca went to tell him about their plan.

"But the trouble is," explained Rebecca, "that people won't come to a store 'way off on a back road."

"That's so," said Silas Bean, puffing at his pipe.

"If we could just get our shop moved over to the signpost on the Turnpike," Will went on, "lots of cars would stop."

"That's so," said Silas.

"You moved Joneses' ice-house half a mile away and it's five times as big," Will reminded him. "Besides, we've got an old cart to hoist our shop on."

"That's so," said Silas Bean again, but this time he uncrossed his legs and put away his pipe. "Well, I'll be over in the morning and see what I can do about it."

When Silas Bean said he would see what he could do about anything, it always meant business, so in a day or two the neighbors were startled to see the little yellow shop mounted on blue wheels and creaking down the road behind Silas Bean's white horse.

"Sakes alive!" cried Miss Peters, who

had dropped in to chat with Mrs. Winterbottom. "Do you see what's going by?"

"Well, I never!' exclaimed Mrs. Winterbottom. "Next thing we know meeting house will change places with county jail and then where'll we be?"

"It's all those children's devilment," agreed Miss Peters, "and I think Roxanna Robbins might be more considerate of her neighbors. But then what can you expect, adopting two young ones at her age?"

Just before the Turnpike reached Cranberry Common four roads met. Where they crossed there was a small three-cornered island of grass holding a sign-post. The letters on the signboards were not very clear. People often found it hard to know which road to take. It was here that Will and Rebecca had decided to set up shop.

"You see," Will told Silas Bean, "they 'most always stop to ask the way and if we're right here they may buy something too."

"That's so," said Silas Bean, backing the horse in neatly.

The yellow shop with its two big blue wheels just fitted in comfortably with enough grass to spare all around and the signpost rising above it like a tree. Silas Bean had promised not to send any bill for moving them till the end of the season, so they had been able to invest in tea, lemons, sugar, peppermint sticks, and lemon drops. Besides this they had bought a geranium for the window. It just matched the red in the curtains and Rebecca's apron, which Miss Roxanna had

made out of the bolt of checkered gingham.

She had made them molasses drops like the kind her brother Timothy had sold, and a batch of sugar cookies. Will had picked cherries off their tree to go in the little paper boxes Rebecca had made and lined with rhubarb leaves.

After the blue glass jars were filled, they squeezed lemons and made a big pail of lemonade with a piece of ice floating in it and a dipper all ready for their first customer.

Then they sat down in the open door and waited for business to begin. It seemed a long time before any of the scudding cars slowed down, but at last one did. It was a very.big green and black one with a driver in front and a lady sitting behind with a little dog beside her. They wanted to know which road went to Oldport. Will told them as politely as he could. Then he summoned up courage and said,

"You wouldn't like anything today, would you? We have very nice candy and lemonade and cookies."

"And everything's home-made," added Rebecca.

The Lady smiled and her little dog put out his pink tongue as if he had understood.

"Well," she said, "it's a little early in the morning for me, but Sandy here would like a drink of water and a cookie."

So Rebecca went in to get the cookie

and Will dipped out some water from the pail he had carried from their well. Sandy seemed to enjoy it very much and

the Lady said they would surely stop again soon.

"Look," said Will, staring down at the dime in his hand, "she gave us the same as if it had been tea or lemonade."

"I never thought our first customer would be a dog," she said.

It happened that Fourth of July came along during their very first week. This was fortunate and they both felt relieved when fine weather was predicted. By noon on the third, cars were spinning along at such a rate that Will and Rebecca decided to invest most of the three dollars and fifty-seven cents they had cleared so far in a large supply of lemons and bottles of ginger ale, root beer, and sarsaparilla. They added more molasses drops and peppermints, till the old jars were full to the top, and their Aunt Roxanna had made an extra-large batch of cookies. These, with the last of the cherries, carefully arranged in the paper boxes, made them feel ready for any number of customers.

They were up almost before the sun rose over Tumbledown Mountain, and breakfast and chores were done before the dew had dried off the grass in the dooryard. Off they set with their pails and bundles. Soon they were hard at it. Rebecca squeezed lemons and set out their wares on a little table by the door while Will went over to the store for a piece of ice. Even before he was back with it, cars were beginning to stop and ask directions. Soon he and Rebecca were so busy filling glasses and answering questions they hadn't time to notice how hot it was getting. Sometimes they heard distant pops from the direction of the town, and they knew that meant that many of their schoolmates were setting off torpedoes and firecrackers.

"They're making a big noise on the common," Will remarked after one very loud burst, "but I'd lots rather be doing this, wouldn't you?"

"Oh, my, yes," Rebecca said. "How much money have we taken in so far?"

"Two dollars and five cents," Will told her proudly. "And it's not twelve o'clock yet. I shouldn't wonder if we made as much as five by tonight."

Just then they saw a cloud of dust and in the middle of it a Motorcycle Policeman, keeping an eye out for speeding cars. The sight of his uniform made the children feel a little sober, even though they felt sure he wouldn't be interested in a shop that stayed perfectly still in one place.

"There he comes again," said Will, pointing.

"He must be pretty hot chasing round in the sun after cars," said Rebecca. "Maybe we ought to give him some lemonade."

"I guess he'd drink it, all right," Will said, "and we give some to Old Man Jenkins 'most every time he goes by with the mail."

The Motorcycle Policeman seemed very glad to stop a few moments. He had a pleasant smile and looked much less old and terrifying when he took off his goggles.

"Well," he said, looking the little Yellow Shop and its owners over, "nice place you've got here. Business good?"

"Oh, yes," they told him, "we've had lots of customers already."

"I have to go chasing after my customers," he explained with a grin.

"Have you arrested lots?" Will couldn't help being curious.

"I've done pretty well so far, and this afternoon I expect to do better."

Presently, with the pleased feeling that they were on speaking terms with a person of great importance on the road, they watched him ride away.

They had sold all their stock of food and drink by six o'clock and their cash box was heavy with five dollars and eighty-seven cents.

"If we keep on at this rate," Will and Rebecca told each other as they closed the Shop door and started home again, "we'll be almost rich by September."

But September is a long way from July. A good many things can happen in between, as they soon discovered. In fact it was the very next day that unpleasant rumors began to reach them.

Old Man Jenkins was the first to give them any warning. He stopped as usual on his way out with the mail. His dog Nellie sat beside him on the front seat of his dilapidated Ford car, with the Rural Free Delivery mail bags piled behind. Nellie was one of their best dog customers and Old Man Jenkins was glad to stop and chat on his way coming and going. It was from him that Will and Rebecca learned how Tony, the Hot-Dog-Stand Man, was feeling about them.

"Yes, sir," he told them one morning

302

soon after the Fourth, "Tony's got it in for you two, all right."

"What—what's the matter?" asked Will and Rebecca together.

"You've run off with all his trade, that's what," Old Man Jenkins explained between gulps of lemonade. "He says you catch all the cars 'fore they get to his stand on the Bridge."

"He's mad because we thought of coming here first," said Will. "He could have put his stand here long ago if he'd wanted to."

"Oh, he's mad, all right." Old Man Jenkins wagged his head and helped himself to another cookie. "Swears he's goin' to get you out of here."

"But he couldn't do that, could he?" asked Rebecca with a worried frown.

"Well,"—Old Man Jenkins wiped his mustache thoughtfully with his blue spotted handkerchief—"I don't say as he could, and then again I don't say as he couldn't. He's tricky, Tony is, and mean, so you watch yourselves."

Will and Rebecca were rather sober after he drove off, but they had a good many customers, because it was a very warm day and lemonade was in demand. They squeezed more lemons and ladled it out into glasses carefully, but their thoughts were busy with wondering whatever they would do if Tony, the Hot-Dog-Stand Man, started to make trouble.

"I don't know what Aunt Roxanna will say when we tell her," sighed Rebecca to Will.

Miss Roxanna Robbins said a great many things when she heard about it from them that night. But she had also heard about Tony and his threats from Miss Peters and Mrs. Winterbottom earlier in the day.

"They say he's going to the Selectmen about it," she told them, "and he claims he can put you off because that little piece of land the signpost stands on is public property."

They were very quiet for a long while after that, and none of them ate much supper or slept very well that night.

Next morning Will was very thoughtful and Rebecca's eyes looked as if she had been crying.

"You ask Silas Bean when he goes by if he'll come and move us back after his supper tonight," Will said without looking at his Aunt's face.

"Well, I guess that's the best thing to do," she answered with a sigh. "It seems a pity with you and the Yellow Shop all fixed there so nice. Still, we can't afford to have any trouble and maybe we can find some other way to get the roof mended."

It was beginning to rain by the time the twins reached the crossroads, but they felt too miserable to remember that this would mean fewer customers.

They opened the Shop door and began watering the geranium and set about their duties for the last time.

Old Man Jenkins came by presently and looked sympathetic when they told him.

"Well, now, that's too bad," he said, "but I can see how your Aunt feels about it. She don't want to get in no hot water with the law."

"That's it," nodded Rebecca, and she and Will gave him extra cookies because it was the last time.

After he had gone they sat indoors by the windows and watched cars scudding by in the rain.

"Let's light the fire and make some tea," said Rebecca at last. "It looks so nice to see the smoke coming out the chimney and perhaps someone would like a cup."

Just as they had the tea steaming and ready to pour out of the china teapot, they heard a car stopping.

"It looks like that big green one with the Lady and Sandy in it," Will said, peering through the rain-splashed window.

Sure enough when he opened the door, there they were.

"Good afternoon," said the Lady from the back of the car. "Sandy would like another cookie. But no water," she added with a laugh, "there's too much coming down already." She spoke to the driver before she turned to Will again. "And I think if you have room for us, Sandy and I will come in and wait in your shop while John takes the car to the nearest garage. We've been having some trouble with it since we left home."

So presently the Little Yellow Shop was as full as it could be, with Rebecca pouring out tea for them all on the counter. The Lady sat on the one chair, drink-ing hers out of their only cup and saucer, and admiring the curtains and the blue glass jars. In fact all the time she talked about other things her eyes kept going back to the shelf where they stood.

Sandy could sit up and beg and "speak" for bits of cookie, and this pleased Will and Rebecca so much they almost forgot their own troubles. It was only when the Lady said what a very nice shop they had that they remembered it would not be there very much longer.

"It won't be here after today maybe," Will told her.

"No," explained Rebecca, passing the cookies, "we've got to go because Tony, the Hot-Dog-Stand Man at the Bridge, is going to make trouble."

"It's a pity, too," Will added, "for there's no place on the road as good as this and we were going to make enough money to get the roof sh——" He stopped just in time, knowing that Aunt Roxanna would not like them to mention such a thing before strangers.

"I'm very sorry to hear it," said their visitor, setting her cup down on the counter, "especially when I can't remember ever having a better cup of tea." Then, after she had looked at the shelf for a long time, she continued, "I wonder if you'd let me have a look at those blue glass jars?"

Rebecca reached them down from the shelf and stood them on the counter beside her. Their customer took each one up carefully, turning it slowly this way and that in her hands.

"They look like old ones," she said.

"Yes, they are," Will told her. "They belonged to Aunt Roxanna's brother Timothy and he's been dead for years."

But the Lady kept rubbing the glass with her handkerchief and the children watched her curiously. After a while she looked up and smiled at them.

"Do you know," she said, "I've been looking for just such a pair of blue glass jars for more years than you two are old? Do you think your Aunt would let me buy them?"

Will and Rebecca had to go behind the counter to talk this over in whispers.

"What do you think?" Rebecca asked Will. "Maybe she wouldn't like for us to sell Uncle Timothy's glass jars."

"Still," Will reminded her, "you know she'd forgotten all about them till we opened the Shop."

"Do you think we'd dare ask as much as a dollar apiece for them?"

"Let's ask her," decided Will.

The Lady did not think a dollar apiece was too much. In fact she opened her bag and took two right out. Then she began to write something on a slip of paper with her fountain pen.

"I want you to give this to your Aunt, please," she told them when she had finished and folded it. "She will know what to do with it."

Just then John came back with the car and soon she and Sandy and the two glass jars were inside, driving away down the Turnpike.

"Well, we've made almost as much money as if it had been a pleasant day," Will told Rebecca.

They were quite happy for a few moments till they recollected it was their last day under the signpost.

"Oh, dear," sighed Rebecca for the twentieth time that day, "I do wish something would happen to make things all right again."

"So do I," Will answered, just as he had every other time she had said it.

Just as the last spark had died out of the fire and they were gathering up their things to go home, they heard the sound of wheels and a voice calling.

It was Silas Bean and their hearts sank, for this must mean that he had come to move them back.

He stood in the door looking very tall in his rubber boots and sou'wester.

"No, I ain't come to move you today," he told them. "Get in the wagon and I'll drive you home."

"But—but didn't Aunt Roxanna tell you?" they questioned him as they jogged along behind his white horse under the big yellow umbrella Silas Bean always put up when it rained.

"Let's see," said Silas Bean, "seems to me she did say something 'bout it when I drove by this noon."

"About Tony, the Hot-Dog-Stand Man," Rebecca prompted, "and how he's going to make trouble?"

"Why, yes, that was what she said." Silas shook the water off the reins before he went on: "But I told her not to bother her head over it."

"But he's going to complain to the Selectmen," said Will.

"Well, let him," said Silas Bean. "I just come from makin' a little call on the head Selectman myself."

"You did!" The twins both stared up at him in amazement.

"Yes, sir, him and me used to go to school together down in the brick schoolhouse. So he's glad to do me a good turn every now and then."

"And you asked him to let us stay by the signpost all the rest of the summer?" they both asked him in the same breath.

"That's right, and he said there wouldn't be any trouble from Tony, leastways if there is, they'll tell him he can't have his stand by the Bridge, for that's public property, too."

"Why, so it is!" exclaimed Will. "I never thought about that."

Miss Roxanna was beaming when she met them at the door. She had made a new batch of molasses cookies and she invited Silas Bean to stay for supper.

"Well, I don't mind if I do," he agreed and went off to put the horse in the barn.

It wasn't till they were all through and the dishes done that Rebecca remembered about Uncle Timothy's glass jars and the slip of paper the Lady had given them, which was still in Will's pocket. When Miss Roxanna put on her spectacles and read what was written on it her cheeks grew very red.

"Oh, my," she said, "I guess there must be some mistake. Nobody could possibly pay as much as all that for two old glass jars."

"Let's see," said Silas Bean. He turned the slip of paper over several times, scrutinizing every letter carefully. "Looks all right to me," he said at last, "and I guess fifty dollars will come in sort of handy to you right now. Want me to buy some shingles and start in on your roof tomorrow?"

"Oh, yes," cried Will and Rebecca, "because we'll have lots more by the end of the summer."

Only Miss Roxanna hesitated.

"I hope it's all right to take it," she said a little doubtfully. "I don't believe your Grandfather and Uncle Timothy would mind, but I don't know what Miss Peters and Mrs. Winterbottom will say."

"I know," said Rebecca. "They'll say, 'This is what comes of taking two children at your age, Roxanna Robbins!'"

"That's so," said Silas Bean.

Singing Games and Favorite Songs

You have probably played the Singing Games on the next several pages, no matter in what country you happen to live, for they are played and sung by children in almost every country in the world.

The Songs that follow the Singing Games come originally from here, there, and everywhere. Some, like the Negro Spirituals and the American patriotic songs and ballads, are typically American. Others may have come from France, England, Ireland, Italy, or any number of other countries, and you may have heard your parents and grandparents singing them.

How to Play A Tisket, A Tasket

Form a ring. One of you stays outside and runs around, dropping a handkerchief quietly behind someone who is part of the ring. The one who drops the handkerchief keeps on running. Whoever is standing in front of the dropped handkerchief picks it up and runs in the opposite direction. Whichever one of the two reaches the empty place in the ring last has to stay outside and run around the circle and drop the handkerchief again.

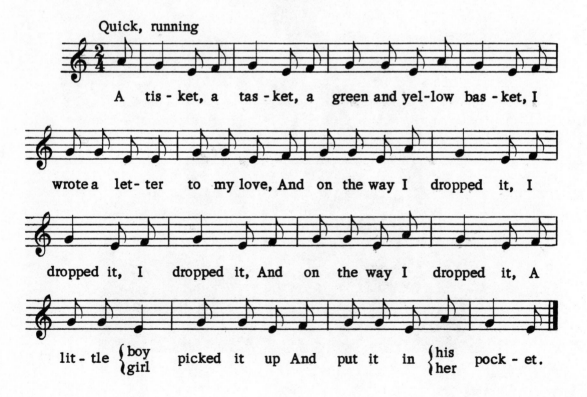

Quick, running

A tis-ket, a tas-ket, a green and yel-low bas-ket, I wrote a let-ter to my love, And on the way I dropped it, I dropped it, I dropped it, And on the way I dropped it, A lit-tle {boy/girl} picked it up And put it in {his/her} pock-et.

308

How to Play London Bridge

Two of you stand with hands joined and raised to form an arch. The others pass through as you sing the words of the song. When you come to the words, "My Fair Lady" the two forming the arch swing down their arms and capture whoever happens to be going through at the time. This one must answer the question: "Which do you choose —gold or silver?" (Or it could be "An emerald ring or a pony?" or any other choices you can think of.) Each side stands for one of the choices. The prisoner goes to the right or left of the arch depending on the choice he or she makes. The game ends with a tug of war between the two sides.

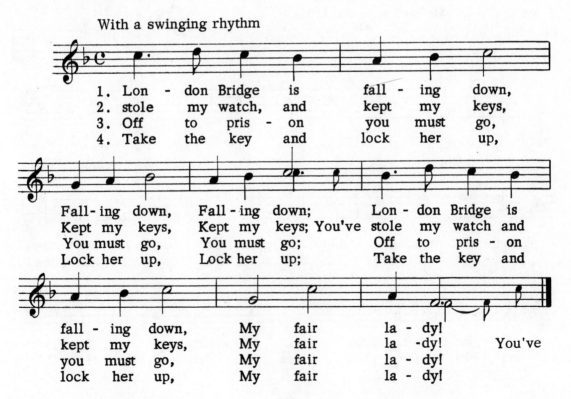

309

How to Play
The Muffin Man

All form a circle around one who stays in the center. You all skip to the left as the one in the center chooses a partner, holding out both hands at the words, "Oh, yes, we've seen the Muffin Man" in the second verse. The two who are now inside the circle skip around in the opposite direction, singing "Two have seen the Muffin Man," and finish the verse. At the beginning of the next verse, these two each choose a partner and the four now in the center sing "We four have seen the Muffin Man", and so on until you are all in one circle again. Then you sing "All have seen the Muffin Man."

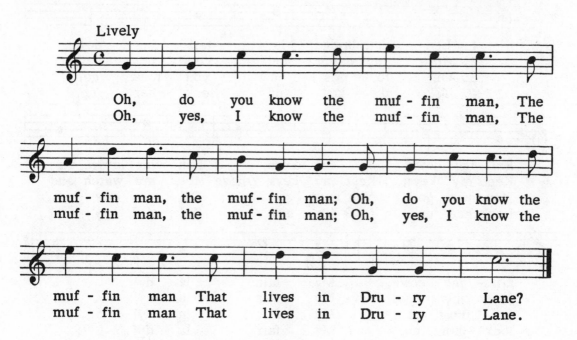

Lively

Oh, do you know the muf - fin man, The
Oh, yes, I know the muf - fin man, The

muf - fin man, the muf - fin man; Oh, do you know the
muf - fin man, the muf - fin man; Oh, yes, I know the

muf - fin man That lives in Dru - ry Lane?
muf - fin man That lives in Dru - ry Lane.

How to Play
The Farmer in the Dell

All of you form a ring except one, who stands in the center. This one is the Farmer. You skip or dance around to the left as you sing the first verse of the song. When you sing the second verse, the Farmer picks out someone for a Wife. In the third, the Wife chooses a Child, and so on until you come to the Cheese verse. The "Cheese" starts all over again as the Farmer.

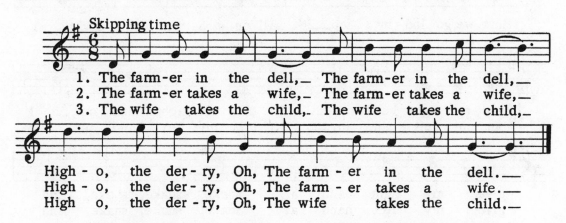

Skipping time

1. The farm-er in the dell,— The farm-er in the dell,—
2. The farm-er takes a wife,— The farm-er takes a wife,—
3. The wife takes the child,— The wife takes the child,—

High - o, the der - ry, Oh, The farm - er in the dell.—
High - o, the der - ry, Oh, The farm - er takes a wife.—
High o, the der - ry, Oh, The wife takes the child.—

4. The child chooses the nurse,
   The child chooses the nurse,
   High-o, the derry, Oh,
   The child chooses the nurse.

5. The nurse chooses the dog,
   The nurse chooses the dog,
   High-o, the derry, Oh,
   The nurse chooses the dog.

6. The dog chooses the cat,
   The dog chooses the cat,
   High-o, the derry, Oh,
   The dog chooses the cat.

7. The cat chooses the rat,
   The cat chooses the rat,
   High-o, the derry, Oh,
   The cat chooses the rat.

8. The rat chooses the cheese,
   The rat chooses the cheese,
   High-o, the derry, Oh,
   The rat chooses the cheese.

9. The cheese stands still,
   The cheese stands still,
   High-o, the derry, Oh,
   The cheese stands still.

How to Play Looby-Loo

Skip around in a circle with hands joined and sing this song until you come to the words "Saturday Night." Now all stretch out your right hands into the circle. Then turn half way around and stretch your right hands to the outside of the circle. Give your right hands a little shake and swing back to face the circle. For the other verses, do what the words say.

Here we go loo-by loo,— Here we go loo-by light,—

Here we go loo-by loo,— All on a Sat-ur-day night.— I

put my right hand in,— I take my right hand out,— I
put my left hand in,— I take my left hand out,— I

give my right hand a shake, shake, shake, And
give my left hand a shake, shake, shake, And

turn my-self a - bout.—
turn my-self a - bout.—

How to Play
Round the Village

Form a ring as you sing this game.

First Verse: One of you runs around and around the Village (the ring).

Second Verse: All join hands and raise your arms high, making "windows". The one outside the ring runs in and out the windows.

Third Verse: He or she chooses a partner.

Fourth Verse: The partners walk hand in hand around inside the circle, ending up in the center. They shake hands and separate.

The chosen partner now stays inside the circle and the game starts over again.

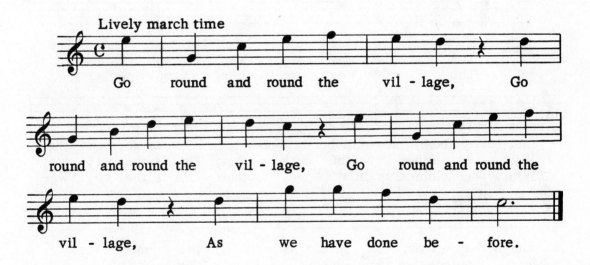

Lively march time

Go round and round the vil - lage, Go round and round the vil - lage, Go round and round the vil - lage, As we have done be - fore.

Go in and out the windows,
Go in and out the windows,
Go in and out the windows,
As we have done before.

Now stand and face your partner,
Now stand and face your partner,
Now stand and face your partner,
And bow before you go.

Now follow me to London,
Now follow me to London,
Now follow me to London,
As we have done before.

Now shake his hand and leave him,
Now shake his hand and leave him,
Now shake his hand and leave him,
And bow before you go.

How to Play
Round the Mulberry Bush

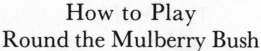

While you are singing this song, you all act out what the words tell you to do.

Skipping time

(Chor.) Here we go round the mul-ber-ry bush, The
1. This is the way we wash our clothes,
2. This is the way we iron our clothes,

mul-ber-ry bush, the mul-ber-ry bush, __ Here we go round the
Wash our clothes, wash our clothes;_ This is the way we
Iron our clothes, iron our clothes;_ This is the way we

mul-ber-ry bush, So ear-ly in the morn-ing.
wash our clothes, So ear-ly Mon-day morn-ing.(Chor.)
iron our clothes, So ear-ly Tues-day morn-ing.(Chor.)

3. This is the way we scrub the floor,
   Scrub the floor, scrub the floor;
   This is the way we scrub the floor,
   So early Wednesday morning.(Chor.)

4. This is the way we mend our clothes,
   Mend our clothes, mend our clothes;
   This is the way we mend our clothes,
   So early Thursday morning.(Chor.)

5. This is the way we sweep the house,
   Sweep the house, sweep the house;
   This is the way we sweep the house,
   So early Friday morning.(Chor.)

6. Thus we play when our work is done,
   Our work is done, our work is done;
   Thus we play when our work is done,
   So early Saturday morning.(Chor.)

314

How to Play
Oats, Peas, Beans and Barley Grow

One of you is the Farmer. The Farmer sings the first three lines of the song while the others march around him in a ring. All stop and sing and act the next four lines, scattering seeds, standing at ease, clapping hands, and turning around. March around again, sing-ing the next verse. As you come to the words "Open the ring and send one in", the Farmer chooses a partner from the ring. All sing the last verse, and at the end the Farmer becomes part of the ring. The game starts again with the partner as Farmer.

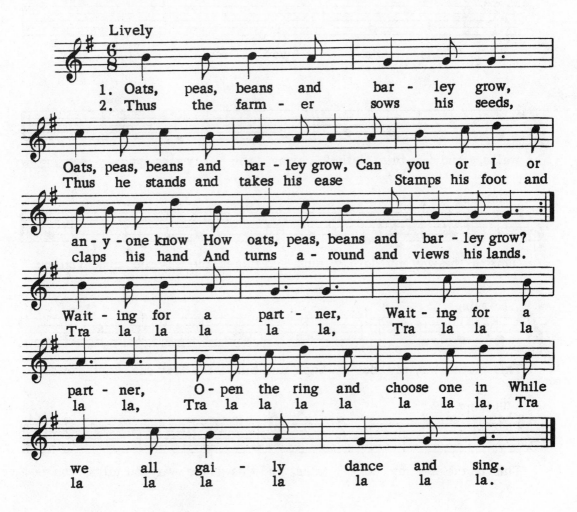

Lively

1. Oats, peas, beans and bar-ley grow,
2. Thus the farm-er sows his seeds,

Oats, peas, beans and bar-ley grow, Can you or I or
Thus he stands and takes his ease Stamps his foot and

an-y-one know How oats, peas, beans and bar-ley grow?
claps his hand And turns a-round and views his lands.

Wait-ing for a part-ner, Wait-ing for a
Tra la la la la la, Tra la la la

part-ner, O-pen the ring and choose one in While
la la, Tra la la la la la la la, Tra

we all gai-ly dance and sing.
la la la la la la la.

How to Play
My Dolly

You all walk around in a circle, stiffly, like dolls, while you sing the first verse. You run while you sing the second verse, and you hop while you sing the third verse. When you come to the fourth verse you talk as your dolly talks, pressing on your own chests at each word the way you press on your dolly's chest to make her talk.

Walking

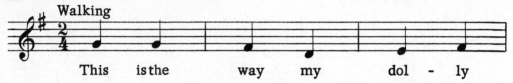

This is the way my dol - ly

walks, And this is the way she walks, you see,

Running

This is the way my dol - ly runs, and this is the way she runs, you see.

Hopping

This is the way my dol - ly hops, and this is the way she hops, you see.

Talking

This is the way my dol - ly talks, and this is the way she talks, you see.

316

How to Play
Did You Ever See a Lassie?

Form a circle with one of you in the center. You all sing the song. When you come to the words "Go this way and that," the one in the center does an imitation of someone sleeping, dancing, reading, or doing any of the things people do in ordinary life. During this last part of the verse you all imitate these actions.

Waltz time

Did you ev-er see a {las-sie, a {las-sie, a {lad-die, {lad-die,

{las-sie, Did you ev-er see a {las-sie go this way and {lad-die, {lad-die

that? Go this way and that way and this way and

that way? Did you ev-er see a

{las-sie go this way and that? {lad-die

How to Play
I'm Very, Very Tall

One of you is chosen to be blindfolded, and the rest form a circle around this child. At the end of the song one of those in the circle is chosen to say which each child shall be—"very, very tall" or "very, very small."

When you sing, very slowly, "I'm very, very tall" you make yourselves as tall as possible. And when you sing, very slowly, "I'm very, very small," you make yourselves as small as possible.

When you get the signal to be either tall or small you sing quickly, "Guess which I am now!"

The blindfold child guesses. If more of his guesses are wrong than right he loses and someone else is chosen to be the blindfolded guesser for the next game.

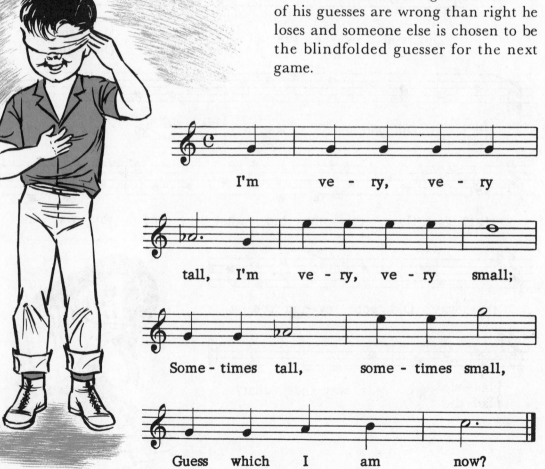

I'm ve - ry, ve - ry

tall, I'm ve - ry, ve - ry small;

Some - times tall, some - times small,

Guess which I am now?

Cradle Song

Music by
FRANZ SCHUBERT

Arr. by Oscar Catsiff

English Words by
F.R.R.

1. Sweet - ly slum - ber 'neath the or - chard shad - ows,
2. Sweet - ly slum - ber o'er thine eye - lids - ten - der,
3. Sweet - ly slum - ber while I bear thee home - ward;

near thee murm - 'ring soft the brook - let flows;
or - chard blos - soms waft their fra - grant snows;
heav'n grows dark - er, cold an east wind blows;

winds of spring - time gen - tly lull thee
may they wake not may they bring thee
in these arms sleep soft - ly, dar - ling

moth - er's dar - ling, moth - er's op - 'ning rose.
an - gel vi - sions, dew - y deep re - pose.
moth - er's love, no change no cold - ness knows.

Lullaby

JOHANNES BRAHMS

Arr. by G. M. Groene

1. Lul - la - by and good night! With ros - es be - dight, creep in - to thy bed, There pil - low thy head. If God will, thou shalt wake when the morn - ing doth break, If God will, thou shalt wake, when the morn - ing doth break.

2. Lul - la - by and good night; Those blue eyes close tight; bright an - gels are near, So sleep with - out fear. They will guard thee from harm with fair dream-land's charm, They will guard thee from harm with fair dream-land's charm.

1. *Gu - ten A bend, gut' Nacht, mit Ro - sen be - dacht, mit Näg - lein be - steckt, schlumpf' un - ter die Deck; Mor - gen früh, wenn Gott will, wirst du wie - der ge - weckt Mor - gen früh wenn Gott will, wirst du wie - der ge - weckt.*

2. *Gu - ten A bend, gut' Nacht, von Eng - lein be - wacht, die zei - gen im Traum dir Christ - kind - leins Baum: Schlaf' nun se - lig und süss, schau 'im Traum's Pa - ra - dies. Schlaf' nun se - lig und süss, schau 'im Traum's Pa - ra - dies.*

Sweet and Low

ALFRED TENNYSON

JOSEPH BARNBY

321

Polly Wolly Doodle

Lively

Arr. by G. M. Compagno

Solo or Unison

1. Oh, I went down South for to see my Sal,
2. Oh, my Sal she am a ___ maid - en fair;

CHORUS

Sing Pol - ly wol - ly doo - dle all the day;

Solo

My ___ Sal - ly am a spunk - y gal,
With ___ laugh - ing eyes and curl - y hair,

CHORUS

Sing Pol - ly wol - ly doo - dle all the day.

Fare thee well, Fare - well, fare thee well, fare - well, fare thee

well my fair - y fay, For I'm goin' to Loui - si - a - na, For to

see my Su - sy - an - na, Sing Pol - ly wol - ly doo - dle all the day.

Row, Row, Row Your Boat

Arr. by George Snowhill

Old MacDonald Had a Farm

Arr. by
Arthur Fields and Fred Hall

1. Old Mac Don-ald had a farm E-I-E-I-O! And on this farm he
2. Old Mac Don-ald had a farm And on this farm he

had some chicks, E-I-E-I-O! With a chick, chick, here, and a chick, chick there,
had some ducks, With a quack, quack, here, and a quack, quack there,

Here a chick, there a chick, Ev-'ry-where a chick, chick, Old MacDonald had a farm E-I-E-I-O!
Here a quack, there a quack, Ev-'ry-where a quack, quack,

3. And on this farm he had some turks, E-I-E-I-O!
With a gobble, gobble, here, and a gobble, gobble there,
Here a gobble, there a gobble,
Ev'ry-where a gobble, gobble, etc.

4. And on this farm he had some pigs, E-I-E-I-O!
With a oink, oink, here, and a oink, oink there,
Here a oink, there a oink,
Ev'ry-where a oink, oink, etc.

5. And on this farm he had a Ford, E-I-E-I-O!
With a rattle, rattle, here, and a rattle, rattle there,
Here a rattle, there a rattle,
Ev'ry-where a rattle, etc.

6. And on this farm he had some mules, E-I-E-I-O!
With a he-haw here, and a he-haw there,
Here a he-haw, there a he-haw,
Ev'ry-where a he-haw, etc.

7. And on this farm he had some sheep, E-I-E-I-O!
With a baa, baa, here, and a baa, baa there,
Here a baa baa, there a baa baa,
Ev'ry-where a baa, baa, etc.

8. And on this farm he had some cows, E-I-E-I-O!
With a moo, moo, here, and a moo, moo there,
Here a moo moo, there a moo moo,
Ev'ry-where a moo, moo, etc.

9. And on this farm he had some dogs, E-I-E-I-O!
With a bow-wow here, and a bow-wow there,
Here a bow-wow, there a bow-wow,
Ev'ry-where a bow-wow, etc.

10. And on this farm he had a wife, E-I-E-I-O!
With a gimme, gimme, here and a gimme, gimme there,
Here a gimme, there a gimme.
Ev'ry-where a gimme, gimme, etc.

Aloha Oe

By H. M. QUEEN LILIUOKALANI

Moderato

Proud - ly swept the rain - cloud by the cliff___ As
Ha - a - heo ka u - a i - na pa - li Ke

on it glid - ed thro' the trees___ Still fol - low - ing with grief the
nihi a - e - la ka - na - he - le E ha - ha - i a - na i - ka

li - ko The a - hi - hi - le - hua of the vale___
li - ko Pu - a a - hi - hi - le - hu - a o u - ka

ff

Fare - well to thee, fare - well to thee Thou charm - ing one who dwells a - mong the
A - lo - ha oe a - lo - ha oe E ke o - na - o - na no - ho i - ka

bow - 'rs One fond em - brace be - fore I now de - part Un - til we meet a - gain.
li - po One fond em - brace a ho - i a - e au Un - til we meet a - gain.

La Cucaracha

English Words by
STANLEY ADAMS

Arr. by G. M. Compagno

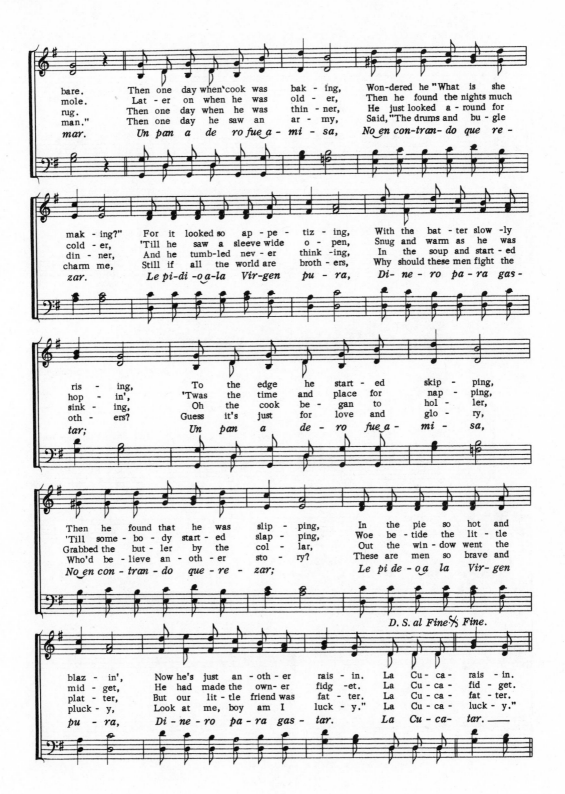

bare. Then one day when cook was bak - ing, Won-dered he "What is she
mole. Lat - er on when he was old - er, Then he found the nights much
rug. Then one day when he was thin - ner, He just looked a - round for
man." Then one day he saw an ar - my, Said, "The drums and bu - gle
mar. Un pan a de ro fue a - mi - sa, No en con-tran- do que re -

mak - ing?" For it looked so ap - pe - tiz - ing, With the bat - ter slow -ly
cold - er, 'Till he saw a sleeve wide o - pen, Snug and warm as he was
din - ner, And he tumb-led nev - er think - ing, In the soup and start - ed
charm me, Still if all the world are broth - ers, Why should these men fight the
zar. Le pi-di -o a-la Vir-gen pu - ra, Di - ne - ro pa-ra gas-

ris - ing, To the edge he start - ed skip - ping,
hop - in', 'Twas the time and place for nap - ping,
sink - ing, Oh the cook be - gan to hol - ler,
oth - ers? Guess it's just for love and glo - ry,
tar; Un pan a de - ro fue a - mi - sa,

Then he found that he was slip - ping, In the pie so hot and
'Till some - bo - dy start - ed slap - ping, Woe be - tide the lit - tle
Grabbed the but - ler by the col - lar, Out the win - dow went the
Who'd be - lieve an - oth - er sto - ry? These are men so brave and
No en con - tran- do que re - zar; Le pi de -o a la Vir- gen

D. S. al Fine 𝄋 Fine.

blaz - in', Now he's just an - oth - er rais - in. La Cu - ca - rais - in.
mid - get, He had made the own - er fidg - et. La Cu - ca - fid - get.
plat - ter, But our lit - tle friend was fat - ter. La Cu - ca - fat - ter.
pluck - y, Look at me, boy am I luck - y." La Cu - ca - luck - y."
pu - ra, Di - ne - ro pa - ra gas - tar. La Cu - ca - tar. ____

327

Ach Du Lieber Augustin

English Version by
DON TITMAN

Arr. by G. M. Compagno

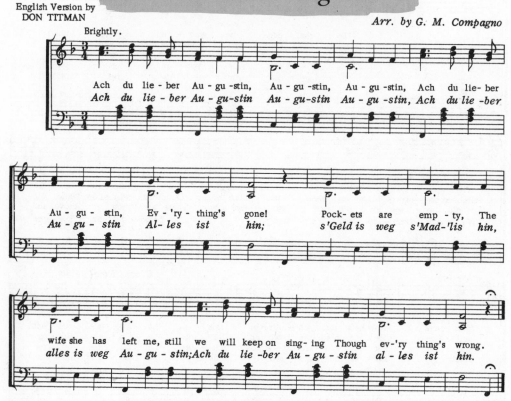

Funiculi, Funicula

English Words By
EDW. OXENFORD

Music by LUIGI DENZA
Arr. by G. M. Compagno

Frère Jacques

French Round

331

Tit Willow

W. S. GILBERT

SIR ARTHUR SULLIVAN
Arr. by George Snowhill

Moderato

1. On a tree by a riv-er a lit-tle tom-tit Sang
2. He __ slapped at his chest as he sat on the bough, Sing-ing
3. Now I feel just as sure as I'm sure that my name Isn't __

"wil-low, tit-wi-low, tit-wi-low!" And I said to him," Dick-y bird,
"wil-low, tit-wi-low, tit-wi-low!" And a cold per-spi-ra-tion be-
wil-low, tit-wi-low, tit-wi-low, __ That 'twas blight-ed af-fec-tion that

why do you sit Sing-ing wil-low, tit-wi-low, tit-wi-low? __ Is it
span-gled his brow, Oh, __ wil-low, tit-wi-low, tit-wi-low. __ He
make him ex-claim "Oh, __ wil-low, tit-wi-low, tit-wi-low!" __ And if

weak-ness of in-tel-lect, bird-ie," I cried, "Or a rath-er tough worm in your
sobbed as he sighed and a gur-gle he gave, Then he threw him-self in-to the
you re-main cal-lous and ob-du-rate, I shall per-ish as he did and

lit-tle in-side?" With a shake of his poor lit-tle
bil-low-y wave, And an ech-o a-rose from the
you will know why, Though I prob-ab-ly shall not ex-

head he re-plied: "Tit - wil-low, tit-wil-low, tit - wil-low!"
su - i-cide's grave, "Oh, wil-low, tit-wil-low, tit - wil-low!"
claim as I die: "Oh, wil-low, tit-wil-low, tit - wil-low!"

Good Night, Ladies

Not too slow

1. Good - night La-dies!   Good- night La-dies!   Good - night La-dies!   We're
2. Fare - well La-dies!   Fare - well La-dies!   Fare - well La-dies!   We're
3. Sweet dreams La-dies!   Sweet dreams La-dies!   Sweet dreams La-dies!   We're

going to leave you now
going to leave you now   Mer-ri- ly we roll a -long, Roll a - long, roll a - long,
going to leave you now

Mer - ri - ly we roll a - long,   O - ver the dark blue sea.

333

The Blue Bells of Scotland

(WHERE HAS MY HIGHLAND LADDIE GONE?)

Traditional
Arr. by G. M. Compagno

Moderately

1. O where, and O where is your High-land lad-die gone? O
2. O where, and O where does your High-land lad-die dwell? O-
3. Sup-pose, and sup-pose that your High-land lad should die? Sup-

where, and O where is your High-land lad-die gone?
where, and O where does your High-land lad-die dwell?
pose, and sup-pose that your High-land lad should die?

He's gone to fight the foe, for King George up-on the throne; And it's
He dwelt in mer-ry Scot-land at the sign of the Blue Bell; And it's
The bag-pipes shall play o'er him, and I'd lay me down and cry; But it's

oh! in my heart, how I wish him safe at home.
oh! in my heart, that I love my lad-die well.
oh! in my heart, that I wish he may not die.

334

Flow Gently, Sweet Afton

Words by ROBERT BURNS

Music by J. E. SPILMAN

Andante con moto.

1. Flow gen-tly, sweet Af-ton, a - mang thy green braes; Flow gen-tly, I'll sing thee a song in thy praise; My Ma-ry's a - sleep by thy mur-mur-ing stream, Flow gen-tly, sweet Af-ton, dis - turb not her dream. Thou stock-dove, whose ech-o re - sounds from the hill, Ye wild whist-ling black-birds in yon thorn-y den, Thou green-crest-ed lap-wing, thy scream-ing for-bear, I charge you, dis-turb not my slum-ber-ing fair.

2. How loft-y, sweet Af-ton, thy neigh-bor-ing hills, Far marked with the cours-es of clear wind-ing rills; There dai-ly I wan-der, as morn ris-es high, My flocks and my Ma-ry's sweet cot in my eye. How pleas-ant thy banks and green val-leys be-low, Where wild in the wood-lands the prim-ros-es blow! There oft, as mild eve-ning creeps o - ver the lea, The sweet-scent-ed birk shades my Ma-ry and me.

3. Thy crys-tal stream, Af-ton, how love-ly it glides, And winds by the cot where my Ma-ry re - sides! How wan-ton thy wa-ters her snow-y feet lave, As gath-'ring sweet flow'r-ets, she stems thy clear wave! Flow gen-tly, sweet Af-ton, a - mang thy green braes, Flow gen-tly, sweet riv-er, the theme of my lays: My Ma-ry's a - sleep by thy mur-mur-ing stream, Flow gen-tly, sweet Af-ton, dis - turb not her dream.

335

Loch Lomond

Words by LADY JOHN SCOTT

Marching time

1. By yon bon-nie banks an' yon bon-nie braes, The sun shines bright on Loch
2. 'Twas there that we part ed in yon shad - y glen, On the steep, steep side o' Loch

Lo - mond, Where me and my true love were ev - er wont to gae, On the
Lo - mond, Where pur - ple in hue, the High-land hills we view, An' the

bon-nie, bon-nie banks o' Loch Lo - mond. O ye'll take the high road, an'
moon com-in' out in the gloam - in'. O ye'll take the high road, an'

I'll take the low road, An' I'll be in Scot-land a - fore ye, For
I'll take the low road, An' I'll be in Scot-land a - fore ye, For

me an' my true love will ne - ver meet a-gain On the bon-nie, bon-nie banks o' Loch Lo - mond
me an' my true love will ne - ver meet a-gain On the bon-nie, bon-nie banks o' Loch Lo - mond.

Annie Laurie

WILLIAM DOUGLASS

LADY JOHN SCOTT

Moderately

Max - wel - ton's braes are bon - nie, Where ear - ly falls the
Her brow is like the snow - drift, Her throat is like the

dew, And twas there that An - nie Lau - rie Gave
swan; Her ___ face it is the fair - est That

me her prom - ise true; Gave me her prom - ise
e'er the sun shone on; That e'er the sun shone

true, Which ___ ne'er for - got will be, And for
on; And ___ dark blue is her e'e, And for

bon - nie An - nie ___ Lau - rie, I'd ___ lay ___ me down and dee.

Killarney

MICHAEL BALFE
Arr. by G. M. Compagno

1. By Kil-lar-ney's lakes and fells, Em-'rald isles and wind-ing bays,
2. In-nis-fal-len's ru-ined shrine, May sug-gest a pass-ing sigh,

Moun-tain paths and wood-land dells Mem-'ry ev-er fond-ly strays.
But man's faith can ne'er de-cline, Such God's won-ders float-ing by.

Boun-teous na-ture loves all lands, Beau-ty wan-ders ev-'ry-where,
Cas-tle Lough and Gle-na bay, Moun-tains Tore and Ea-gle's Nest,

Foot-prints leave on man-y strands, But her home is sure-ly there!
Still at Muck-cross you must pray, Tho' the monks are now at rest.

An-gels fold their wings and rest, In that E-den of the west,
An-gels won-der not that man, There would fain pro-long life's span,

Beau-ty's home Kil-lar-ney, Ev-er fair Kil-lar-ney.
Beau-ty's home Kil-lar-ney, Ev-er fair Kil-lar-ney.

The Wearing of the Green

Arr. by
Arthur Fields and Fred Hall

Allegretto

Oh__ Pad-dy dear and did you hear the news that's go-in' 'round The
Saint Pat-rick's day no more we'll keep his col-or can't be seen For

sham-rock is for - bid-den for to grow on I - rish ground.
there's a blood-y law a - gin the wear-in' of the green.

I__ met with Nap-per Tan-dy And he took me by the hand And he

said "How's poor old Ire - land and__ how__ does she stand?" She's the

most dis-tress-ful coun-try, sir, that ev - er you have seen They're

hang-ing men and wo-men For the wear-ing of the green.

Comin' thro' the Rye

Words by ROBERT BURNS

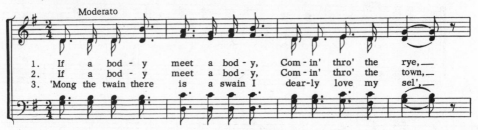

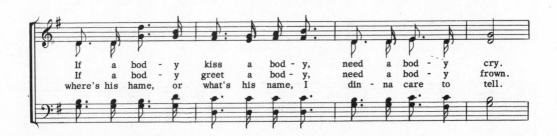

1. If a bod - y meet a bod - y, Com - in' thro' the rye, ___
2. If a bod - y meet a bod - y, Com - in' thro' the town, ___
3. 'Mong the twain there is a swain I dear - ly love my sel', ___

If a bod - y kiss a bod - y, need a bod - y cry.
If a bod - y greet a bod - y, need a bod - y frown.
where's his hame, or what's his name, I din - na care to tell.

Ev - 'ry las - sie has her lad - die, Nane they say have I Yet

all the lads they smile on me, When Com - in' thro' the rye.

Cockles and Mussels

Simply, *with tenderness*

Arr. by George Snowhill

1. In Dub - lin's fair cit - y where girls are so pret - ty, 'Twas
2. She was a fish - mon - ger, but that was no won - der; Her
3. She died of the "fa - ver" and no one could save her, Sure,

there that I met with sweet Mol - ly Ma - lone; She drove a wheel-bar - row through
fa - ther and moth - er were fish - mon - gers too. They drove their wheel-bar - row through
that's how I lost my sweet Mol - ly Ma - lone. Now her ghost drives her bar - row through

mf 1st time: *sweetly*
f 2nd time: *cackling*
p 3rd time: *gently*

rit.

streets old and nar - row
streets old and nar - row } Cry - ing: "Cock - les and mus - sels, a - live, a - live, O!"
streets old and nar - row

a tempo　　　　　　　　*same as above*

A - live, a-live, O, — A - live, a-live, O, — Cry-ing: "Cock-les and mus-sels a - live, a - live, O!"

341

Deck the Halls

Welsh Air

Joyfully

1. Deck the halls with boughs of hol - ly!
2. See the blaz - ing Yule be-fore us, Fa la la la la la la la la
3. Fast a - way the old year pass - es,

'Tis the sea - son to be jol - ly,
Strike the harp and join the chor-us, Fa la la la la la la la la
Hail the new, ye lads and lass - es,

Don we now our gay ap - par - el,
Fol - low me in mer - ry meas-ure, Fa la la la la la la la la
Sing we joy - ous all to - geth - er,

Troll the an - cient Yule - tide car - ol,
While I tell of Yule - tide trea - sure, Fa la la la la la la la la.
Heed - less of the wind and weath - er,

Home, Sweet Home

JOHN HOWARD PAYNE

HENRY BISHOP

The Harp that Once thro' Tara's Halls

THOMAS MOORE

Air "Gramachree"
Arr. by G. M. Compagno

1. The harp that once thro' Ta-ra's halls, The soul of mu-sic shed; Now
2. No more to chiefs and la-dies bright, The harp of Ta-ra swells; The

hangs as mute on Ta-ra's walls As if that soul were fled: So
chord, a-lone, that breaks at night, Its tale of ru-in tells: Thus

sleeps the pride of form-er days, So glo-ry's thrill is o'er, And
free-dom now so sel-dom wakes The on-ly throb she gives, Is

hearts that once beat high for praise, Now feel that pulse no more.
when some heart in-dig-nant breaks, To show that still she lives.

Au Clair de la Lune

J. B. LULLY

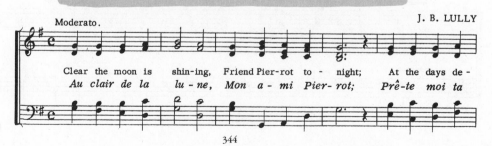

Clear the moon is shin-ing, Friend Pier-rot to-night; At the days de-
Au clair de la lu-ne, Mon a-mi Pier-rot; Prê-te moi ta

cli - ning, I've no fire nor light. Pen and pa - per lend me, Just one word to
plu - me pour e' - crire un mot. Ma chan-delle est mor - te Je n'ai plus de

write, _____ Pray you, do not send me, From your door this night.
feu; _____ Ou - vre moi ta por - te, Pour l'a - mour de Dieu.

La Marseillaise

ROUGET DE LISLE

Arr. by G. M. Compagno

Majestically

Ye sons of France a - wake to glo - ry! Hark! Hark! what my - riads bid you
Al - lons, en - fants de la pa - tri - e! Le jour de gloire est ar - ri -

rise! Your child- ren, wives, and grand-sires___ hoar-y, Be-hold their tears, and hear their
vé! Con - tre nous de la ty - ran - ni - e L'é - ten - dard san-glant est le -

cries! Be - hold their tears, and_hear their_ cries! Shall hate- ful ty - rants, mis-chief
vé! L'é - ten - dard san-glant est le - vé! En - ten-dez - vous, dans les cam -

breed-ing With hire-ling hosts, a ruf-fian— band, Af-fright and des-o-late the

pa - gnes, Mu-gir ces fé-ro-ces sol - dats? Ils vien-nent jusque dans nos

land;— When— peace and lib-er-ty lie bleed-ing? To arms, to arms ye

bras— E — gor -ger nos fils, nos cam - pa-gnes! Aux ar - mes, ci-to-

brave, Th'a - veng - ing sword un - sheath! March on,— march

yens! For - mez — vos ba-tail - lons! Mar - chons,— mar-

on,— All hearts— re - solved On lib - er - ty or death!

chons! Qu-un sang— im - pur A - breuve nos sil - lons!

Drink to Me Only with Thine Eyes

BEN JONSON

Arr. by G. M. Compagno

1. Drink to me on - ly with thine eyes, and I will pledge with mine;
2. I sent thee late a ro - sy wreath, not so much hon - 'ring thee

Or leave a kiss with - in the cup, And I'll not ask for wine; The
As giv - ing it a hope that there It could not with - ered be; But

thirst that from the soul doth rise Doth ask a drink di - vine;
thou there - on didst on - ly breathe, And sent'st it back to me,

But might I of Jove's nec - tar sup, I would - not change for thine.
Since when it grows and smells I swear, Not of it - self, but thee.

A Wand'ring Minstrel

W.S. GILBERT

SIR ARTHUR SULLIVAN
Arr. by George Snowhill

A wan-d'ring mins-trel I, A thing of shreds and patch-es, of bal-lads, songs and snatch-es, And dream-y lul-la-by! My ca-ta-logue is long, through ev'-ry pas-sion rang-ing, And to your hum-ours chang-ing I tune my sup-ple song! I tune my sup-ple song!

America the Beautiful

KATHERINE LEE BATES

SAMUEL A. WARD
Arr. by Harry Henneman

1. O beau - ti - ful for spa - cious skies, For am - ber waves of grain, _____ For pur - ple moun - tain maj - es - ties a - bove the fruit - ed plain. _____ A - mer - i - cal A - mer - i - cal God shed His grace on thee, _____ And crown thy good with broth - er - hood from sea to shin - ing sea. _____

2. O beau - ti - ful for pil - grim feet whose stern im - pas - sion'd stress, A thor - ough - fare for free - dom beat a - cross the wil - der - ness. _____ A - mer - i - cal A - mer - i - cal God mend thine ev - 'ry flaw, _____ Con - firm thy soul in self - con - trol, Thy lib - er - ty in law. _____

3. O beau - ti - ful for pa - triot dream That sees be - yond the years _____ Thine al - a - bas - ter cit - ies gleam un - dimmed by hu - man tears. _____ A - mer - i - cal A - mer - i - cal God shed His grace on thee, _____ And crown thy good with broth - er - hood from sea to shin - ing sea. _____

The Star Spangled Banner

FRANCIS SCOTT KEY

stream - ing? And the rock - et's red glare the bombs burst - ing in
- clos - es? Now it catch - es the gleam of the morn - ing's first
na - tion! Then con - quer we must, when our cause it is

air, Gave__ proof thro' the night that our flag was still there.
beam, In full glo - ry re flect - ed now shines on the stream;
just, And__ this be our mot - to: "In God is our trust!"

O__ say, does that Star - span - gled Ban - ner yet
'Tis the Star - span - gled Ban - ner, O long may it
And the Star - span - gled Ban - ner in tri - umph shall

wave,__ O'er the land__ of the free and the home of the brave?
wave,__ O'er the land__ of the free and the home of the brave!
wave,__ O'er the land__ of the free and the home of the brave!

351

The Maple Leaf Forever

O Canada

French Text by
ADOLPHE B. ROUTHIER

C. LAVALLEE
Arranged by Felix Guenther

Maestoso

O Can - a - da, Our home and na - tive land, True pa - triot
O Can - a - da, Where pines and ma - ples grow, Great prai - ries
O Can - a - da! Ter - re de nos ai - eux, Ton front est

love in all thy sons com - mand: With glow - ing hearts we
spread and lord - ly riv - ers flow. How dear to us thy
ceint de fleu - rons glo - ri - eux! Car ton bras sait por - ter l'é-

see thee rise, The true North, strong and free. And
vast do - main, From East to West - ern sea, Thou
pé - e, Il sait por - ter la croix! Ton his-

stand on guard, O Can - a - da, Stand aye en guard for thee.
land of hope for all who toil, Thou true North, strong and free!
toire est une é - po - pé - e Des plus bril - lants ex - ploits.

CHORUS

O Can - a - da! O Can - a - da! O Can - a - da! We stand on
Et ta va - leur, de foi trem - pée, Pro - té - ge - ra nos foy - ers

guard for thee, O Can - a - da! We stand on guard for thee.
et nos droits, Pro - te - ge - ra nos foy - ers et nos droits.

353

Home on the Range

Arr. by H. S. Krouse

1. Oh give me a home where the buf - fa - lo roam, Where the
2. Where the air is so pure, the zeph - yrs so free, And the
3. How oft - en at night when the heav - ens are bright, With the
4. Then I would not ex - change my home on the range, Where the

deer and the an - te - lope play,_____ Where sel - dom is heard a dis-
breez - es so balm - y and light;_____ I would not ex - change my
light of the glit - ter -ing stars,_____ Have I stood there a - mazed and
deer and the an - te - lope play,_____ Where sel - dom is heard a dis-

cour - ag - ing word, And the skies are not cloud - y all day, (all the day.)
home on the range, For___ all of your cit - ies so bright,
asked as I gazed, If their glo - ry ex - ceeds that of ours.
cour - ag - ing word, And the skies are not cloud - y all day.

REFRAIN

Home, home on the range, Where the deer and the an - te-lope play,_____ Where

sel -dom is heard a dis - cour- ag-ing word and the skies are not cloud-y all day, (all the day.)

Old Folks at Home

STEPHEN C. FOSTER
Arr. by P. Gallico

Carry Me Back to Old Virginny

By JAMES A. BLAND
Arr. by George Snowhill

My Old Kentucky Home

Words and Music by STEPHEN C. FOSTER
Arranged by P. Gallico.

Poco adagio.

The sun shines bright in the old Ken-tuck-y home, 'Tis sum-mer, the young folks are gay. The corn-top's ripe and the mead-ow's in the bloom, While the birds make mus-ic all the day; The young folks roll on the lit-tle cab-in floor, All mer-ry, all hap-py and bright, By'n by Hard Times comes a knock-ing at the door, Then my old Ken-tuck-y home, Good-night!

The Bear Went Over the Mountain

Arr. by L. Anthony

The Blue Tail Fly

Arr. by Florence White

CHORUS
Gaily.

Jim crack corn, I don't care,— Jim crack corn, I don't care,—

Jim crack corn, I don't care,— My mas-ter's gone a - way.

Fine

With mock drama.

1. When I was young I used to wait on mas-ter and hand him his plate, And
2. When he rode out in the af - ter noon, I'd fol - low with a hick-'ry broom, The
3. One day he rode a - round the farm, The flies so num-'rous they did swarm, One

pass the bot-tle when he got dry, And brush a - way the blue tail fly.
po - ny be - ing ve - ry shy, When bit - ten by the blue tail fly.
chanced to bite him on the thigh, The de - vil take the blue tail fly.

D. C.

4. The pony run, he jump, he pitch,
He threw old master in the ditch,
He died and the jury wondered why,
The verdict was the blue tail fly.

5. Old master's gone now, let him rest,
They say all things are for the best;
But I'll never forget 'til the day I die
Old master and that blue tail fly.

359

Upidee

Allegretto.

mf

1. The shades of night were fall-ing fast, Tra, la, la, Tra, la, la, As
2. His brow was sad, his eye Be-neath, Tra, la, la, Tra. la, la, Flash'd
3. "Oh stay," the maid-en said, "and rest Tra, la, la, Tra, la, la, Thy

thro' an Al-pine vil-lage passed, Tra la, la, la, la! A youth, who bore, 'mid snow and ice, A
like a fal-chion from its sheath, Tra la, la, la, la! And like a sil-ver clar-ion, rung The
wea-ry head up-on this breast!" Tra la, la, la, la! A tear stood in his bright blue eye, But

ritard.

ban-ner with the strange de-vise:
ac-cents of that un-known tongue: U-pi-dee-i, dee-i, da, U-pi-dee, U-pi-da,
still he an-swered with a sigh:

(Imitating a watchman's rattle.)

U-pi-dee-i, dee-i-da, U-pi-dee-i da! r-r-r-r-r-r-r-r-r-r-r-r yah! yah! yah! yah!

U-pi-dee-i-dee-i-da, U-pi-dee, U-pi-da, U-pi-dee-i, dee-i-da, U-pi-dee-i-da!

360

Clementine

By PERCY MONTROSE
Arr. by Harry Henneman

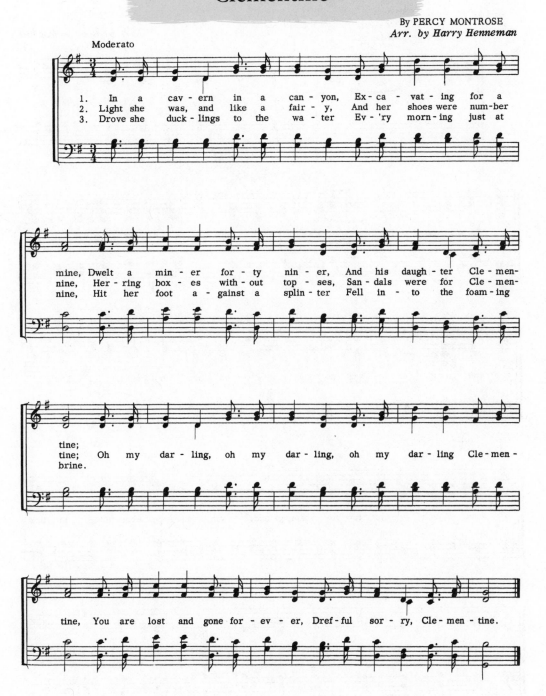

Moderato

1. In a cav-ern in a can-yon, Ex-ca-vat-ing for a
2. Light she was, and like a fair-y, And her shoes were num-ber
3. Drove she duck-lings to the wa-ter Ev-'ry morn-ing just at

mine, Dwelt a min-er for-ty nin-er, And his daugh-ter Cle-men-
nine, Her-ring box-es with-out top-ses, San-dals were for Cle-men-
nine, Hit her foot a-gainst a splin-ter Fell in-to the foam-ing

tine;
tine; Oh my dar-ling, oh my dar-ling, oh my dar-ling Cle-men-
brine.

tine, You are lost and gone for-ev-er, Dref-ful sor-ry, Cle-men-tine.

Deep River

Arr. by George Snowhill

Andante quasi Lento

Deep ——— Ri - ver, My home is o - ver

Jor - dan, ——— Deep ——— Ri - ver, Lord, I want to cross o - ver in - to

camp - ground, Lord, I want to cross o - ver in - to camp ground, ——— Lord, I

want to cross o - ver in - to camp ground. Oh, don't you want to go to that

Gos - pel - feast, That Prom - ised Land, where all is peace? Oh,

don't you want to go to that Gos-pel-feast, That Prom-ised Land, where

all is peace? Deep _____ Ri - ver, My home is o - ver

Jor - dan, ____ Deep _____ Ri - ver, Lord, I

want to cross o - ver in - to camp ground, Lord, I want to cross o - ver in - to

camp ground, ____ Lord, I want to cross o - ver in - to camp ground.

Swing Low, Sweet Chariot

Arr. by George Snowhill

Little David, Play on Your Harp

Negro Spiritual
Arr by J. Rosamond Johnson

365

Go Down, Moses

Negro Spiritual
Arr. by
J. Rosamond Johnson

Majestic (well sustained)

Go down Mo-ses, Way down in E-gypt land ___

Tell ole Pha - a - a -roah, To let my peo-ple go.

When Is - rael was in E - gypt's land,
Spoke the Lord, bold Mo - ses said: Let my peo-ple go. Op -
If

Humming

pressed so hard they could not stand,
not I'll smite your first born dead, Let my peo-ple go. Thus go.

Oh Dem Golden Slippers

By JAMES A. BLAND
Arr. by George Snowhill

Nobody Knows de Trouble I See

Slowly (with feeling)

Arr. by George Snowhill

No-bod-y knows de troub-le I see, No-bod-y knows but Je-sus;

No-bod-y knows de troub-le I see, Glo-ry hal-le-lu-jah! Oh,

No-bod-y knows de troub-le I see, No-bod-y knows but Je-sus;

No-bod-y knows de troub-le I see, Glo-ry Hal-le-lu-jah! Some-

times I'm up Some-times I'm down, Oh, yes, Lord; Some-

Steal Away

Arr. by George Snowhill

Steal a-way, steal a-way, Steal a-way to Je-sus!

Steal a-way, steal a-way home, I ain't got long to stay here.

Steal a-way, steal a-way, Steal a-way to Je-sus.

Steal a-way, steal a-way home, I ain't got long to stay here.

My Lord, He calls me, He calls me by the thun-der, The trump-et sounds— with-in — a my soul I ain't got long to stay here.

Green trees a' bend-ing, po' sin-ner stand a trem-bling, The trump-et sounds— with-in — a my soul I ain't got long to stay here.

D. C. al Fine

Joshua Fit de Battle of Jericho

Arr. by J. Rosamond Johnson

All God's Chillun

Arr. by Florence White

1. I got shoes, you got shoes, All God's chil-lun got
2. I got wings, you got wings, All God's chil-lun got
3. I got a harp, you got a harp, All God's chil-lun got a

shoes; When I get to heav-en, gon-na put on my shoes; I'm gon-na
wings; When I get to heav-en, gon-na put on my wings, I'm gon-na
harp; When I get to heav-en, gon-na play on my harp, I'm gon-na

walk all o-ver God's heav-en, Heav-en, Heav-en;
fly all o-ver God's heav-en, Heav-en, Heav-en;
play all o-ver God's heav-en, Heav-en, Heav-en;

Ev-'ry-bod-y talk-in' 'bout heav-en ain't go-in' there,

Heav-en, Heav-en, Gon-na walk all o-ver God's heav-en.

Rocked in the Cradle of the Deep

Andante

By JOSEPH P. KNIGHT

1. Rock'd in the cra - dle of the deep,_ I lay me down_ in peace to sleep; Se -
2. And such the trust that still were mine,_ Tho' storm-y winds_ sweep o'er the brine, Or

cure I rest up - on the wave,_ For Thou, O Lord,_ hast pow'r to save. I
though the tem-pest's fier-y breath,_ Roused me from sleep_ to wreck and death. In

know Thou wilt not slight my call, For Thou dost mark the spar-row's fall!
o - cean's wave still safe with Thee, The germ of im - mor-tal - i - ty; And

calm and peace-ful is my sleep, Rock'd in the cra-dle of the deep, And

rit.

calm and peace-ful is my sleep, Rock'd in the cra-dle of the deep.
rit.

Joy to the World

ISAAC WATTS

GEORGE F. HANDEL

With spirit

1. Joy to the world! the Lord is come; Let earth re-ceive her King; Let ev-'ry heart pre-pare Him room, And heav'n and na-ture sing, And heav'n and na-ture sing, And heav'n, and heav'n and na-ture sing.

2. Joy to the earth! the Sav-ior reigns; Let men their songs em-ploy; While fields and floods, rocks, hills and plains Re-peat the sound-ing joy, Re-peat the sound-ing joy, Re-peat, re-peat the sound-ing joy.

3. He rules the world with truth and grace, And makes the na-tions prove The glo-ries of His right-eous-ness, And won-ders of His love, And won-ders of His love, And won-ders, and won-ders of His love.

1. And heav'n and na-ture sing,

And

heav'n and na-ture sing,

Away in a Manger

MARTIN LUTHER

Tenderly

1. A - way in a man - ger, No crib for a bed, The
2. The cat - tle are low - ing, The Ba - by a - wakes, But
3. Be near me, Lord Je - sus, I ask Thee to stay Close

lit - tle Lord Je - sus Laid down His sweet head; The
lit - tle Lord Je - sus, No cry - ing He makes; I
by me for - ev - er, And love me, I pray; Bless

stars in the sky —— Looked down where He lay, The
love Thee, Lord Je - sus! Look down from the sky, And
all the dear chil - dren In Thy ten - der care, And

lit - tle Lord Je - sus, A - sleep on the hay.
stay by my cra - dle, 'Till morn - ing is nigh.
take us to heav - en, To live with Thee there.

376

O Come, All Ye Faithful

(ADESTE FIDELES)

JOHN READING

Majestically

O come, all Ye Faith-ful, Joy-ful and tri-um-phant, O
A - des - te, Fi - de - les, Lae-ti tri-um - phan-tes, Ve-

come ye, O come ye to Beth - le - hem. Come and be-hold Him,
ni - te, ve - ni - te, in Beth - le - hem. Na-tum vi - de - te,

Born the King of An - gels: O come, let us a-dore Him, O
Re - gem an - ge - lo - rum. Ve - ni - te, a-do - re - mus, Ve -

come let us a-dore Him, O come let us a-dore Him,— Christ— the Lord.
ni - te, a-do - re - mus, Ve-ni - te a-do-re - mus,— Do - mi - num.

377

Hark! the Herald Angels Sing

CHARLES WESLEY

FELIX MENDELSOHN - BARTHOLDY

Moderately fast

1. Hark! the her - ald an - gels sing, — "Glo - ry to the new - born King!
2. Christ, by high - est heav'n a - dored, — Christ, the ev - er - last - ing Lord:
3. Hail, the heav'n-born Prince of Peace! — Hail, the Sun of Right-eous - ness!

Peace on earth, and mer - cy mild; — God and sin - ners rec - on - ciled!"
Long de - sired, be - hold Him come, — Find-ing here His hum - ble home.
Light and life to all He brings, — Ris'n with heal - ing in His wings.

Joy - ful, all ye na tions, rise; — Join the tri - umph of the skies;
Veiled in flesh the God-head see, — Hail th' in - car - nate De - i - ty!
Let us then with an - gels sing, — "Glo - ry to the new - born King!

(2nd time)

With th' an - gel - ic hosts pro - claim, "Christ is — born in Beth - le - hem!"
Pleased as man with men to dwell, Je - sus — our Im - man - u - el.
Peace on earth and mer - cy mild; God and — sin - ners rec - on - ciled!"

378

God Rest You Merry, Gentlemen

Traditional
Arr. by Sir John Stainer

The Twelve Days of Christmas

Arr. by George Snowhill

Tenderly with growing wonder

On the first day of Christ-mas my true love gave to me a

par-tridge — in a pear tree. On the sec-cond day of Christ-mas my

true love gave to me two tur-tle doves and a par-tridge in a pear - tree.

On the third day of Christ-mas my true love gave to me three French-hens,
On the fourth day of Christ-mas my true love gave to me four col-ly birds;

two tur-tle doves and a par-tridge in a pear - tree.

On the fifth day of Christ-mas my true love gave to me five gold-en rings,

four col-ly birds, three French hens, two tur-tle doves, and a par-tridge in a pear tree.

On the sixth day of Christ-mas my true love gave to me six geese a - lay-ing,
On the sev-enth day of Christ-mas my true love gave to me se - ven swans a - swim-ming,
On the eighth day of Christ-mas my true love gave to me eight maids a - milk-ing,
On the ninth day of Christ-mas my true love gave to me nine pip-ers pip-ing
On the tenth day of Christ-mas my true love gave to me ten drum-mers drum-ming
On the 'lev-enth day of Christ-mas my true love gave to me 'lev-en Lords a - leap-ing
On the twelfth day of Christ-mas my true love gave to me twelve la-dies danc-ing

five gold - en rings, four col - ly birds, three French hens,

two tur - tle doves and a par - tridge in a pear - tree.

381

Lead, Kindly Light

J. H. NEWMAN

J. B. DYKES

1. Lead, kind-ly Light, a-mid th'en-cir-cling gloom,
2. I was not ev-er thus, nor prayed that Thou
3. So long Thy pow'r has blest me, sure it still

Lead Thou me on; The night is dark, and I am far from home;
Shouldst lead me on; I loved to choose and see my path; but now
Will lead me on O'er moor and fen, o'er crag and torrent, till

Lead Thou me on.— Keep Thou my feet; I do not ask to see.
Lead Thou me on.— I loved the gar-ish day, and spite of fears,
The night is gone.— And with the morn those an-gel-fac-es smile,

The dis-tant scene one step e-nough for me.
Pride ruled my will: Re-mem-ber not past years.
Which I have loved long since, and lost a-while. A-men.

Good King Wenceslas

Arr. by Felix Guenther

4. "Sire, the night is darker now,
   And the storm blows stronger;
   Fails my heart, I know not how,
   I can go no longer."
   "Mark my footsteps, good my page,
   Tread thou in them boldly;
   Thou shalt find the winter's rage
   Freeze thy blood less coldly."

5. In his master's steps he trod,
   Where the snow lay dinted;
   Heat was in the very sod
   Which the saint had printed.
   Therefore, Christian men, be sure,
   Wealth or rank possessing,
   Ye who now will bless the poor,
   Shall yourself find blessing.

Abide with Me

H. F. LYTE   W. H. MONK

1. A - bide with me: fast falls the e - ven - tide;
2. Swift to its close ebbs out life's lit - tle day;
3. I need Thy pres - ence ev - 'ry pass - ing hour:
4. Hold Thou Thy cross be - fore my clos - ing eyes,

The dark - ness deep - ens; Lord, with me a - bide:
Earth's joys grow dim, its glo - ries pass a - way,
What but Thy grace can foil the tempt - er's pow'r?
Shine thro' the gloom, and point me to the skies:

When oth - er help - ers fail, and com - forts flee,
Change and de - cay in all a - round I see:
Who like Thy - self my guide and stay can be?
Heav'n's morn - ing breaks, and earth's vain shad - ows flee

Help of the help - less, O a - bide with me!
O Thou who chang - est not, a - bide with me!
Through cloud and sun - shine, O a - bide with me!
In life, in death, O Lord, a - bide with me!